THE ASCENDANT ORGANISATION

By the same author

THE ROAD TO NISSAN
MANAGEMENT IN THE FAST TRACK
LEAN PRODUCTION AND BEYOND
SCHLÜSSEL ZUR WELTKLASSE-PRODUKTION
  (*with Franz Lehner*)

The Ascendant Organisation

Combining commitment and control for long-term sustainable business success

Revised and updated paperback edition

Peter D. Wickens, OBE

First edition 1995
Reprinted three times
Revised edition 1998

Published by
MACMILLAN PRESS LTD
Houndmills, Basingstoke, Hampshire RG21 6XS
and London
Companies and representatives throughout the world

ISBN 0–333–73580–3

A catalogue record for this book is available from the British Library.

This book is printed on paper suitable for recycling and made from fully managed and sustained forest sources.

Copy-edited and typeset by Povey–Edmondson
Tavistock and Rochdale, England

10 9 8 7 6 5 4 3 2 1
07 06 05 04 03 02 01 00 99 98

Printed and bound in Great Britain by
Antony Rowe Ltd
Chippenham, Wiltshire

*To **Brian** and **Gaye***
who cared
when it mattered

Contents

PART II 'KNOW-HOW'

List of Figures

List of Tables

Acknowledgements

The first edition of this book was researched over a three-year period while I was still a Director of Nissan Motor Manufacturing (UK) Limited. After leaving Nissan in mid-1995 and becoming a so-called portfolio person I was asked by Macmillan to prepare a paperback version. Little did I realise that revisions take a huge amount of time with every word being scrutinised a dozen times or more and my thanks go out yet again to my wife Helga for tolerating the disruption to family life.

In addition to the thanks recorded in the first edition to Terry Hogg, Keith Jones, Peter Hill and Helen Murlis I must add special thanks to Professor Franz Lehner, head of the Institut Arbeit und Technik, Gelsenkirchen, Germany who, in offering me a Visiting Professorship in 1996, allowed me to use the superb resources of the Institut to research much of the latest thinking regarding Japan and lean production.

John Monks, General Secretary of the Trades Union Congress, kindly commented on Chapter 13, 'Trade Unions in the Ascendant Organisation', and, as ever, I am grateful to him for his openness and constructive thinking. Keith Sissons, of Warwick University's Industrial Relations Research Unit, provided excellent advice on this chapter.

Ian Gibson, Chief Executive Officer of Nissan, and I worked together for ten years; and he, John Cushnaghan and Colin Dodge provided much of the debate and practical experience which permeates this book. I was remiss in not acknowledging this in the first edition and am glad of the opportunity to do so now.

My friend and colleague, Barry Venter, Managing Director of Organisation Development International, has, as always, provided mental stimulation at just the right time and I am grateful to him not only for this, but also for providing the opening for me to work in and discover the delights of South Africa. Dieter Lange was primarily responsible for developing the Ascendant Organisation Questionnaire and I greatly value and appreciate his talents as an occupational psychologist.

Since becoming a consultant and lecturer I have met with and helped people at all levels in companies of all sizes and stages of development. Everywhere you go you learn something, and I am grateful to everyone who, often unknowingly, has contributed to my developing thinking –

more of their influence will be found in my next book, *Energise Your Enterprise*.

One of my positions on leaving Nissan was a two-year appointment as Professor of Industrial Management and President of the Centre for Achievement in Manufacturing and Management at the University of Sunderland. This built on my previous work for the university and I remain grateful to the Vice Chancellor, Dr Anne Wright, for allowing me to experience at first hand the value as well as the tribulations of working with first-class academic minds.

In the acknowledgements in the first edition I referred to the influence of Toshiaki Tsuchiya, Nissan's first Managing Director. The further in time I move away from him and the more I experience some of the problems of other Japanese companies, both in Japan and in the West, the more I recognise his wisdom. When I left Nissan I was told that in any disagreement between the British and the Japanese, if he felt that the Japanese were about 70 per cent right and the British about 30 per cent right, he would opt for the British way. That requires great strength, and together we built a company that has become, in many respects, *the* benchmark. Thank you, Tsuchiya san.

I will be delighted to hear from readers. Please contact me as follows:

10 Kingsclear Park
Camberley
Surrey, England
GU15 2LS
Fax 01276 23968
e-mail ProfPeterDWickens@msn.com

PETER WICKENS, OBE

Introduction to the Revised Edition

Nissan in Sunderland is regularly rated as one of the 'best companies to work for' and is also the most productive car manufacturing plant in Europe. The relationship is no accident. From the very beginning its first British executives determined that the company would be both well managed and a good place to work, that it would be both highly effective and a company of which everyone would be proud.

One of the advantages of a greenfield site is that you necessarily build from scratch but, critically, we sat down and asked ourselves not only the practical questions but also the strategic and philosophical. We were deeply concerned about our style of management as well as achieving our goals. On many occasions, visitors would point to the advantages of a greenfield site but I never tired of pointing out that every company was a 'greenfield' at some point in time and that many contemporary 'greenfields' were unsuccessful. Similarly, there are many traditional companies which are succeeding in turning themselves around.

The common element is not a greenfield site but a greenfield mind.

It is the willingness to ask the fundamental questions, to get back to first principles, to understand the thinking and concepts that lie behind the practices, to get down to the basics of what motivates people, to learn from the best wherever it may occur, to recognise that there are potentially best practices which no one has yet achieved. Whenever I am asked the question, 'What was the most important factor making for success?' I always respond that it was approaching the challenge with a greenfield mind.

In putting this book together I was very conscious that there are thousands of business books, most of which are written by conceptual thinkers who cannot do or by doers who cannot think conceptually. I have always found it irritating that there is a ready market among business practitioners for books written by academics who have never managed anything in their life. They trawl around a few companies (usually the same names are quoted time and time again), produce a model which purports to be new but usually only repackages old wine in a new bottle, give it a fancy name and then launch the latest panacea on the bookshop shelves and conference circuit.

It is equally disturbing that so few practitioners are prepared to make the time to write about their experiences in ways which can provide transferable lessons. Books by 'inspirational' business leaders are often ghost-written and, while their biographies make for good anecdotes, only rarely are their lessons transferable to lesser mortals.

The first edition of *The Ascendant Organisation* was an attempt to combine the practical and the conceptual and, judging by the sales and feedback, it succeeded. This second edition is structured in the same way but I have tried to make it even more practical, cutting out much of the 'big picture' analysis. It incorporates practical experience gained over thirty years with British, American and Japanese companies (and adds my new experiences as a non-executive director in German, South African and British companies), understanding gleaned through research and lecturing, knowledge accrued by working with academics and trade unionists and learning gained from consulting and advising companies from all over the world. It takes a multi-dimensional approach – theory and practice, strategy and tactics, hard and soft issues, historical and contemporary analysis – uses examples from a variety of nations and examines the perspectives of both critics and advocates.

It is structured like an egg-timer. Into the top half, Part I, I pour 'knowledge', in particular the work of earlier thinkers and an analysis of Japan, its successes, its failures and its response to the bursting of the financial bubble. This knowledge leads to the neck of the egg-timer in which I draw twenty provisional conclusions leading to the concept of the ascendant organisation and other organisation types. Part I of this edition is now tighter and I have been able to bring Chapter 3 (Japan – right or wrong) up to date, using many examples from that country's recent difficulties. I have extended the debate on 'lean production' and, in introducing the concepts of 'the pressure equation' and 'operator care', point the way out of the problems that the excesses of leanness can cause. I have greatly extended the Japanese 'target', a model which attempts to show on one page all the influences impacting on the behaviour of Japanese companies, while also showing the changes that are taking place. This has been developed over several years and has gone through many iterations. I have been greatly encouraged by comments from Japanese colleagues many of whom have said that it has greatly helped their understanding of their own country.

The other major addition is The Ascendant Organisation Questionnaire© which was developed primarily by colleagues in Organisation Development International (ODI) and is intended to help readers discover the 'footprint' of their own organisation. Following publication of the first edition we found many people who were trying to work out their own position on the map, and in order to make this systematic ODI colleagues spent months preparing and validating the questionnaire and its analysis which I now share with you.

Part II ('Know-How') is the bottom half of the egg-timer into which 'knowledge' runs and is primarily concerned with practices. It offers many examples of success and some failures and provides guidance on how to behave if you wish to be 'ascendant'. But there is no magic formula. All we can do is to learn and then apply that knowledge intelligently in our own organisation; but continually I emphasise the need to *understand* before acting.

Again, I have made Part II tighter than in the first edition, editing out much of the 'big picture' material. Every chapter has been refined and, where necessary, updated. The major changes are in Chapter 10 (Customer–supplier partnerships), Chapter 12 (Recognition and reward) and Chapter 13 (Trade unions in the ascendant organisation). I have modified Chapter 14 (Becoming ascendant) to introduce the Ascendant Organisation Questionnaire as a tool in the change process.

The ascendant organisation is no panacea. It does not seek to replace other initiatives but provides guidelines and parameters into which other initiatives can fit and which will make them more likely to succeed. However, it is not neutral. It takes a firm position which, if followed, will enable you to lead and manage your business in a way that is more likely to lead to long-term sustainable success. If I were an American academic, I would be likely to present you with the new miracle cure. As primarily a British practitioner I know that *there are no miracle cures*. Long-term sustainable success comes about only by long-term application of a few simple, basic guidelines. There is no rocket science about them. They just need hard work, consistency, sustained attention and continuous improvement.

At the heart of this book is the combination of commitment of people and control of the processes, the soft and the hard. There is also the recognition that an organisation is no more than the people in it. But I reject the hypocritical statement that 'our people are our greatest asset', so frequently uttered by senior executives who, in any case, rarely act that way. The words imply that 'our people' belong to 'us' and subconsciously perpetuate the 'them and us' distinction which remains prevalent in most companies, however much it may be denied. I also use the word 'people' throughout instead of pandering to the fashionable 'human resources'. People are people when they get up in the morning, relax in the evening and enjoy their recreation. They do not suddenly change to 'human resources' for that part of the day when they are at work!

Incidentally, following the example of the British government where there is now a Department *for* Education and Employment, why can we not retitle our positions, Director *for* Personnel or, if you must have it, Director *for* Human Resources? Think of the messages it sends out!

I have taken care lately, when talking with top executives, to ensure that there is a bottle on the table. So often top executives complain of the bottleneck in their organisation, meaning that in the middle management group there are people who are preventing things from 'getting through'. I ask them to look at the bottle. Where is the neck? It is not in the middle; *it is at the top*. We are all someone else's top manager. We are all a 'bottleneck at the top' so, first, we must remove our own personal bottleneck.

As you read *The Ascendant Organisation*, to mix the metaphors, aim to remove your personal bottleneck and create your own greenfield!

PART I

'Knowledge'

1 The Ascendant Organisation

> The ascendant organisation combines high levels of commitment of the people with control of the processes to achieve a synthesis between high effectiveness and a high quality of life leading to long-term, sustainable business success.

The basis of what I have come to call 'the simple model' of the ascendant organisation was initially developed during a bar-room discussion one late evening in Düsseldorf in 1992. I still have the scrappy piece of paper on which I first drew the quadrant with its two axes and four organisation types. It took many months, though, for the term 'ascendant' to emerge.

However, having suffered from a plethora of business fads I have never seen the ascendant organisation as yet another miracle cure nor as a brand-new concept breaking entirely new ground. It recognises that business managers have to attend to a host of issues, many of which conflict with each other. It forms part of a continuum, preceded by many eminent thinkers and, no doubt, will be followed by many more.

For example, in 1985 I was much influenced by Richard Walton's *Harvard Business Review* article, 'From Control to Commitment in the Workplace', in which he explained the shift from the Taylorist 'control' model to the human relations 'commitment' model as a main reason for the significantly improved performance of a number of American companies. Under his commitment model:

> Jobs are designed to be broader than before, to combine planning and implementation and to include efforts to upgrade operations, not just maintain them. Individual responsibilities are expected to change as conditions change and often teams, not individuals, are the organisational units accountable for performance. With management hierarchies relatively flat and differences in status minimised, control and lateral co-ordination depend on shared goals and expertise rather than formal position-determined influence. (Walton, 1985)

Walton was essentially correct in his analysis and, coming at the time when we were establishing the Nissan culture in Sunderland, greatly reinforced my own thinking. However, having worked with American, Japanese and British companies for some thirty years and having experienced the problems and successes of each of them I am now convinced that Walton went too far in his rejection of the 'control' model. If we are to achieve long-term sustainable business success we need the right balance between the commitment of the people and control of the processes.

This is the essential concept of the ascendant organisation. During the course of the next chapters I shall present the 'knowledge' which led me to this conclusion and then discuss the more complex model. Let me though at this stage introduce 'the simple model' (see Figure 1.1). Throughout, we should remember that the value of such models lies not in their accuracy – most are unproveable – but in their utility.

Most writers, with the honourable exception of Eric Trist (see Chapter 2), have concentrated on just one axis; the 'scientific management' school on control of the processes and the 'behaviouralists' on commitment of the people. Many believe that the Japanese strength lies in the latter but they are also the most effective of controllers.

'Control' is externally imposed. It is the top-down imposition of standards, rules, procedures and processes. Command and direction are the normal methods of determining behaviour and achieving results. 'Commitment', however, is internal, with people believing in their own

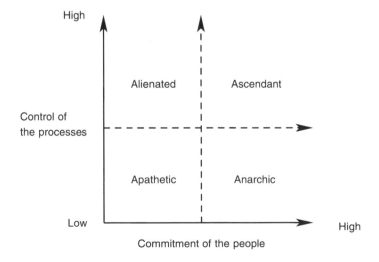

Figure 1.1   Organisation Types: The Simple Model

values. Committed people are highly motivated to work to achieve their own goals and, hopefully, those of the organisation.

As with all such models, while focusing the mind, it is too simple and for this reason I subsequently developed a more complex model, the Nine Alpha Organisation Map, which, following the analysis in Part I, will be fully explored in Chapter 4. However, in order to put the analysis into a framework I now briefly discuss the simple model.

The first quadrant I describe as *anarchic* – high levels of individual commitment combined with low levels of control which, at the extreme, can lead to people doing what they, individually, think is right for them and/or their organisation.

A classic example of this was the selling of personal pension plans in Britain in the late 1980s and early 1990s. A basically good product was released on to the market and the enthusiastic sales people either had no guidelines or, if they did, were allowed to ignore them. As a result, personal pensions were sold to thousands of people already in excellent occupational pension schemes and who lost out as a result. An investigation in 1993 by the Securities and Investment Board (SIB) found only 9 per cent of cases complied with industry guidelines on giving best advice and 83 per cent of records examined were unsatisfactory. The sales agents had simply failed to enquire properly into the benefits of the customer's existing pension scheme. As a result the insurance companies now have bills of hundreds of millions of pounds, either to buy back their customers into their old schemes or to pay compensation.

The most celebrated individual case is that of the highly empowered Nick Leeson of Baring Brothers fame. Leeson was a highly committed individual, operating out of Singapore, intent on doing what he considered best for himself and his bank but, as subsequent investigations showed, there was no control over his actions. The apparent profits he built up were sufficient for the people back in London to encourage him to continue; they were totally unaware of his subsequent attempts to cover his losses and, when these losses mounted to hundreds of millions of pounds bringing down Britain's oldest bank, the most prevalent emotion, apart from horror, was surprise! Total freedom without control leads to anarchy.

The opposite effect, high control and low commitment results in the *alienated* organisation. Douglas McGregor's Theory X company was based on the view that the average person dislikes work, and management has to rely on control and coercion to generate effort. In such organisations, people are controlled *by* the processes – management determines what should be done and how. The classic examples are line-paced production, or office work in which people are told what to do with little consideration as to whether they can have a constructive input. In such organisations, people are controlled *by* the processes. Many workers in local government have told me how alienated they feel, and shop workers, piece-rate workers and agricultural workers often feel the same. Alienation can exist in any business, large or small, private or public, service or manufacturing.

The lower left segment is low commitment and low control and applies to the type of organisation in which management has given up trying, has abdicated its responsibility or is simply of low calibre. People broadly do what they want but without any shared objectives or sense of direction. It may be the large, fat, private sector company, comfortable in its markets and sure of its profits, for example ICI before Lord Hanson came along and purchased 2 per cent of the shares – an action which eventually led to the total restructuring of the company; or the public sector organisation which does not really have to try. 'Low commitment, low control' is the *apathetic* organisation. In such an organisation neither management nor the people really care what happens and, generally, if you do not care what you get, you are not disappointed! In discussing this model I was surprised how many university audiences placed their institutions in this lower left quadrant.

The objective must, therefore, be to progress to the upper right quadrant, a high level of commitment of the workforce and high control *of* the processes. Individuals, instead of having every task determined for them, are able to influence or determine how the job is done, and often what that job should be. Changing from people being controlled *by* the processes to people having control *of* the processes is a fundamental and very difficult task.

Jack Welch, CEO of General Electric, recognised the need to change:

> The old organisation was built on control, but the world has changed. The world is moving at such a pace that control has become a limitation. It slows you down. You've got to balance freedom with some control, but you've got to have more freedom than you ever dreamed of. (Tichy and Sherman, 1993, p. 21)

In such an organisation the best of scientific management combines with the behavioural scientists; the best from Japan combines with the best of the West; and the hard and soft areas of management are pulled together. In addition a significant amount of practical experience, understanding and plain common sense is thrown into the pot.

I spent a long time trying to determine the right word for that upper right quadrant. Having realised that the first three began with the letter 'A' (which was not deliberate) it was essential in the nature of these things that the fourth also began with 'A'. After searching *The Concise Oxford Dictionary* my conclusion was 'Ascendant', one definition of which is:

Rising towards the zenith

and 'zenith' is defined as:

The highest point, time or place of greatest power, or prosperity or happiness.

This was my 'Eureka' moment – a definition which felt so right that afterwards it seemed amazing that it took such a struggle.

Translating these dictionary definitions into a business context:

The ascendant organisation combines high levels of commitment of the people with control of the processes to achieve a synthesis between high effectiveness and a high quality of life leading to long-term, sustainable business success.

I choose 'effectiveness' rather than 'efficiency' for the latter is too narrow. 'Effectiveness' combines productivity, quality and profitability and means that you can sell what you provide! It reaches out to suppliers and to the market place. It requires high-quality investment, engineering, research and product development. Above all, it requires high-calibre, highly motivated people and leaders committed to these goals. 'Quality of life' is deliberately chosen to take us beyond the workplace. Many in the West would regard the Japanese quality of life as low, both in the workplace and beyond, and if all we do is concentrate on the workplace we are missing something. It is no good working hard to achieve prosperity if you are unable to use that prosperity in the way you prefer, whatever that might be.

The quadrant is also simplistic. There is no room for the maverick organisation, or for the autocratic, the authoritative or the numerous other organisation types. The more complex model in Chapter 4 has four axes, not two, allowing nine organisation types to be developed.

However, before exploring the more complex model it is necessary to explain how I arrived at this concept and to emphasise that it is not yet another business fad. The ascendant organisation can sit beside most other concepts. It does not seek to replace anything, aiming to build on everything in a way that will enable them to work better than would otherwise be the case. To put it into this context I begin by briefly looking at the influence of the 'thinkers' before turning a critical eye on Japan.

2 The Fundamentals of Behaviour

No number of men, when once they enjoy quiet, and no man needs to fear his neighbour, will be long without learning to divide and sub-divide their labour.

Mandeville, *Fable of the Bees*, 1729

Add to the fact that to have conscientiously studied the liberal arts refines behaviour and does not allow it to be savage.

Ovid, 43BC–17AD

The purpose of this book is to attempt to achieve a better understanding of the underlying principles and the practices which make for long-term sustainable business success. Short-term success is easy, but an unthinking and superficial application can leave an organisation in a far worse state than it would have been had it never started the process. An understanding of these underlying principles and a judicious application of the concepts can lead to an accumulation of experience and knowledge which can have a beneficial effect throughout an organisation.

At its heart lies the conviction that an organisation is no more than the people in it. By itself, an organisation structure achieves nothing; processes, practices and procedures are devised by people for people; financial investment achieves nothing until it is used for creative purposes by people; machinery and equipment left alone for long breaks down; products and services do not create themselves and it is only people who improve on what is currently done. If the people in an organisation are committed to its success and they are properly led and motivated then everything is possible. If not, then failure is the most likely outcome.

Most readers will have some knowledge of so-called 'scientific management' and the teachings of the behavioural scientists. However, I make no apologies for including this short chapter which pulls together some of the relevant thinking. The names of F. W. Taylor, Henry Ford, Elton Mayo, Frederick Herzberg and others will be familiar. Others such as Victor Vroom will be less so. Our problem is that we are always hypnotised by the new and forget that several decades ago people were writing sensible things about behaviour in organisations. While many academics have criticised their writings as being non-provable and simplistic, their continuing importance lies in the fact that their lessons are fundamental and profound. If only we paid more attention to some of this thinking many mistakes would be avoided, particularly when seeking to implement change.

In Chapter 1 I referred to Richard Walton and his use of the words 'control' and 'commitment'. In using these words Walton was echoing two of the fundamental long-term trends in business thinking and I will continue to use them.

'CONTROL'

Adam Smith wrote in 1776 of his celebrated pin factory:

> The greatest improvement in the productive powers of labour and the greater part of the skill, dexterity and judgement with which it is anywhere directed, or applied, seem to have been the effects of the division of labour.

Since that time the debate over what makes for effective work organisation has been almost unceasing.

F. W. Taylor argued against the waste of human effort; sought to gather in 'the great mass of traditional knowledge which in the past has been in the heads of the workmen' and reduce it to laws, rules and formulae so as to produce more work of better quality. For Taylor, there was only 'one best way' and it was management's responsibility to define it. The workman was simply a pair of hands with no real need to use his brain.

His principles of scientific management pre-dates the Japanese concept of *kaizen* (continuous improvement) which recognises that the person doing a job knows more about that job than anyone else, and their emphasis on the 'one best way', the standard operation. Taiichi Ohno, the genius behind what came to be called the Toyota production system, expressed his debt to the work of F. W. Taylor.

Henry Ford when seeking to move from the craft-built motor cars of his early years to the Model T was faced with what he regarded as an 'ill-educated immigrant workforce' which did not have the ability to assimilate a lengthy assembly process at the pace demanded for mass production. The critical building blocks for him were, therefore, components which were built to a rigorous specification and were easy to fit together, and a short job cycle. The training time was about ten minutes, planning and control were given to specialist functions and the workers were paid to 'do', not to 'think'. When these concepts were in place the moving assembly line completed the picture.

The combination of division of labour, the one best way, the separation of thinking from doing, short and repetitive job cycles and the moving assembly line led to an environment in which:

- Brains were left at the factory gate unless used to thwart the system.
- The gathering in of the mass of traditional knowledge became 'expropriation of the workers' knowledge', taking from them any semblance of influence over their working lives.
- Top-down control and coercion led to alienation, conflict and restrictions of output.
- Workers were only able to express themselves and gain any form of recognition and representation through their membership of trade unions.

The brain power of the workers went into finding ways of beating the system, of scoring victories over their foreman, of doubling up and getting additional rest breaks. Their trade unions were forced into militancy. Mike Judge, Personnel Director of Peugeot, tells of his early days as a personnel officer in a car plant:

> We only needed two men to fit the roof lining, but as it was a difficult job at some time someone had agreed to four: two on and two off. One day we had a claim that they needed two more and if they didn't get them there would be a stoppage. Those were the days when we needed all the cars we could get, so we gave in. We subsequently found that they needed two more because they had become enthusiasts at playing bridge and always needed four off the job at any one time to make sure the game continued! Anyway, we eventually designed a rigid roof liner and put a stop to that!

Such stories are legion throughout the automobile industry. The brain power goes into thwarting the system.

Like all such extremes it led to the pendulum swinging in the opposite direction.

'COMMITMENT'

The fifty years from the mid-1920s when Elton Mayo conducted his investigations into the behaviour of people employed at the Hawthorne Plant of the Western Electric Company were the golden years of the behavioural scientists. The work of Mayo, Douglas McGregor (Theory X and Theory Y), Frederick Herzberg (motivation and hygiene factors), Abraham Maslow (needs hierarchy) and so on, has been taught to several generations of managers, although their behaviour frequently suggests that the lessons were not well learned.

There are considerable overlaps between the work of the various behavioural scientists, and in lectures and workshops since the publication of the first edition of *The Ascendant Organisation* I have found it convenient, rather than listing the conclusions of individual researchers, to summarise the most important collective lessons. It is, perhaps, a tribute to the influence of their work that despite academic criticism based on their 'unprovability' much of what follows now seems obvious. The problem in many organisations is that we forget the obvious in favour of the new and trendy. They are:

Stimulating/significant work gives most satisfaction
If my work is stimulating and I feel that it is of value then I am much more likely to feel good about it than if it is boring and seems to me to be of little value. When I have genuine responsibility and am fully involved in what I do I gain considerable satisfaction.

Special attention gives a positive response and poor treatment or neglect gives a negative response
If my efforts are recognised and valued I feel good about my work, my colleagues and my organisation. Conversely, if I am treated badly or neglected my feelings will be just the opposite.

Get the basics right then develop the higher needs
Abraham Maslow's 'hierarchy of needs' posited that basic needs have to be satisfied before an individual can move to higher needs. His hierarchy begins with physiological needs (food, water, air, shelter), and moves on to social needs (belonging, acceptance, giving and receiving friendship), esteem needs (self-confidence, achievement and recognition, and respect from others), and self-actualisation (self-fulfilment, realisation of one's potential, continuous self-development).

Individuals who are regarded as having only low-level needs and are managed in this way will behave accordingly. They will develop their own anti-company norms of behaviour. At best, they will switch off and, at worst, use their capabilities against the organisation. If the needs hierarchy has any meaning it must be that it becomes a managerial responsibility to facilitate the development and growth of individuals.

Achieving an acceptable level does not necessarily motivate people
Frederick Herzberg classified events into those which cause satisfaction (motivators) and those which cause dissatisfaction (hygiene factors). The motivators are positive – achievement, recognition, the work itself, responsibility and advancement. Hygiene factors – company policies, supervision, salary, working conditions, relationships – are more complex. If they are not perceived to be right they will cause dissatisfaction, but if they *are* right they will not necessarily cause satisfaction. For example, if I feel that my salary is inadequate I will be demotivated, but if it is acceptable I will not necessarily be motivated.

The link between the social and technical factors is profound
Based on his studies of the impact of new technology and the resulting changes in working arrangements in coal mines, Eric Trist found that the new methods totally changed the attitudes of the miners. Trust disappeared and anti-social practices grew. This led him to the view that the working group is neither solely a technical nor a social system but an interdependent socio-technical system in which the social and technical requirements are interactive and dynamic, not only within the group but also in relation to the environment within which it operated. He recognised that the hard and soft areas of managing businesses are inextricably linked and that management ignores this link at its peril.

Informal group norms are stronger than those imposed from the outside
Every group develops its own patterns of behaviour and unless the group is committed to change it will resist all attempts by outsiders to impose change upon it. This applies to everyone at every level and to both the social and work environment.

Goals and responses differ depending on experience
People's perspectives depend on the sum total of their experiences. A senior executive who meets people with different backgrounds and disciplines, from many different organisations, and gains a wide spectrum of business experiences is likely to have a different perspective from

someone who has spent his or her working life within the four walls of the organisation, face down to a machine or desk. The higher the mountain the grander the view.

Participation leads to commitment

While I resist externally imposed change in which I have had no say, I am enthusiastic about something in which I have participated. If I have been involved and think of a change as my idea I want it to happen quickly, I am committed to the goal and will work to achieve it, particularly when I receive effective feedback.

Effort is related to anticipated outcomes

This is from Victor Vroom and for our purpose is one of the most important insights. In simple terms, if I believe my efforts will result in outcomes that are beneficial to me I will put in considerable effort, whereas if I believe the outcomes will be to my detriment I will not try very hard. For example, if I believe that a productivity improvement or a re-engineering programme will result in me losing my job I will not work hard to make it happen. In even simpler terms, it is 'What's in it for me?'

If the initiators of such changes realised that the people who are needed to implement it are the very people who are most likely to lose their jobs, they should not be too surprised that so many do not achieve the hoped for results!

Maximise the discretionary work

In 1961 Elliott Jacques used the terms 'prescribed' and 'discretionary' work when developing his concept of 'time span of discretion' to establish the value of different jobs. While his job evaluation system never really caught on I use his terminology as the basis for a different concept.

All work can be divided into two elements, the 'prescribed' and the 'discretionary'. Prescribed elements are those which have to be done in a specific way at a specific place often in a specified time. Discretionary elements are those over which the individual can have some flexibility and choice over whether, how and when they are done.

The balance between the discretionary and the prescribed for a variety of positions is illustrated below (see box). These examples are for illustration – they have no analytical basis – but for every job there are prescribed and discretionary elements. It is essential, however, to make the discretionary work as meaningful as possible for those who have only a small mount. The line-paced assembly operator may be initially trained to perform the prescribed tasks well, and may (or may not) get

Position	Prescribed (%)	Discretionary (%)
Senior executive	5	95
Line paced assembly operator	95	5
Shop sales assistant	75	25
Customer service staff	60	40
Dentist	50	50
Maintenance worker	50	50

satisfaction from a job well done, but it is the opportunity to influence the way the job is done that really motivates, and that opportunity lies in the 5 per cent of discretion. But if we go in the opposite direction and reduce the discretionary element, that can have a dramatic effect on those who have only a small element of discretion. If the senior executive loses 5 per cent, then his or her discretionary proportion drops to 90 per cent, but if the line-paced operator loses 5 per cent there is no discretion left. The result is alienation.

The great thing, however, is that change can take place. The operator can take responsibility for preventive maintenance, improvement activities and reordering and be involved in projects and other assignments; the hotel porter can be encouraged to use discretion to assist guests with their problems; retail assistants can be given responsibility for displays, promotions or customer service, and so on. The possibilities are endless and all expand the discretionary at the expense of the prescribed. And by so doing both the individual and the organisation can grow.

Influence is not a zero-sum game
Arnold Tannenbaum's great contribution was to argue that influence is not a zero-sum game. Traditionally, 'bosses' believe that they exercise authority and influence over their 'subordinates' by controlling them, and think that if they give additional influence to the subordinate, then their own influence will automatically reduce. This is illustrated in Figure 2.1 which shows the progression from the zero-sum influence pie.

Figure 2.1a illustrates the traditional relationship – the 'boss' has 80 per cent of the responsibility and the 'subordinate' 20 per cent. The boss believes that by giving additional responsibility to the subordinate then his or her own responsibility will be reduced, thus moving from the 80–20 relationship to, say, 70–30. Because the boss sees this as changing the balance of responsibility in favour of the subordinate, he or she resists the

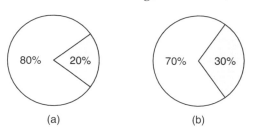

Figure 2.1 (a and b) The Zero-Sum Influence Pie

change, but the subordinate is likely to be in favour because it removes part of the oppressive regime. The problem is that everyone sees it as a zero sum.

Tannenbaum argued that it is not a zero sum. If, for example, my boss is a command and control authoritarian allowing me neither responsibility nor discretion but is persuaded to give me real responsibility for quality, continuous improvement, reordering, etc., then that increases my segment of the pie but it also changes his or her job. The boss's responsibility becomes one of equipping me to perform my new responsibilities, and when I am capable and can further develop myself my boss is freed up to concentrate on the bigger picture – planning for the future, multi-functional initiatives, improving the linkages between the different stages of the procedure, and so on. Both of our jobs have grown and the responsibility pie is larger. There will be a different relationship but we both have additional responsibilities.

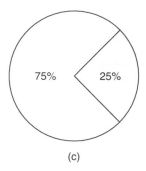

(c)

Figure 2.1 (c) Influence is Not a Zero Sum

All of the above seems no more than obvious common sense. Unfortunately, sense is not always obvious nor is it common! While I will not continually refer to the teachings outlined in this chapter, their influence permeates everything that follows.

3   Japan – Right or Wrong?

The Japanese out-Taylor us all.
    Richard J. Schonberger, *Japanese Manufacturing Techniques*, 1982

Both the sword and the chrysanthemum are part of the picture. The Japanese are to the highest degree both aggressive and unaggressive, both militaristic and aesthetic, both insolent and polite, rigid and adaptable, submissive and resentful of being pushed around, loyal and treacherous, brave and timid, conservative and hospitable to new ways.
    Ruth Benedict, *The Chrysanthemum and the Sword*, 1982

DEEP DOWN AND WAY BACK

Learning processes are never solely one way. F. W. Taylor's *The Principles of Scientific Management* was translated into Japanese in 1912 and sold 1.5 million copies as *The Secret of Saving Lost Motion*. Thirty-three years later, during the American occupation of Japan, one of General Douglas MacArthur's first acts was to call in American staff from AT&T to rebuild the nation's communications system. Frank Polkinghorn, Charles Protzman and Homer Sarasohn are now virtually unknown, but they were the real pioneers of modern manufacturing in Japan and paved the way for the subsequent visits of W. Edwards Deming who has received most of the credit.

Until then, the Japanese had little idea about effective manufacturing. Homer Sarasohn described what he found when visiting the Hayakawa Electric Company:

> The manager wanted to show me he understood my lectures about having a clean workplace. He hired a man specifically to keep the place clean. This fellow had a stick with a string coming from the end of it, and on the end of the string were a couple of pieces of ribbon. He was going round the assembly benches flicking this stick, using the ribbons to push the dust around a bit. The plant manager looked on proudly, thinking that his man was cleaning the plant and that I would be impressed.

The Hayakawa Electric Company has since changed both its ways and its name – it is now Sharp Electronics!

(I am grateful to Will Hopper, chairman of the CCS Institute, for his research and insights into this almost forgotten story of the impact of the American occupation of Japan prior to the Deming visits.)

Taiichi Ohno (who, with Shigeo Shingo, developed in Toyota virtually all the techniques of contemporary manufacturing) acknowledged his debt to Henry Ford, arguing that his successors did not adapt his system to changing times. Said Ohno, 'I for one am in awe of Ford's greatness. I think that if the American king of cars were still alive today he would be headed in the same direction as Toyota.'

Visitors on the three-day study tour of Japan often seek the miracle cure and return thinking that it is all down to lifetime employment, consensus, seniority and enterprise-based trade unions, but they could do well by starting with the writings of Taiichi Ohno and Shigeo Shingo. They will find that Japan is not some sort of industrial Lourdes and that their *manufacturing* success comes from a complex inter-linking of their history and culture which led to their national characteristics and corporate practices – all of which made possible Ohno's continuous improvement cycle.

Many attempts to understand Japan confuse these relationships and Figure 3.1 (and the more detailed version shown in Appendix One which also includes symbols indicating the depth of change which is taking place) is an attempt to clarify, showing a model of Japanese behaviour which led to the successes of the 1970s and 80s, before the bursting of the financial bubble.

Lying outside of this model are the numerous long-term historical and cultural factors and values (shown in full in Appendix One). The Japanese ethical system built on the teachings of Confucius clearly has an influence, but so too does the fact that, historically, Japan was a nation of mutually dependent farmers with the person who disrupted the village harmony being ostracised. The practice of interdependent allegiance between servant and master no doubt plays a part. The code of the warrior – *bushido* – emphasised winning, but also honour in personal relationships. The first true constitution of Japan, promulgated in AD 604, stipulated that the principle of all societies and communities was *wa* harmony. No doubt the fact that Japan is probably the most homogeneous of industrialised nations helps achieve an intuitive under-standing within a unified culture; so that *Ishin Denshin* (feelings conveyed without words) is a powerful tool of communication. The practical manifestation of the Japanese aphorism 'Silence is expression' is extremely difficult for voluble Westerners to handle.

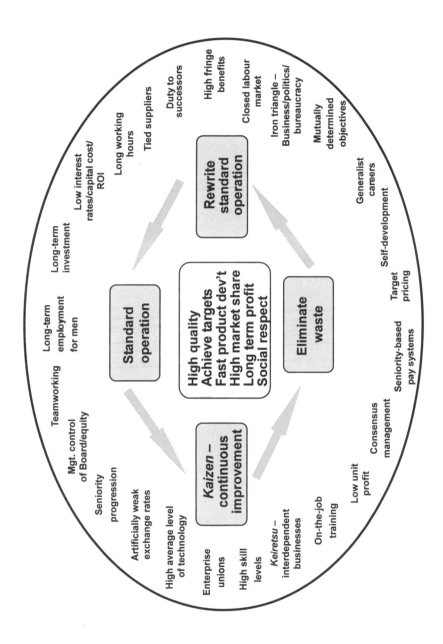

Figure 3.1 Japanese Behaviour

The Japanese tend to value group harmony more than individuality and it is not surprising, therefore, that group-oriented ideas have been adopted in corporate management practices. The Nissan publication, *Things you want to know about Nissan and Japan*, puts it neatly:

> There is a belief in Japan that a person who works diligently will gain social recognition and work is regarded as something of a virtue . . . an integral part of a person's life and consequently that it should be enjoyable; this leads to independent efforts on the part of workers to improve their jobs and to upgrade the quality of their work. In addition, since changing jobs is relatively rare in Japan the work that an individual does within the framework of a single company takes on a great deal of importance in his personal life. Therefore, there is a strong feeling that if one contributes to his company by working hard, his efforts will be rewarded and his private life will be enriched accordingly.

These deeply embedded social and cultural values have created a society in which order, respect, honour, duty, hard work, interdependence, harmony, continuity and spiritual fulfilment are lived on a daily basis. They led not only to Ruth Benedict's chrysanthemum but also to her sword or, as Arthur Koestler expressed it in *The Lotus and the Robot*, (1960), 'Life in Japan may be compared to a scented bath which gives you electric shocks at unexpected moments!' They have clearly impacted on behaviour in the workplace but they are not the *cause* of Japanese manufacturing success, but without them manufacturing success would have been less likely. They are akin to Herzberg's hygiene factors – their presence did not produce success, but without them, success would have been less likely.

Japanese industrial society, reflecting its national culture, is a complex mixture of the chrysanthemum and the sword, the soft and the hard. Unfortunately, early analysts who set the tone, missed this critical relationship. In 1981, William Ouchi's influential *Theory Z* concentrated almost entirely on 'a special way of managing people' and, a year later, Richard Schonberger's *Japanese Manufacturing Techniques – Nine Hidden Lessons in Simplicity* (1982) took the manufacturing technique route. Not only did both present just part of the story but they also failed to notice that not every sector of the Japanese economy was successful. By the 1980s in key exporting industries – automobiles, electronics, ship building, machine tools, and so on – Japan had reached a point where it could produce high-quality goods at high productivity levels, but it is frequently overlooked that these industries form less than a quarter of the

Japanese economy. They are surrounded by a plethora of over-regulated, over-protected, inefficient companies supplying the domestic economy. In agriculture, food processing, domestic manufacturing, distribution, retailing, banking, insurance and the service sector the Japanese economy is hopelessly inefficient and often corrupt. The early writers failed to explore the inefficiencies and excesses of the finance and service sectors which were time-bombs waiting to explode; nor did they notice that the successful blue-chip companies were built on the backs of the small businesses with their low pay and insecurity.

For example, in Britain, a classic complaint used to be the number of men it took to dig a hole in the road. Walking through Tokyo's main thoroughfare in 1995 I came across road works approximately 20 metres long. Eighteen men were 'working' – six of them directing traffic, four in the hole, two operating mechanical diggers, and six, to put it politely, were supervising! Such over-staffing is repeated in every area of non-manufacturing with estimates that there are four to five million too many people employed in the service sector. But it is this expanding service sector that has been able to absorb those displaced from manufacturing. Who is right?

The truth is that Japan's success in its key exporting industries generates the wealth that enables such employment inefficiencies to continue. In the height of the recession, the total number of people employed actually grew!

During their surge of the 1970s and 1980s the Japanese did not learn from the West. They became comfortable, confident, arrogant and complacent. They did not change when they did not *need* to change. Now that they need to change they are realising that it is a little, but not too, late.

The Anglo-American tradition, on the other hand, traces its origins back to the liberal traditions of Adam Smith, who regarded government as a necessary evil which should be restricted to the minimum functions necessary to maintain law and order. In continental Europe, Max Weber argued that the prime influence was the growth of the Protestant ethic and its influence on the pursuit of individual wealth (Weber, 1930). The American frontier thesis based on the individual pushing forward, responsible for only himself and his immediate family, did nothing to encourage a group mentality except for short-term defensive alliances. The cultural development in the West has been centred upon the individual and from this the special Western contributions flow – cost control, product planning, marketing, innovation, top-level drive, the ability to respond rapidly, and so on.

The West has learned from Japan; and the USA, after getting over the trauma of realising that it will not always be number one in everything, has put much of its house in order to an extent that the doomsayers of the 1970s would have thought impossible. The resurgence of the American automobile industry in the mid-1990s is but the most prominent example.

The Japanese achievements were helped by an artificially low exchange rate which, in turn, was supported by low interest rates, low capital costs, low dividend expectations and low wage rates (this latter until the mid-1980s when wage rates took off). Further, the companies, linked together in mutually reinforcing groupings, *keiretsu*, sought long-term growth rather than short-term profitability. No wonder the Japanese economy boomed.

It is vital, however, to appreciate the effect of their artificially weak exchange rates. Throughout the years leading to its boom period Japan enjoyed a protected exchange rate. At key dates the yen/US dollar exchange rate since the end of the Second World War has been:

1946	360:1	1987	145:1
1975	299:1	1995	80:1
1985	264:1	1997	120:1
1986	190:1		

For 22 years the yen/dollar exchange rate was maintained at 360:1 and until the mid-1980s remained very weak. But the Plaza Accord of 1985 aimed to strengthen the yen and weaken the dollar, following which the exchange rate moved from 264 to 190 in one year, and with the further strengthening of the yen, life became much more difficult. But like many clouds there was silver lining, for during the late 1980s many companies embarked on programmes designed to make them profitable at 100 yen/dollar. When it weakened to 120 (and in late 1997 to 127), such companies are now securing windfall profits.

THE CONTINUOUS IMPROVEMENT CYCLE

At the heart of much of Japanese manufacturing success is the four-stage continuous improvement cycle shown in Figure 3.1: Standard operation – *Kaizen* – Eliminate waste – Rewrite the standard operation.

The cycle begins with the standard operation – the current best method for achieving quality, cost and delivery time in a safe manner. It is F. W. Taylor's 'one best way' of doing a job, but adhered to with a rigour beyond anything he conceived. As Richard Schonberger said, 'The Japanese out-Taylor us all.' The standard operation is formalised in a written document which includes all information about a task, including its description, main steps in the correct order, the time allowed, required protective clothing, tools to be used, and so on. Because, by definition, it is the current best known way, any deviation will result in a worsening of quality, productivity or safety and will cause waste. It must be adhered to but it also provides the reference point for continuous improvement – *kaizen.*

okay with standard demand demand varies?

Of all Japanese concepts, *kaizen* has most to offer the West. It can work successfully in all sectors, in all jobs and at all levels – including in service sectors where standard operations are not so easy to pin down (although the Japanese have had success in many back-office jobs). It recognises that the person doing a job knows more about that job than anyone else and that it is management's task to motivate everyone so that this knowledge can be utilised for the benefit of both the individual and the company. It is about seeking the hundreds of 0.01 per cent improvements that, added together, can significantly improve quality, productivity and ease of working and, at the same time, greatly enhance motivation and commitment. In most Western companies such knowledge is at best withheld and at worst is used against the company.

The Japanese contrast *kaizen* with the Western concept of innovation which they see as large incremental steps, often implemented from the top down using significant amounts of capital investment. They believe that Western management is then content to sit back and expect any improved results to be maintained, but, of course, they are not. First, the incremental change has frequently excluded any input from those actually doing the job, they do not own it and therefore it is not as effective as it might have been. Second, if there is no continuing input, any benefits will decay.

Successful *kaizen* is achieved not through some vast bureaucratic process but in the simplest way possible: by an operator saying to the supervisor, 'If we shifted that pallet one metre to the left I wouldn't have to walk so far.' Or in the office, by a clerk suggesting that a couple of tasks be combined to reduce the time and make the job more satisfying. Responds the supervisor, 'That seems a great idea. Why don't you talk with your colleagues to make sure it doesn't give them any problems and if everyone is happy with it we can make sure it happens.' Following the change, the written standard operation sheet is updated.

Within this simple example lie the key ingredients of *kaizen*. It came about as a normal part of the person's work, it was not something special. The supervisor had the authority to agree and readily did so; the individual first made sure that other people affected were happy and then implemented the change without outside help. Finally, the standard operation was amended and the revised method became the new 'best way' waiting for another improvement. The improvement was initiated, owned and implemented without reference to anyone outside the group and there was no specific reward.

Kaizen is *not* a suggestion scheme despite the many apocryphal stories about the hundreds of suggestions made in Japanese companies. No Western company is likely to match Japanese suggestions performance, even though their professed achievements rarely result in significant change on the ground, and Toyota's suggestion scheme in its newest plant in Kyushu has deliberately moved away from the traditional target of 'hundreds per person per year'. Suggestions schemes are bureaucratic, slow and wide open to abuse but the fundamental criticism is that, with their panoply of reviews and awards, they are based on the premise that most people are not paid to think – but if they do, they should receive some sort of additional reward! Suggestion schemes reinforce Taylorism, separating the thinking and doing roles. *Kaizen*, though, is based on the premise that thinking is part of everyone's job and that everyone can contribute better ways. People are not directly rewarded for *kaizen* improvements, although flexibility and innovation can be recognised as part of an overall performance assessment, as we shall see in Chapter 7.

For the Japanese the process is as important as the results. They see it as part of the learning and personal growth which come from all small group activities and which, contribute to the total improvement process. It is long-term and long-lasting and seeks to involve everyone throughout the organisation in low-cost improvements. It can be top-down or bottom-up. Top-down, it is management asking a group to try to find a solution to a problem; bottom-up, it is an individual or group coming up with an idea.

For *kaizen* to be successful it is critical that employees feel secure. No Japanese company ever dismisses people because of *kaizen* improvements; but because the ideal *kaizen* activity not only makes life easier but also improves both quality and productivity there are many instances of individuals' work changing as a result. For a period, the change may result in an individual having less work to do, but for the benefits to accrue to the company the savings must eventually be collected together and either someone is removed or more work is given to the same number of people. This is a basic principle of productivity improvement and the Japanese are relentless in applying it. Non-value adding work is waste and *kaizen* exists to eliminate waste not create it.

Waste, *muda*, is anything which does not add value to the product or service. Taiichi Ohno called it 'the great evil' and Shigeo Shingo believed that searching it out was an unrelenting task:

> Plant improvements demand an unrelenting keen eye and persistent efforts to identify problems. Maintaining this attitude and timelessly observing the job at hand to find problems makes it possible *to wring water even out of dry towels* [my emphasis]. This is how we have to think about total waste elimination. (1988, pp. 27–8)

The biggest waste is over-production but waste also includes pre- and post-production inventories; buffer stocks, i.e. banks of partially finished product between processes; movements such as walking and stretching; processes which, due to poor design, add complexity; transport of materials and components; time spent looking for tools or material or waiting for something to happen; space which is not used for productive purposes; rectification work, and so on. The ideal state is *60 seconds of added value work every minute* from both people and machines.

A clothing manufacturer explained to me why they had large buffer stocks between the various process stages. 'They are there to assist the work flow. If there is a problem upstream, then downstream operators can draw from the buffer stock. If there is a problem downstream, then upstream operators can feed into the buffer stock.' They had created the buffers 'just-in-case' but failed to identify the true causes of the problems. The Japanese response would be, 'Eliminate the buffers, highlight the problems, find the real causes and fix them!' And then, for Taiichi Ohno, if something is working smoothly, throw in some grit – reduce the staffing level or pile in extra work. Problems will arise which then have to be solved and the improvement spiral will take a further turn upwards – or so you hope. Ohno was a perfectionist who had little time for lesser mortals; he was never known to give a word of praise to anyone, and while he believed in the dignity of the workforce, that dignity had to find its expression in efforts to improve production efficiency.

Virtually every step in this process would be recognised by F.W. Taylor. It is the same in almost every respect except for the most important. For Taylor that process belonged to the managers, engineers and foremen. For the Japanese *it belongs to the people doing the job* and, even in companies such as Toyota in which the pressures to improve productivity have been relentless, that difference has been fundamental to Japanese success.

LEAN OR MEAN?

It was this approach which led to the concept of 'lean production', popularised by James Womack, Dan Jones and Daniel Roos (WJR) in *The Machine that Changed the World* (1990). The 'machine' was the Toyota production system.

> Lean production is 'lean' because it uses less of everything compared with mass production – half the human effort in the factory, half the manufacturing space, half the investment in tools, half the engineering hours to develop a new product in half the time. Also, it requires keeping far less than half the needed inventory on site, results in many fewer defects, and produces a greater and ever growing variety of products.

This celebrated statement swept through the world's automobile industry in the early 1990s, penetrated its components supply industry and subsequently reached virtually all areas of manufacturing, before moving into many other areas of business.

Lean production aims for perfection: continually declining costs, zero defects, zero inventories and endless product variety. Womack *et al.* see lean production as a development along the path from craft production and mass production, combining:

> the advantages of craft and mass production while avoiding the high cost of the former and rigidity of the latter. Towards this end lean production employs teams of multi-skilled workers at all levels of the organisation and uses highly flexible, increasingly automated machines to produce volumes of products in enormous variety. (Womack *et al.* 1990)

According to WJR, Japanese lean production has two key organisational features: 'It transfers the maximum number of tasks and responsibilities to those workers actually adding value to the car on the line, and it has in place a system for detecting defects that quickly traces every problem, once discovered, to its ultimate cause.'

But, they warn, 'Lean production is fragile . . . to make a lean system with no slack – no safety-net work at all it is essential that every worker try very hard . . . if management fails to lead and the workforce feels no reciprocal obligations are in force, it is quite predictable that lean production will revert to mass production.' ('Fragile' was, in fact, the original word, to be later discarded in favour of 'lean'.) They argue that while a properly organised lean production system does indeed remove all slack, 'it also provides workers with the skills they need to control their work environment and the continuing challenge of making the work go more smoothly'.

One would be surprised, therefore, if there were critics of such a beneficial system – but there are!

The Japanese critics

Much of the criticism of Japanese working practices has its emotional origins in Satoshi Kamata's account of his experiences as a seasonal worker with Toyota in the mid-1970s. His 1983 book *Japan in the Passing Lane* was published as *Automobile Factory of Despair* in Japan. Kamata, a left-wing, freelance journalist sought employment to obtain material for his writing and was hostile from the start:

> Almost as soon as I begin, I am dripping with sweat. Somehow I learn the order of the work motions but I'm totally unable to keep up with the speed of the line . . . Some skill is needed, and a new hand like me can't do it alone. I'm thirsty as hell, but workers can neither smoke nor drink water. Going to the toilet is out of the question. Who can have invented a system like this?

While Kamata's work is dated, it still remains for Japanese workers to display the 'right' attitude, to work overtime and not take their full holiday entitlement. It was, however, surprising that in February 1992 the Japan Auto Workers Union (JAWU) published *Japanese Automobile Industry in the Future*, in which they highlighted what they called the triple sufferings of the Japanese automobile industry:

> The employees are exhausted, the companies make only little profit and the automobile industry is always bashed from overseas.

While many commentators commend the high level of domestic competition as a factor which contributed to Japan's success, the JAWU argued that the constant demands for innovation placed unacceptable demands on the companies and their work-forces. It emphasised the length of the individual's working year and asked, 'How competitive will we be when we shorten our 2,200 hours to 1,800?'

These figures do not tell the whole story. Many companies have traditionally relied on 'voluntary', unpaid and unrecorded overtime to meet their production requirements. A Ministry of Labour Report in July 1991 showed that the average Japanese had 7.1 days holiday, and in a survey of nearly 1,200 companies, 76 per cent were good enough to say that they would allow employees to take consecutive holidays of three days or more in July and August! But if the Japanese are stressed in their work they accept it. The archetypal Japanese salaryman is the male university graduate destined to stay with one company for life, and I have asked many of them, 'Do you enjoy yourself?'. 'Yes' is the inevitable reply. They know they work hard and long but it is in a good cause. To them it is *seishinshugi*, the victory of the spirit over the material – their spirit triumphs over adversity.

In his annexe to the JAWU report, Professor Haruo Shimada, who was also a contributor to *The Machine that Changed the World* (Womack *et al.*, 1990), said of the Japanese automobile industry:

There is competition for competition's sake and everything is sacrificed to it, wages, working hours, profits, suppliers, traders, the welfare of Japanese employees and job prospects of workers overseas . . . If competition becomes an end in itself and people compete whatever the cost then it will grow into a monster which can destroy life, society and even the economy.

A 1992 Japanese survey of parental attitudes asked 'Would you advise your children to work in the automobile industry?' Only 4.5 per cent answered 'Yes', with the most frequent negative reasons being:

	%
Pay too low for intense work	43
High work intensity	41
Onerous shift system and nightshift	40
Much work on holidays and overtime	36
Unfriendly personnel practices	33

(Nomura, 1992)

Clearly, in Japan there is a perception of the automobile manufacturing industry that is different from that presented overseas by the most extreme enthusiasts.

The German critics

Criticism of Japanese working practices has also come out of Europe. The International Metalworkers Federation, in addition to citing the long working hours, untaken holiday, unpaid overtime and high workloads, emphasised what it saw as other reasons for Japanese success, including major outsourcing of final assembly to subsidiary companies which pay considerably lower wages, supportive government policies, and success 'based on a young and steadily growing market, whereas the North American producers were stuck with ageing plant in a mature and cyclical market' (Unterweger, 1992).

There is no doubt that wages in the supplier sector in Japan are lower than in the assemblers. Werner Sengenberger of the International Labour Organisation has produced comparative information which shows the wage gradient, top to bottom, in the UK and Japan related to the size of firm. (See Table 3.1.)

In the UK, all companies have wages which are close to 80 per cent of the highest, whereas in Japan the gradient slopes steeply downwards with 26.5 per cent of companies paying only 56.4 per cent of the highest. Around 40 million Japanese work in small and medium enterprises against ten million in larger enterprises, and salaries in the small enterprises are little more than half those in the large.

The German metal workers' union, IG Metall, approves of *kaizen* as practised in Japan which, it believes, values human labour, and argues that to be successful in Germany, with its culture which combines social

Table 3.1   Wage Gradient: Japan v. UK

Size of firm	Japan		UK	
	Wage gradient (%)	*Share of employment*	*Wage gradient (%)*	*Share of employment*
1,000+	100.0	40.6	100.0	68.5
500–999	86.2	12.6	79.6	8.8
200–499	76.6	11.8	79.5	8.6
100–199	68.2	8.5	74.7	4.9
1–99	56.4	26.5	78.3	9.2

Source: Sengenberger (1992).

well-being with a highly skilled workforce and powerful protective trade unions, it is necessary to combine economic and social progress for the well-being of all:

> One mark of an intelligent and socially harmonious system of production would most definitely be the avoidance of waste, increase in efficiency and declining costs. This cannot be tied to the goal of achieving competitive advantage through speed up, lay-offs and exploitation of productivity gain . . . A clear rise in efficiency can only be achieved when the workforce can see that all this is bound up with

> - an actual improvement in working conditions
> - fair distribution of gains in productivity
> - stabilisation of employment.

> *It is an illusion to think that employees will readily work for improvements to which they themselves fall victim* [my emphasis]. A production system that requires high morale, qualified workers and a commitment to constant improvement cannot be pushed through against the will of the employees. (Roth, 1992)

This is the corollary of Victor Vroom's teaching that effort will only be expended if the individual feels that the benefits to be gained are worthwhile.

In discussion with numerous German managers, I have found that most have not yet accepted the underlying philosophy. Their direction is all about structures, both physical and organisational. They have failed to grasp that the great change, which must first come at the top, is a recognition that all people at all levels in their organisations are able to contribute effectively to improving the way things are done. Following a visit to a number of manufacturing plants in Britain, including Nissan, the leader of a German delegation commented on the quality and flexibility they had seen: 'The trust and delegation of responsibility needed are not common in Germany – Germany must become flatter, less hierarchical and there must be more teamwork with responsibility pushed downwards.'

The Canadian critics

The Canadian Autoworkers Union (CAW) seems to be the Neanderthal of the international trade union movement. It distinguishes between the interests of capital and labour and remains part of that section of the labour movement which believes that capitalist organisations can only succeed by exploiting the workers. Its first experiences of Japanese production methods were based on CAMI, a General Motors–Suzuki joint venture located in Ingersoll, a small town of 8,500 people.

To the CAW, the objectives of lean production are to:

- reduce the number of labour hours per vehicle
- intensify the work effort
- eliminate non-value-adding functions
- increase managerial flexibility and control
- undermine the independence of trade unions

The critical issue for them is, 'Who controls the shop floor?' They reject a 'logic of production based on competition among workers from different plants. It is the workers who are on the same team, not managers and workers.' They see the move to 'just in time' (JIT) and the elimination of buffer stocks as being against the workers' interests because it requires jobs to be standardised, and imbalances eliminated. But, they argue, it is these imbalances which provide workers with flexibility and the opportunity to create personal time (doubling up, banking, and so on).

> Our willingness to make up after hours the production lost during the shift [means] the buffers are less visible . . . We are the buffers . . . It is not that Japanese production methods have done away with unnecessary buffers; it has simply shifted the cost of these. (Robertson, 1992)

David Robertson, at a conference of the Transport and General Workers' Union in December 1992 said, 'Lean production is intent on taking labour out of production and time out of labour. At the end of the day there will be fewer of us in the plant, and the jobs of those who remain are going to be worse.'

The CAW, with the acquiescence of CAMI, undertook a longitudinal study – a series of six-monthly surveys with unrestricted access to the shop floor – to examine specific workstations, interview managers and, on a random basis, interview 10 per cent of union members. Their stated aim was to find out how lean production and the associated concepts actually operates and how it affects workers. The comparison of the results between rounds one and four (two years apart) are shown in Table 3.2.

Table 3.2   CAMI Attitude Survey

		Round 1 (%)	Round 2 (%)
Do you work harder than in a traditional auto plant?	Yes	Not asked	78
Do you belong to a quality circle?	Yes	56	38
Is CAMI special, designed to change the way people work?	Yes	43	12
Does single status make managers and workers more equal?	Yes	43	6
Is management interested in the welfare of the workers?	Very	28	3
	Mildly	53	48
	Not very	15	35
	Not	4	15

Source: David Robertson, TGWU Conference, December 1992.

The results, with all the caveats that have to be applied when union members are answering a union survey, show an increasing dissatisfaction with their lot, but, corresponding with IG Metall and Victor Vroom, is David Robertson's comment that, 'Workers were more likely to express approval for particular features of Japanese production methods when they could see real possibility for advancing their own objectives or for adapting existing structures to realise specific goals. Thus workers tried to appropriate the *kaizen* process to make work less stressful.' In discussion with Robertson he said, 'Workers will accept *kaizen* if it benefits them – if it makes their job harder or doesn't make any change they don't want it.'

The Canadian Autoworkers Union is right in that the elimination of buffer stocks does mean that on some occasions catch-back is achieved by scheduling overtime at short notice, and it is a practice which if abused by management is justifiably criticised. However, if properly managed and agreed with the people concerned this presents no problems. Nissan in the UK reached a perfectly sensible understanding that small amounts of downtime could be caught-back that same day but larger amounts would be planned for later.

David Robertson and Wayne Lewchuck subsequently undertook a study of 1,670 workers in sixteen workplaces in the Canadian automotive parts industry and questioned people at all levels. Their conclusions were:

Compared with workers in traditional Fordist-style plants, those at lean companies reported their work load was heavier and faster. They reported work loads were increasing and becoming even faster. They did not report it was easier to change things they did not like about their job. They did report that it was becoming more difficult to get time off and were more likely to have to find a replacement worker before they could go to the washroom. They were more likely to report that they would be unable to maintain their current work pace until age 60. The only area where we found any support for the propositions put forward by supporters of lean production was in the area of time needed to train someone to do one's job. Those at lean plants reported it would take longer to train someone to do their job. (Lewchuk and Robertson, 1996)

The value of the CAW arguments is that in taking an extreme position, they illustrate the dangers that abuse might lead to. But the CAW rejects even this, for it believes that abuse is built into the system. When I asked David Robertson 'What went wrong at CAMI?', his response was, 'Nothing, everything that management was supposed to do, it did. And the workforce reacted increasingly against it. That is the lesson!'

David Robertson brings out the great difficulty in translating the vision into reality. He says that, 'Vision becomes illusion', and there can be no doubt that, as in all things, turning the vision into reality is difficult.

The British critics

I have been privileged to have spoken at several seminars organised for officials of the Transport and General Workers' Union. They asked strong questions and were not convinced that management was not simply seeking to screw them into the ground, but they were concerned, above all, that the elimination of waste meant that the easy jobs, to which older workers move when they cannot keep up with the manufacturing pace, are disappearing. They were not resisting change for the sake of it, but they did have a genuine concern for their ageing colleagues – and for themselves in a few years' time. 'The jobs are tough enough now. How are we going to manage when we're in our fifties?' But I did not experience hostility to the concept. Practical people understand the realities of life; they do not have the academics' luxury to criticise from the outside. They have to earn a living and know that they have to compete in the real world.

The most penetrating British academic criticism comes from Karel Williams (now of the University of Manchester) who has taken the statistician's scalpel to the lean production analysis.

The basis for WJR's 'Half of everything' statement was a 1987 comparison of Toyota's Takaoka and General Motor's Framingham plants which showed that Takaoka took 16 hours for the assembly stages of a car against Framingham's 31, while achieving a quality level which was three times better and using only 60 per cent of the space. However, Williams argues that while it was the Framingham–Takaoka comparison which sent shock waves around the world, many lost sight of WJR's qualifying statement that Framingham was the *worst* US plant and Takaoka was the *best* Japanese plant. The average US plants had only half the Takaoka–Framingham gap, and the best US-owned plants in North America were nearly as productive as the average Japanese plants. Further, even in Japan there was a difference of two to one between the best and worst plants in both productivity and quality. They found that some plants in Japan are not particularly lean, and a number of Japanese-owned plants in North America had demonstrated that they, also, could practise lean production.

According to John Krafcik, who really started the whole thing off and was responsible for much of the early research, the true figures are 27.6 hours against 18 hours, a difference of around 50 per cent. But, for Karel Williams, the problem is compounded because at the time of the comparisons Takaoka was overloaded with a considerable amount of 'voluntary', unrecorded and unpaid overtime being worked, whereas Framingham was a demoralised plant, working at 60 per cent capacity and awaiting its notice of closure (It closed in 1989, before *The Machine that Change the World* was published.)

Karel Williams and his colleagues take the argument one step further in presenting an alternative picture. They compare the *whole* of the Japanese and American auto industries (not just the final assembly stages which were the basis of the WJR study) from 1969 to 1988 and calculate the build hours per vehicle over this 20-year period. The results are shown in Table 3.3.

In 1969 the Japanese took 279 hours to build a vehicle, compared with the Americans' 187 hours; they surpassed the Americans in 1975 (176 hours v. 188 hours), and continued to improve until 1981 after which their improvements were only slight. The Americans took 187 hours per unit in 1969 and, while fluctuating around this figure, had improved to 186 hours by 1988! In the same period, the number of vehicles produced per employee per year increased from 8.33 to 17.12 in Japan, whereas in the US it rose (albeit with fluctuations above and below these figures) from 11.54 to 11.95!

Table 3.3   Build Hours per Vehicle 1969 to 1988, US v. Japan

Year	Employees ('000s)	Vehicle output per employee	Hours per employee	Hours per unit of output
United States				
1969	882	11.54	2,158	187
1972	916	12.34	2,174	176
1975	807	11.14	2,096	188
1978	1,061	12.09	2,194	182
1981	791	10.09	2,127	211
1984	865	12.63	2,220	175
1987	944	11.62	2,184	188
1988	921	11.95	2,220	186
Japan				
1969	561	8.33	2,330	279
1972	607	10.37	2,304	222
1975	601	11.55	2,033	176
1978	638	14.53	2,127	146
1981	700	15.97	2,200	138
1984	722	15.78	2,220	141
1987	742	16.51	2,179	132
1988	742	17.12	2,257	132

Note: The hours-worked figures come from the ILO which records a week as being around 43 hours in Japan. This underestimates the actual hours worked and the table therefore flatters Japanese performance.
Source: Karel Williams, Colin Haslam, John Williams and Tony Cutler, *Employment and Society* (1992).

Two major points emerge. First, the 1988 Japanese figure is 132 hours per unit compared with the Americans' 186 hours, showing the Japanese to be 41 per cent better – and even this probably overestimates the Japanese advantage because of the voluntary, unrecorded, unpaid overtime.

Second, and perhaps more important, it confirms the mass production industry's long held conviction that 'It's volume, stupid!' Throughout this 20-year period, the continually increasing Japanese production levels (between 1960 and 1989 the Japanese share of world automobile production rose from 1 to 25 per cent) correlate almost exactly with the ranking order of hours needed to build a unit. In simple terms, the more vehicles that are built the fewer hours per vehicle are needed and each person builds more vehicles per year. As volumes increase, productivity improves. When volumes decline, productivity worsens!

During periods of rapid growth it is comparatively easy to sustain productivity improvements, and young industries, with all the advantages of new facilities and practices, can readily outstrip their more mature competitors. The surprise would be if the Japanese were not more productive than anyone else: the real test comes when the mature industries learn from the newcomers.

For Karel Williams this means that while Japanese labour productivity was, for the most part, better in the assembly areas, the difference, when taking into account *all* stages of manufacturing, is not as great as many of the alarmists would suggest. Garel Rhys of Cardiff Business School calculated that the difference was about 25 per cent ('The Motor Industry: A Wider Vision', SMMT conference, 30 Sept. 1992). This is still substantial – but it is not double.

THE BURSTING OF THE BUBBLE

The research for *The Machine that Changed the World* was undertaken during Japan's boom period of the second half of the 1980s. Economic growth reached a peak of 5.6 per cent in 1990, and while, in the second half of the 1980s the strengthening of the yen was already having an adverse effect on exports this was more than compensated for by growing domestic sales fuelled by the massive profits being made by investors in real estate.

As with all such booms the end came, and though no one can really distinguish cause and effect it was probably triggered in the late 1980s by a combination of the rising value of the yen, a decline in exports and a reduction in domestic demand with a resulting reduction in profitability of the borrowers and their subsequent difficulty in repaying their loans. The banks and loan companies started to call in their loans; the borrowers were unable to repay; investment in property nose-dived; the value of the banks' assets followed; the stock market crashed; seven out of eight of the housing loan associations found they had 'non-performing' loans of 4.2 trillion yen; the value of people's savings dramatically reduced and they stopped buying; companies which had undertaken capital investment based on ever-increasing demand found they had over-capitalised and under-utilised factories; they reduced hiring and stopped spending. In 1992 growth was 0.8 per cent and in 1993 GDP declined by 0.5 per cent.

Faith in the previously rock-solid 'iron triangle' – the link between business, politics and the bureaucracy – nose-dived and many cases of previously covered up corruption came to light The cosy links between the interdependent businesses, the *keiretsu,* came to be challenged as banks put the squeeze on their blue-chip customers who in turn squeezed their suppliers – often small companies were unable to stand the pressure and went under.

The Japanese found that they were no different from other nations – they were not immune to the law of the market which says that when the trade balance is consistently in your favour your currency will strengthen and eventually make it more difficult for you to export. If a currency is artificially held at a weak level during a long period of trade surpluses, the shift, when that protection is removed, will be dramatic. That was America's intention when it sought a major currency realignment during the Plaza discussions of 1988 – and it worked!

The realisation of all this impacted on the Japanese psyche. The 1995 edition of *Contemporary Enterprises* published by *Nikkei,* the financial newspaper, contrasted its current view with that expressed in the first edition, published in 1990:

> the first edition of this book emphasised Japanese management as the source of strength for Japanese firms, and was seen as transferable all over the world. But the prolonged recession revealed that Japan's successful post-war economic system is hardly transferable and that Japanese management is only one of a number of management methods, not *the* management method.

In this they were echoing the earlier expressed views of Masamuchi Shimizu of the Japan Management Association who said, 'There are many admirable managers in Japan but if the working environment continues in the present direction, what Westerners regard as Japanese management style may not be appropriate' (*Financial Times,* 24 September 1992).

All of this had a significant impact on day-to-day corporate behaviour, but most of their central objectives have been remarkably resilient. Referring to the bull's eye of Figure 3.1 the commitments to high quality and target achievement targets remain rock solid. Product development rates have been accelerated, although there has been a significant cut-back in the number of models and options offered. Within the car industry, all companies lengthened model life and introduced far greater standardisation of parts aimed at reducing the variety by 50 per cent. MITI said that customers were no longer fooled by gimmicks and warned manufacturers that frequent model changes are an unnecessary waste of resource and labour time. The sustained desire for social respect is one of the fundamental reasons that Japanese companies have not gone in for mass compulsory redundancies.

The significant changes relate to the balance between their objectives of market share and long-term profitability. The former has long been of greater importance, for when you can sell all you can produce, are satisfied with low unit profits and are experiencing rapid growth, then profit seems to look after itself. Japanese executives (metaphorically – I think!) threw themselves off tall buildings if they lost market share but only slapped themselves on the wrist if profits went down. When life changed it was amazing how quickly profitability assumed an importance not dissimilar to that in the West. Japanese manufacturing companies have responded in the 1990s by making swingeing cuts in their cost base. Not only have they squeezed the dry towel but they have put it through a high pressure wringer!

One of their great problems, however, was that in the 1980s there a realisation that Japanese society needed to relieve the pressure and concentrate on the well-being of the population, socially as well as economically. Many initiatives were begun which started to bear fruit in the 1990s at the very time when the pressure was being released for totally different and unexpected reasons.

The Japanese government's ten-year plan for industrial and social development prepared by MITI has as its theme for the 1990s, 'Creating human values in the global age'. It proposed:

Free time for Japan's citizens to achieve their full potential according to their own choice and individuality and the opportunity to choose what to purchase and the chance to decide what to pay . . . Japan must adopt human-oriented international trade and industrial policies.

This plan does not commit anyone to anything, but it is a significant change of direction from previous plans which concentrated almost solely on industrial development.

Within manufacturing industry, this was reflected in attempts to ensure that technology serves rather than dominates. Tadaaki Jagawa, who supervised Toyota's new plant design, said:

If we don't attract workers, we don't even get to the point of worrying about waste . . . Maybe we made a mistake in designing such gloomy factories. I wish we had used more of our profit to improve working conditions. (*Financial Times*, 30 December 1990)

It was this type of thinking, combined with the increasing difficulty in the boom period of attracting workers to the 'dirty, dangerous and difficult' jobs, that caused manufacturers to begin to question some of their sacred cows.

Toyota was in the vanguard. Its first navel-gazing exercise in 1986, the Committee for Urgent Measures Against the High Yen, looked at the global strategy needed to compete in the new world. Like many Japanese exporting companies they set themselves the target of 'Be profitable at 100 yen/dollar' (in one company, I saw workers wearing '100' badges). For the most part, the pressure wringer on costs achieved this objective. With the yen now consistently above this level they are reaping the benefits. However, they are not satisfied: their long-term strategy is to become immune to exchange rate fluctuations and to this end their 1995 Global Business Plan determined that they would accelerate overseas production, decrease exports and increase the import of cars and components.

Other studies were more concerned with internal behaviour. In mid-1990 a joint management–union committee examined the problems of production workers and questioned everything that was sacred, including the very production system and methods of managing work. They even questioned the nature of production efficiency, the Personnel Department saying, 'If the number of production workers is increased, productive efficiency will be lowered. *But we should not think solely about productive efficiency.*'

The year of this statement, 1990, was the year of publication of *The Machine that Changed the World*. In that year labour turnover was 25 per cent among new recruits, 11.6 per cent of the workforce was temporary and working hours had increased from 2,224 in 1989 to 2,315!

During the 1980s Toyota began to design plants which, it hoped, would begin the move away from the 'dirty, dangerous and difficult', and in 1991, in Tahara, launched a new facility which moved away from the 'no buffer stock' edict of Taiichi Ohno. The spacious, new facility comprises eight mini-lines with a several minutes buffer at the end of each, allowing flexibility and catch-back. But they went further and spent vast amounts of money on large-scale automation, even providing for a conveyor system which can be adjusted in height by the operator to make work more comfortable. Nissan in Kyushu, Mazda in Hofu and Honda in Suzuka all moved in this direction, considerably increasing the automation levels of final assembly up to about 30 per cent. They sought to eliminate the worst of the 'dirty, dangerous and difficult' jobs, allowing, for example, the operators to adjust the height of the production line and to control the body shells to a specific pace with each being capable of being stopped at any desired location, depending on the model carried and the components to be fitted. They also improved the working environment with, variously, air conditioning, quieter working areas, employee lounges, flowers, shrubs and picture windows, even spa-type baths.

A great problem for the Japanese car manufacturers is that in seeking this capital-intensive automation route they initially forgot Taiichi Ohno's teachings about the value of low-cost automation, and certainly did not pay heed to any lessons coming out of General Motor's $50 billion experience when they found that high-tech facilities may release large numbers of plentiful and relatively low-cost workers but require almost as many scarce but high-cost workers to make them work! WJR found that it is not automation that makes for efficiency, estimating that it accounted for only about one-third of the difference in productivity:

> High-tech plants that are improperly organised end up adding as many indirect technical and service workers as they remove unskilled direct workers from the manual assembly tasks. [Frequent breakdowns] reduce the fraction of the total operating time that a plant is actually producing vehicles. (Womack *et al.*, 1990)

Significantly, Toyota's second new plant in Kyushu took the mini-lines concept further, increasing them to eleven with a five-car buffer at the end of each. However, Toyota also realised that its attempts at high-tech automation had gone too far. Operators at Tahara had experienced 'stress, feelings of estrangement and a stagnation of work motivation'. The automated facilities had taken too much space and in the new 'Worker Friendly Factory' at Kyushu they aimed for lower-cost automation which would co-exist with and be controlled by the operators. Also, in Kyushu, Toyota has attempted to humanise its personnel management by abolishing productivity pay in favour of an individual evaluation system and by abandoning its traditional 'suggestions targets' approach.

Unfortunately, these new plants were all planned during the boom and came on stream during the slump. Rarely have any of them been more than 60 per cent loaded – not unlike General Motor's Framingham plant at the time of the 'lean' comparisons. One wonders how they would have come out!

What has been the result? Statements coming from Toyota executives suggest that problems remain. Mikio Kitamo, Director of Production Engineering, said in 1992:

The real intention is how to make work easy for people. We have not been successful in replacing people with machines . . . if we do not make the work easy, we will lose people. If we make work more comfortable for people, people will stay at the plant. (*Financial Times*, 21 December 1992)

And, most significantly because he has his name above the door, Shoichiro Toyoda, chairman of Toyota Motor Corporation, wrote in the company's weekly newspaper in 1993:

In the production shops . . . [we need to consider] the development of a *new production system* . . . where it is possible to feel attraction towards manufacturing and a sense of fulfilment in connection with manufacturing.

But there is also a realisation on the part of the trade unions that in the post-bubble economy they, also, must be more circumspect. Earlier, I referred to the Japan Auto Workers Union 1992 publication, *Japanese Automobile Industry in the Future*, in which they highlighted what they called the 'triple sufferings' of the Japanese automobile industry. This 'triple sufferings' promotion was short-lived. Formulated during the boom period at a time of great labour shortages it was published when the bubble had burst. Subsequent research conducted by the Mitsubishi Research Institute on behalf of the JAWU resulted in the union recognising that the key to the future is a stable yen – but that this is beyond the union's control. Instead the JAWU is examining other measures (see box).

- Transfers within the auto industry and with other companies
- Reduced working hours
- Creation of businesses by developing new technologies
- Creation of businesses by developing high value adding products
- Deregulation of the Japanese system
- Reform of the tax system applied to automobiles
- Non-filling of vacancies caused by retirement

There is little that is new in these ideas. However, the important fact is the change of tack by the union and its recognition that times have changed. In their different ways the companies and the trade unions are coming together.

To me, the biggest manufacturing challenge of the twenty-first century, in Japan and elsewhere, will not be finding ways to replace people with machines – that will be easy – it will be to find means of combining people and machines in ways which remove the drudgery but allow people to contribute effectively to achieving high quality and improving continuously the product and the process.

Accompanying this, will be changes to Japan's 'sacred treasures'. Soichiro Honda died in August 1991 and with him went the concept eulogised in *The Honda Book of Management* (Mito, 1990) whereby the directors sat together is an open-plan office theoretically making decisions on a basis of consensus and teamwork. Yet it ended up with no one taking responsibility for decisions and a growing number of layers of middle management, with decision-making being passed up the tree. Honda's Soichiro Irimajiri said, 'We find that we have become very slow.' As with many elements of Japanese management practices, they worked very well in times of rapid growth and assured profits but when the market demands a rapid response they are less effective.

Having worked with Japanese people for thirteen years, it is clear that they do not really understand the Western ability to make rapid decisions with defined and assigned responsibility. The argument for consensus is that as everyone is involved there is commitment to the decision. While the decision might not be ideal and takes a long time to reach you can be certain that it will be fully and rapidly implemented once it has been signed off through the *ringi* process. However there are hidden problems. First, at heart, Japan remains an authoritarian society and utilises top-down decision-making, *kono,* and, as it was once put to me, consensus can be defined as, 'A method of reverential enquiry to determine that your plan is in line with what your boss desires.' Ian Gow, one of the few Japanologists who really understands Japan, emphasises the critical difference between consensus *producing* a decision and consensus *around* a decision.

Consensus can lead to the lowest common denominator solution. Because it is difficult to say 'No', the final product or solution includes a little of what everyone wanted – which is why Japanese products and solutions are often over-complex. The critical point is to have consensus before action, but once action has been taken, and something then goes wrong, it is very difficult to change. There is no clear responsible person and so many people have been involved who subsequently have to be consulted, that the reaction is slow and often indecisive. Consensus is often an excuse for inaction.

Lifetime employment (LTE) is also threatened. Interestingly, the term did not exist until 1958 when James Abegglen in his book, *The Japanese Factory*, used the words 'lifetime commitment' which were translated into Japanese as *shushin koyo* and then back into English as 'lifetime employment'!

However, LTE has never been contractual and only ever benefited adult males working full-time for a large blue-chip company, and even here, for most people, it seldom lasted beyond the age of 55. It is surrounded by a large amount of unstable peripheral employment comprising people working for small companies, sub-contractors, home-workers, casuals, and so on who can be turned off and on at the whim of the blue-chip company. A Ministry of Labour survey found in 1991 that in firms employing more than 1,000 people, half had left by age 29 and only half of university graduates stayed with their company throughout their working life. A survey on Japanese youth conducted by the Nikkei Research Institute (1990) found that 37 per cent of the Japanese workforce under 30 years of age had changed jobs at least once. Between two and a half and three million Japanese change their job every year.

In the post-boom years of the 1990s 'voluntary' retirement has been reintroduced with the target often being the 40–45-year-olds, although Japanese companies go to great lengths to protect their staff. Activities include the elimination of overtime, increased holidays, reduction in bonuses (up to 30 per cent of total earnings), bringing sub-contract work in-house and subsequently removing sub-contract labour. Temporary, seasonal and day labourers are not re-hired; regular employees are retrained and may be sent out to sell the product; many are sent to subsidiaries or sub-contractors; some are temporarily released with government subsidies paid for 'employment adjustment'; top managers take pay cuts or retire to take responsibility for the catastrophe. Following this, those who are to go are identified by the personnel department and are approached by management. None refuse!

What none of this says is that many of those who are kept on with little to do subsequently choose to resign 'voluntarily.' Those who move to sub-contractors or subsidiaries find that LTE no longer applies and, being the staff with the shortest service, they are the first people to go when the next turn of the screw comes round. The blue-chip company has maintained its policy of no compulsory redundancy but a year or so later the transferred person is just as redundant!

Virtually all of these actions were taken by Nissan when in 1993 it made the previously unheard of decision to close a major manufacturing plant, Zama, which employed some 4,500 people. It took Nissan three years to accomplish and at the end only a handful were made compulsorily redundant – everyone else accepted transfers to other plants or took voluntary retirement. The critical issue was not only to treat people well but to maintain confidence in the company. If it had been seen to be acting hastily and outside of the Japanese way, public confidence would have been lost, with disastrous consequences. Unlike the Anglo-Saxon world where a quick decision is seen as a sign of positive management, the Japanese see it as a sign of panic; and if a company panics consumer confidence rapidly disappears, bringing about the very end it seeks to avoid.

In 1994, Honda classified managers who are unable to win promotion as 'special staff' with a salary cut of 10 to 30 per cent. For those who could not accept the loss of face there were incentives to take early retirement or go to work elsewhere. In April 1993 Japanese Airlines (JAL), faced with a massive decline in international air travel, extended its early retirement programme to employees aged 35–44 and offered one year's leave of absence to managers aged over 50 to encourage them to consider a second career, but with no obligation to leave the company. However, said a JAL representative, 'We have no intention of changing our basic policy of lifetime employment.' As long as lifetime ends at the age of 44!

The main impact of the changing circumstances is, however, likely to fall on future employees who are far less likely to be offered lifetime employment. The Japanese Federation of Employers' Associations published its proposals in 1995, *Japanese Management in a New Era – Direction and Concrete Policies,* advocating that employees should be divided into three categories: – long-term employees, i.e. managers, salarymen and core production workers; professionals, i.e. those whose professional ability is valued for immediate use but without the expectation of long-term employment; and rotating employees, i.e. part-timers and temporary workers who are paid hourly to perform simple tasks.

Long-term employees and rotating employees already exist but the idea is to gradually reduce the number in the first group and create a group of highly specialised personnel such as researchers, financial analysts and so on who, it is thought, will be mobile from one company to another. The problem with this proposal is that, correctly, Japanese companies believe that these specialised jobs require detailed knowledge of the company which can only be accumulated over a long period. They have found, as have companies throughout the world, that mobile employees do not have the same allegiance and take their acquired knowledge with them to their next company. The proposal will be very difficult for the blue-chip companies to accept and, as yet, there is little evidence that it is being taken up. The subject is, however, on the agenda.

Closely linked to LTE are the seniority progression and pay systems whereby salarymen (the university graduates), expecting to stay with one company throughout their working lives, could progress upwards at regular intervals, almost irrespective of ability. Both are now severely threatened. A 1993 survey conducted by *Nihon Keizai Shinbun* on 450 major listed companies found that 80 per cent of top managers wanted to see the seniority system abolished and one-quarter wanted to do away with LTE. Takuma Yamamoto, chairman of Fujitsu, suggested that the seniority promotion system had been losing ground for several years, giving way to performance-based systems.

Seniority based pay, *nenko,* originated in the 1920s and became compulsory in the Second World War when the government insisted that all companies pay a living wage which should increase with age. At the insistence of the trade unions, ability pay was added later, as was its extension to white-collar workers and the practice that the salary gap between the highest and lowest paid should not be large. Under the *nenko* system there is no difference in base pay between skilled, semi-skilled and unskilled workers. Their view is that they all work for the same company, therefore they should all receive the same pay. However, twice yearly personal assessments can result in increases of up to 30 per cent of basic pay and do result in individual differences in salary.

The difficulty is that because the difference between the highest and the lowest paid is small neither *nenko* nor performance bonuses provide any great incentive for individual performance and often the unions negotiate the bonus which then applies to everyone irrespective of individual performance. To counter this in the post-Bubble economy some companies, for example, Honda, Fujitsu. Sony and Nissan, are introducing salary systems which comprise, for managers and white-collar workers, basic pay plus a strongly fluctuating bonus element based on individual performance. But these initial attempts have not been extended to production workers. While the slogan, 'From *nenko*-based pay to ability-based pay' is constantly pushed, there are, as yet, few companies which have gone very far down this road. Particularly at a time when there have been considerable reductions in overtime, anything that can cause even greater variability in pay is resisted by the trade unions.

Nobuhiko Kawamoto, Honda's President, recognises that Japanese business must change:

The traditional Japanese system is now in direct conflict with the competitiveness system of the Western world. Therefore, we have to survive through this period of harsh competition and yet maintain the good features of the Japanese tradition. We want to give the next generation something to hope for! (*Financial Times*, 19 July 1994)

But the next generation is impatient. Japan has seen the emergence of the s*hinjinru*, the younger generation, who did not experience the post-war privations and now want to share the benefits.

Perhaps the greatest indication of change though is that until very recently few had heard a Japanese equivalent of the Western idiom, 'Thank God it's Friday', or POETS – 'Push off early, tomorrow's Saturday'. In late 1993 a Japanese colleague told me there was now a Japanese equivalent, *Hana no kinyobi* – Friday's the greatest. Maybe there is hope for the West!

THE WAY FORWARD

There remains considerable strength in the Japanese manufacturing system. 'Leanness' is a valuable concept from which the West can greatly benefit. It does result in increases in labour productivity but by nowhere near as much as the extreme advocates would claim. It does place strains on the workforce but by nowhere near as much as the extreme antagonists would argue. It *is* possible to criticise lean production constructively while at the same time answering many of the extreme criticisms; and it *is* possible to find a way through so that both the company and all the people who work for it can experience the potential benefits without too much of the potential pain.

Leanness is, however, much more than simply eliminating waste. The whole value stream has to be integrated and organised on lean principles, bringing products and services from initial concept to delivery to the customer, across all the different organisations, activities and functions that may be involved. It requires developing the concept of partnership sourcing leading to much greater supplier capability particularly in the field of product development and engineering. It requires a sharing of the profit and the pain; being prepared for open book costing and working together for mutual benefit. Exactly the same principles extend forward to the distribution chain and eventually to the end customer so that the whole system is driven by end customer orders which are quickly incorporated into the production schedules.

These latter themes were subsequently developed by two of the authors, James Womack and Dan Jones, in their second book, *Lean Thinking* (1996). The principles are not greatly different but the value in this second book is the emphasis they place on *kaikaku,* radical improvement, which adds to the concept of *kaizen.* Though using a Japanese term, radical improvement is normally associated with the West; it is the initial radical change that can give immediate benefits and, perhaps, inspire the people to greater things.

The real strength comes from a combination of *kaikaku* and *kaizen.*

THE IMPACT ON PEOPLE

WJR say very little about the impact of lean production on people but they recognise that you cannot have a dynamic work team undertaking these responsibilities unless there is a genuine sense of reciprocal obligations. Management must value its workers, make sacrifices to retain them in the difficult times and be willing to delegate responsibility. In contrasting lean production with mass production, they also say, 'While the mass production plant is often filled with mind-numbing stress, as workers struggle to assemble unmanufacturable products and have no way to improve their working environment, lean production offers a creative tension in which workers have many ways to address challenges.'

But the heart of the people issues is contained in their comments on teamworking:

The truly lean plant has two key organisational features: It transfers the maximum number of tasks and responsibilities to those workers actually adding value to the car on the line, and it has in place a system for detecting defects that quickly traces every problem, once discovered, to its ultimate cause.

This in turn, means teamwork among line workers and a simple but comprehensive information display system that makes it possible for everyone in the plant to respond quickly to problems and to understand the plant's overall situation . . .

So in the end, it is dynamic teamwork that emerges as the heart of the lean factory. Building these efficient teams is not simple. First, workers need to be taught a wide variety of skills – in fact, all the jobs in their work group so that tasks can be rotated and workers can fill in for each other. Workers then need to acquire many additional skills: simple

machine repair, quality checking, housekeeping, and materials ordering. Then they need encouragement to think actively, indeed
*pro*actively, so they can devise solutions before problems become
serious. (Womack *et al.*, 1990)

Current thinking and practice in many countries seeks to involve the
workforce in determining how their work is done, implementing
teamworking, devolving responsibility to the front-line staff, and so on,
but such concepts are not unique to lean production. The heart of lean
production is not teamworking but the elimination of waste.

Central to the WJR thesis is the view that lean production is different
from mass production, and while it is true that in many industries flexible
production is the order of the day the physical task for the vast majority
of people either does not dramatically change or, if it does, it is a result of
technological change rather than any change in managerial concepts and
practices. The front-line worker may have a greater responsibility for
influencing how the job is done, may have greater responsibility for
quality, may be involved in small group activities and group working but
by far the greatest percentage of that person's time must be spent in the
routine task. Jobs and responsibilities may have expanded and forward-
thinking managers speak of using people's brains as well as their hands
but the schedule must be met and the best way to achieve the schedule at
the required quality is by insisting on specific tasks to be performed in a
specific way in a specific place in a specific time. This is the Japanese way;
it is Taylorism writ large except that, as we have seen, the Japanese way
seeks to use the brain as well as the hands.

But having said that, a very small proportion of the worker's time is
spent improving the way the job is done. By far the greatest proportion,
well in excess of 95 per cent, is spent actually doing it. Despite the fact
that an individual may have been responsible for achieving an
improvement in productivity he or she must follow the standard
operation, the clearly defined one best way.

In fact, it is not unreasonable to say that lean production is simply
mass production – but smarter. The extreme critics would add, 'and
harder'! And there is some truth in this. The Japanese certainly do work
at a steadier pace and have fewer 'breathers' than their Western
counterparts.

There can be no doubt that in the vast majority of companies
throughout the world a dose of leanness is absolutely necessary. I referred
earlier to the Japanese objective of ensuring 60 seconds of added-value
work every minute, and when companies are achieving less than 30

seconds of added-value a minute – as is the case in much of the world's industry – vast improvements are there to be gained. However, when a company is already at very high levels of efficiency, as is the case with the Japanese and a small number of US and European plants, marginal improvements are not only very difficult to attain but often can only be achieved at the expense of the operators.

For example, a person with a 60-second job cycle may spend five seconds walking to collect a component, five seconds selecting it from a pallet and ten seconds walking back, before spending 40 seconds actually fitting the component. Of that 40 seconds, some 10 seconds might be 'waste' in that the operator conned the industrial engineer while he was being studied. Thus, of the 60-second cycle only 30 seconds is genuinely adding value.

The task is to eliminate the 30 seconds waste.

By relocating the stock and placing it at waist height the 20 seconds may be reduced to five; and because the operator is committed to improving efficiency, he voluntarily gives up 'his' ten seconds; therefore the total waste may be reduced from 30 seconds to five. Then, through the *kaizen* process it may be possible to identify improvements that can be made to the 'real' work by, for example, designing a shuttle whereby the material is automatically placed in the required position without being handled at all. This may eliminate the remaining five seconds of handling so that 'real' work now comprises the desired 60 seconds in a minute. The whole team may be involved in similar activities and while for a short period this 'free' time will accrue to the individuals the principle of the elimination of waste requires that 'savings' be gathered together, the work reallocated and the team either takes on more work or loses a member.

The end result is that each element of the cycle may be 'easier' but that each operator ends up with more of the 'easier' elements. Thus, they now have far more elements and the resulting pressure is no less, and may be greater. A mistake of the advocates of the elimination of waste is to believe that it always makes the jobs easier. They do not appreciate what I call the 'pressure equation':

$$\textbf{Pressure} = \textbf{Effort} \times \textbf{Incidence}$$

In simple terms, if I have a difficult task it may take me two minutes to complete and I can perform thirty cycles an hour. If the degree of difficulty is reduced it may become possible to complete the task in one minute. For a while I may enjoy the benefit of the newly available time, but eventually I will be required to increase the number of cycles to sixty per hour. Effort has reduced but incidence has increased and the 'pressure' may well be the same. The end result will depend on the balance between the two. Of course, life is much more complex – the additional work I am given may be either easier or harder, but the principle is valid. The failure to recognise and act on this 'pressure equation' can lead to increasing levels of high intensity repetitive work which can physically damage those subject to increasing levels of leanness.

I have no truck with those critics who equate teamworking with 'management by stress', but I do understand those who are concerned that one of the potentially most serious problems associated with leanness is the growing incidence of physical disorders, generally under the headings of repetitive strain injuries, work-related upper-limb disorders or cumulative trauma disorders. In the United States the writings of the Fucinis published in 1990 highlighted experiences in Mazda's Flat Rock, Michigan plant where in its early days carpal tunnel syndrome injuries were running at a level three times higher than at comparable American plants.

Nissan in the UK is one of the leanest automobile manufacturers in the world and builds more cars per employee than any other car plant in Europe (73.2 against Toyota's 66.9, Fiat Melfi's 50.0 and Rover Longbridge's 28.2. Source: Economist Intelligence Unit 1997). I will always regard one of my most significant contributions as being the early recognition of these potential problems associated with leanness – particularly as in Japan the issue was not seriously addressed until around 1994. As a result we determined that the potential problems should not become actual problems and established a formal policy that:

> The ergonomics of building a car will be a fundamental factor in the original design, engineering and specification of the product, facility, tooling and processes. Such factors will be included in all changes, improvements and *kaizen* activities.

Of course, establishing a policy, by itself, achieves nothing. It is only when that policy is translated into action that its impact is felt and those actions have to be both preventive and remedial.

The key is prevention and this is achieved by attention to all of the following actions:

- *Design for ease of manufacture,* eliminating the potentially difficult tasks at the design stage. In particular, this requires the design engineers to understand the manufacturing process, to be there on the line to appreciate how it feels to perform the repetitive task hour after hour. But it also requires a procedure whereby the manufacturing staff have an input into the design process, identifying difficult tasks in a particular model and ensuring that such tasks are not carried over to the next. Once a product is designed, marginal changes can be made to current models but some 90 per cent is fixed and rarely are fundamental changes possible.

- *Design the facilities for ease of working* so as to ensure that they are as easy to operate as possible and do not place unnecessary strains on the operators. Tools, jigs, material, working heights, etc. must always be carefully thought out and balanced so that strain is minimised Again, the facilities engineers need an appreciation of the way the job is done and the manufacturing people need an input into the design process. One of the great deficiencies in the training of engineers is an appreciation of ergonomics – this has to be remedied if the demands of lean production are not to be so great that its full potential is unrealised.

- *Design the tasks ergonomically* so that they are easy to perform. This can only be properly achieved by fully involving the people doing the job but to be successful they need to have an understanding of ergonomics. At one stage we involved a professional ergonomist but found that his analytical tools were so complex that only a professional ergonomist could use them. The solution was to ask a small group comprising engineers, production supervisors, safety people and trainers to come up with a tool which was sound but also sufficiently user-friendly that it could be used by 250 supervisors, not by one ergonomist. It took them more than six months to get it right but they achieved a result which is now in wide use throughout the company.

- *Education is vital,* for many people take a delight in performing the tough jobs. Often, in the early days, aids and devices would be introduced to make the job easier but would not be used, often because it took time to learn to use them properly or because they had been designed without a full understanding of user requirements. The employment of physiotherapists was vital, not simply to correct actual

[handwritten margin note: job rotation to stop rep. strain injury]

problems but to educate the supervisors and operators in the impact of tasks on the people.

Prevention is better than cure but you have to deal with both the current situation and the problems that slip through the net. Remedial activities include ergonomic analysis and modification of difficult tasks; regular job rotation so that individuals are not constantly using one set of muscles to the exclusion of others; movement away from the repetitive tasks and hiring mainly on to the repetitive tasks. These latter actions challenged some of Nissan's sacred cows. It was originally thought that people had to stay on a specific job for a long time to develop the ability to perform it consistently at the right quality and speed. We subsequently found that rapid (around two-hour) rotations work just as well, provided that the rotation pattern is determined by the people doing the jobs, because only they fully understand the problems and personalities.

It was always a sacred cow that supervisors had the right to select their own teams from external applicants but it was determined that we should externally hire mainly on to the repetitive, line-paced jobs and that supervisors in the more desirable areas should select people who were already employed and who had spent a long time on these jobs. The initial view of these supervisors was that their freedom of choice was being restricted – and so it was – but a realisation that someone who has performed well on a line-paced job for several years must be pretty good, plus a little 'encouragement' when needed, quickly integrated the new concept.

The essential point is that lean production systems can lead to problems and it is no use a management pretending otherwise. The trick is to realise this and to take action to prevent the potential problems becoming actual problems.

So, what comes out of all this?

Lean production is not some fiendish plot dreamt up by capitalist managers out to screw the workforce, nor is it the answer to Western manufacturing ills. It must be managed sensibly, not by squeezing out every last drop of blood but by genuinely involving the people doing the job in ways which not only enhance performance but also make their working lives more fulfilling; by demonstrating that their views count and that management has a genuine concern for all the people. By showing respect for everyone and offering security. By providing for the continuous development of everyone in the company.

To me that is all simple common sense.

4 Conclusions – and Beginnings

If a man will begin with certainties he shall end in doubts, but if he will be content to begin with doubts, he shall end in certainties.
Francis Bacon [1561–1626], *Advancement of Learning*

CONCLUSIONS – SO FAR

Mature industrial societies are subject to many long-term and fundamental macro changes – global competition, accelerating technological change, a shift from manufacturing to service and from the collective to the individual, a changing employment structure – all of which are having a major impact on the behaviour of organisations. Competitive advantage based on products or technology is rarely sustainable and high quality is now taken for granted. These economies cannot compete with the emerging countries on cost and price and are increasingly producing or buying where costs are lowest while maintaining their established brand names. Continuing success for the mature economies depends increasingly on quality *plus* service *plus* price *plus* innovation *plus* speed. Those who are content to continue in the same old way, will, with a few exceptions, lose out. But even those few – Rolls Royce, Scottish malt whiskey distillers, French vineyards, Italian ceramicists and the like – are having to change many aspects of their purchasing, manufacturing and marketing.

There is, no longer, any place to hide. We are all subject to the performance of the best, wherever it my occur in the world. As a result there is no longer any right size or structure for an organisation – there are only well or badly managed organisations, be they large or small, diversified or centralised with current fashion dictating that diversification is 'in'.

Employment is more volatile with the growth areas being in the service sectors – however defined. The growth of small businesses is accelerating as large companies divest themselves both of non-core activities and of people who, if they are unable to find new employment, increasingly establish their own business. Developments in personal computers and telecommunications allow people to work from home and still maintain contact with colleagues and customers. Full-time, 'nine to five' permanent employment is now a minority activity. Those who lack the necessary skills to be employable or self-employed will join the growing ranks of the non-employable dependent on state benefits.

The emerging consensus is that the ability to create employment depends on a balance between high-quality education and training, entrepreneurship and a dynamic labour market. Success in organisations is dependent on the leadership, quality and motivation of people.

If this is the case, what conclusions emerge so far that will help us in managing our organisations?

1. Taylorism is not dead, for we still have division of labour, standard operations and the 'one best method'; in short, control of the processes. Taylor (1911) emphasised the elimination of waste, so did Taiichi Ohno. Taylor advocated 'The deliberate gathering in of all the great mass of traditional knowledge' and so does *kaizen*. In such an environment people are expected to use their hands, not their brains, leading to alienation and institutionalised conflict. The workplace can become a battleground with many adversarial groups, none of whom work together for the common good.

2. The Japanese continuous improvement cycle is fundamental to their success. Many elements of this cycle are similar to Taylorism but the critical difference is that under Taylorism the process belongs to management whereas under the Japanese it belongs to the people doing the job. *Kaizen* is built on the fact that the people doing a job know more about that job than anyone else and it is a management responsibility to create the environment in which that knowledge is brought out and used for the benefit of the people and the organisation. Waste has to be eliminated, wherever it occurs, and it is the people doing the job who are best equipped to achieve this.

3. However, *kaizen* by itself is not enough. For poor-performing companies, regular, small-step improvements will not get them out of the basement. They need radical improvements, *kaikaku*. Equally, even good companies require radical changes which will break the mould.

4. 'Control of the processes' has to go beyond the physical process and reach into the business processes. Whether the business processes are about the recruitment of staff, the sequence of developing and introducing product changes, the arrangements for the supply and delivery of components or the method of assessing the performance

of suppliers, they must be under control. However, it is not unthinking control. The individual must be able to influence the way the job is done. Different people have different ways and the trick is to achieve the right balance.

5. Companies have to improve both radically and continuously, to always be evolutionary and, periodically, revolutionary. Fundamental questions have to be asked about the organisation structure, systems, processes and products, but once changes are made they must be continuously developed – if not, there will be decline.

6. The moving assembly line is still with us and, for mass production, no one has yet found an alternative which, economically, can achieve both the same quality and productivity.

7. Technological advances are, however, allowing moves away from line-paced assembly work, except for the most intensive mass-produced products. Flexible manufacturing cells can expand the range of responsibilities and are allowing individual workers to have more control over their work. Flexible manufacturing processes are allowing customised production at almost the same cost as mass production. 'One of a kind' or mass customisation is technically possible and will increasingly become the norm.

8. The work of the behavioural scientists demonstrates that people are not motivated by bread alone. Once a person has a job then actual pay levels are not the prime motivators. Being able to contribute, exercise discretion and to influence become important, and people respond positively when their efforts are recognised. The corollary is that people who are not trusted will behave accordingly. Different people have different goals and react in different ways. Many now wish to move beyond 'self-actualisation' and give of themselves to the wider community. The link between the social and technical factors in the workplace and their relation to their external environment is profound. If people are not positively led and stimulated, it is easy for them to regress and adopt norms of behaviour which are not conducive to the mutual success of the individual and the enterprise. Imposed change is invariably resisted. The work of Victor Vroom (1964) teaches us that people will work hard if they see that they will benefit. If not, their enthusiasm will be greatly diminished.

9. Work can be divided into the 'prescribed' and the 'discretionary' and it is a managerial task to ensure that the prescribed elements are performed with the maximum effectiveness and the discretionary elements are optimised. Japanese practices add a new dimension to

the prescribed tasks. Teamworking, problem-solving, continuous improvement and quality built in at source, allow us to move from the alienated worker and create more fulfilling, meaningful jobs. Involving people beyond the routine provides an essential stimulus to high levels of co-operation.

10. For many the basic task is unchanged, and while there may be significant modifications to the way work is structured, and the involvement of employees greatly expanded, the fact of the routine, repetitive job has not gone away. We are moving into an era of lean, volume production. I use the word 'volume' deliberately because new technology allows us to produce numerous varieties from a common base.

11. Automation of complex or troublesome manual processes as the solution for the problems may lead to expensive failures. Simplification before automation may eliminate the need to automate, but if the need remains then at least the automated process stands a greater chance of success. Use the most appropriate technology, not necessarily the most advanced. Low-cost automation can work wonders. Always have regard to the interface between the people and the technology so that the people are able to influence what goes on. Consider also that great benefits can come from restructuring the processes before automation is even considered.

12. The introduction of new technology can mean the elimination of much difficult and tedious physical work but can also de-skill, creating another type of routine task. On the other hand, it can create an environment in which the operator is able, if allowed, to contribute way beyond the routine and in so doing develop and utilise new levels of knowledge and capabilities. Lean, volume production can develop into lean, people-centred, volume production. Far too often, technology is introduced without thinking of the people who will use it or without providing proper training. As a result fear sets in and it is resisted. When introduced properly, new technology becomes just another tool. The biggest manufacturing challenge of the twenty-first century will not be finding ways to replace people with machines, it will be to find means of combining people and machines in ways which remove the drudgery but allow people to contribute effectively to achieving high quality and to improving continuously the product, the process and the quality of their life.

13. Japanese production systems have over the last thirty years or so achieved higher quality and productivity levels than those of the

West but in many respects the West has now learned from the best of Japanese practices and is catching up. Japan is not an industrial Lourdes where a few days worshipping at the shrine will bring about the miracle cure. The West, when it sought uncritically to emulate Japan, was aiming at a target which in many respects was moving towards it. The Japanese, however, have not yet learned from the West's specific expertise, particularly financial control, the clear definition of responsibility, the importance of product planning and marketing and the ability to make rapid decisions when necessary.

14. The elimination of waste does stretch the system and, if undertaken in isolation and taken to extremes, can create unacceptable pressures. This is true whether the waste is excessive people, activities, space, time or stock. Just-in-time systems are sensitive and fragile, and susceptible to delays and interruptions when small problems can have a disproportionate effect on the whole operation. The elimination of waste, in removing the easy jobs, can create problems for the future as operators become less capable of handling those jobs which remain. There is, increasingly, no place to hide.

15. Much of Japanese success is due to factors such as their long working hours, the pressure to conform, the previously undervalued yen and a tied supplier base which does not offer the benefits of the blue-chip companies but provides a cushion in the hard times. However, in design for manufacture, employee involvement, work-force experience and continuous improvement they are well ahead of the West. In many areas, particularly in the <u>service sector</u> and administration, Japan's efficiency and effectiveness are way behind the West. There are high levels of disguised unemployment.

lean needs to be able for service.

16. Japan's manufacturing is subject to new financial, cultural and social pressures and is undergoing significant changes. The sacred treasures of lifetime employment, seniority progression systems, enterprise trade unions and consensus are under strain and, while they will remain for a long time to come, there will be gradual modifications. At the same time Japanese workers, particularly the young, are seeking the fruits of their labours, but are doing so at a time when corporate Japan is least able to satisfy them.

17. The critics are right when they highlight the problems if management attends solely to the short-term productivity and financial goals of what is a holistic system. However, those who denigrate the total system appear to do so from a political point of view which wishes to see capitalism collapse. Further, when they argue that these techniques are simply attempts to undermine trade unions,

they fail to realise that their loss of influence is not due to anti-unionism on the part of management but their own failure to adjust to the new environment.

18. In some respects trade union influence will be strong in the short term when they seek to criticise but, as employees come to recognise that their success and security are integrated with that of the company, the role of the unions needs to change. Long-term influence can best be achieved if they recognise that the prosperity and security of the company and employees are bound together and that they should work within the system, seeking to minimise the potential excesses and ensuring that the benefits are properly shared. They are more likely to participate constructively if they are brought into the change process than if they are left outside.

19. Most managers are ill-equipped to cope with these changes. They fear to devolve responsibility because they believe that if they do, their own responsibility will diminish. Those who have been brought up to control find it difficult to motivate. Therefore, they frequently seek to suppress initiative. If they are to facilitate the change process they must learn that devolving responsibility may alter their role but not necessarily diminish it. It becomes a top management responsibility to equip middle managers to handle the change process and this can best be achieved if they are intimately involved.

20. There will always be mavericks – that is, organisations and people who break all the rules. Many fail and a few succeed, but those who do succeed, often do so spectacularly. They are the small groups given their head within a large organisation, or it may be the whole organisation. Virgin Atlantic, Body Shop, Microsoft and 3M are organisations which in their various ways have done things differently and succeeded. People Express and Laker Airways failed, not necessarily through their own fault.

These conclusions are, at this stage, simplifications and the detail will emerge as we progress through subsequent chapters. However, it is these conclusions, together with the long-term changes taking place in Western industrial society, which led me to the simple model of the ascendant organisation described in Chapter 1. However, life is not that simple, and my second 'Eureka' moment came when my friend and colleague, Barry Venter, Managing Director of Organisation Development International, suggested that the model needed four axes. Together, we developed what we came to call the Nine Alpha Organisation Map as shown in Figure 4.1.

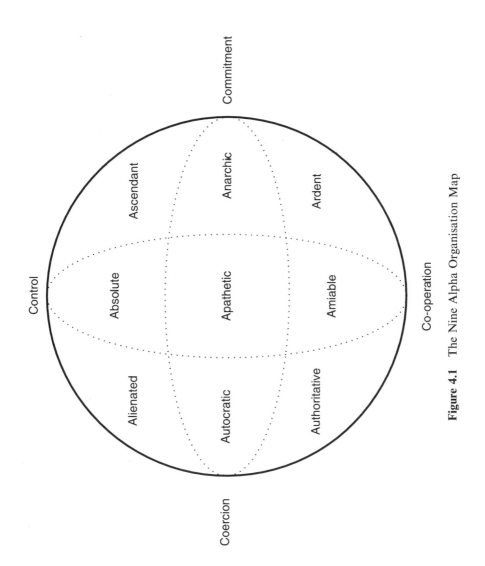

Figure 4.1 The Nine Alpha Organisation Map

THE NINE ALPHA ORGANISATION MAP

Because I had started with four 'A's in the simple model, we sought to continue the alliteration and with just a little licence believe we succeeded, but as Humpty Dumpty said to Alice, 'When I use a word it means just what I choose it to mean – neither more nor less.'

The positions on the map are still simplifications. They are not absolutes, do not sit precisely on the axes, they overlap, and their shapes will not be precisely as shown. 'Apathetic', for example, is most likely to be an irregular oval, off-centred to the upper left.

Just as there are no straight lines in nature so there are few direct links between the organisation types. It is not necessary to pass through an adjacent type to reach your destination. The map suffers from the deficiencies of all two-dimensional representations when a more realistic representation would be a globe with routes both around the surface and through it.

The Axes

Turning to the map, there are four axes: Control, Coercion, Co-operation and Commitment. The central point is 'low' and the intensity increases as the organisation progresses to the outer point of each axis. The definitions of the axes are:

Control	Top-down imposition of standards, rules, procedures and processes. Command and direction are the normal methods of determining behaviour and achieving results.
Coercion	Exercise of authority, and pressure to conform with the demands of those in 'superior' positions. Compels obedience, often with the threat of sanctions.
Commitment	Internalised individual belief in the values and objectives of the organisation and/or self. Highly motivated to work to achieve these objectives.
Co-operation	Working with others to achieve shared goals which will normally be those of the organisation.

The axes are, in part, a reflection of the work of the behavioural scientists. McGregor in his 'Theory Y' assumed a commitment to objectives and contrasted it with control. 'If [commitment] is large, many conventional external controls will be relatively superfluous and to some extent self defeating.' In his studies at the Hawthorne Plant Elton, Mayo contrasted the previous coercion with the co-operation of the operators who 'became a team and the team gave itself wholeheartedly and spontaneously to co-operation in the experiment'.

The Organisation Types

Organisation types are determined by the balance between the axes. Definitions become clearer the further out to the extremes the balance lies.

Apathetic

There is virtually no commitment or co-operation. There may be some attempt at control and, perhaps, a little coercion by someone who seeks unsuccessfully to be strong. But because of the arbitrary nature of such attempts and the lack of commitment, the organisation is switched off. There is no central respected authority. Such organisations may include large public sector organisations in which there is no pressure to perform and, as long as you are not caught with your fingers in the till, you have a job for life (before public sector readers complain, remember this is a general observation and it does still apply in many countries); comfortable private sector companies sure of their market and profits, and any organisation which lacks leadership, a sense of direction and clear goals. Neither the management nor the workforce greatly cares, either about the organisation or each other.

Some organisations which consider they are already very good do not know or understand the standards that are being achieved by their competitors let alone appreciate what the very best in other spheres are doing. They kid themselves that they are 'world-class' when the world has left them behind. Over-confidence breeds apathy. IBM in the 1970s was the supreme example.

Absolute

An absolute organisation requires a high level of control by the rules and procedures, with little room for flexibility: for example, an organisation in which there is a high risk potential – a nuclear power station; or externally imposed standards – an audit practice, or a requirement for consistent standards such as a microchip manufacturer. High levels of technical training to clearly defined standards are evident. Such an organisation can extend out to alienation if it combines with high levels of coercion and zero discretion, or can move to ascendant if individual contributions are allowed and valued.

Alienated

The alienated organisation combines high levels of coercion and control. From the top it imposes rules and procedures with no attempt to involve people or obtain their co-operation except by edict. Its management style overlaps with the autocratic but those in charge do not have the individual power of the true autocrat. It often leads to staff indulging in activities aimed at restricting individual performance or undermining the organisation. Examples include line-paced assembly work where individual contributions are ignored, a textile factory based on piece-work, time-driven project groups and organisations in which low-calibre managers care only about results and little about people. Labour turnover is high and skills development low.

Autocratic

Autocratic organisations display a high level of coercion with some rules and procedures but little commitment. Enforcement depends on bullying and the whim of those in charge. In its milder versions it may move towards apathy or, if there is an attempt to restrict the excesses by having the bullies operate within rules, to authoritarianism. Autocratic organisations may include those with an owner-manager or a strong chief executive who seeks to ignore formal structures or change them to suit their preferences. They retain the right to hire and fire. Most car manufacturers have in the past been autocratic and some still are. Large organisations with corporate bureaucracies now temper the excesses of potentially extreme chief executives and in the late 1990s such an organisation is more likely to be small or medium-sized and can exist in any sector.

Authoritarian

The authoritarian organisation achieves a good level of co-operation based on legitimate authority and respect resulting from an acceptance of the knowledge and position of the leaders. This legitimacy may, however, lead to an element of coercion on the basis of 'the boss knows best' but not necessarily in a vindictive way. It may include organisations dependent on the knowledge and capability of the founder/leader. Authoritarian organisations can be 'benevolently autocratic' and can combine this with strong elements of ascendancy or shift to the autocratic depending on the behaviour of the leaders. Margaret Thatcher's government began by being authoritarian and then drifted to the autocratic.

Amiable

The amiable organisation has a high level of co-operation, and is more likely to tend to commitment than to coercion, although in some such organisations the pressures of a few might result in a small amount of 'acceptable' coercion. It may include the voluntary caring organisation or club led by enthusiasts, in which participants' dedication is more to the activity and colleagues than to the bureaucracy. At one extreme there may be few rules, in which case it is easy to drift to anarchy; at the other the rules may be absolute, for example, the golf club. In the business world the amiable organisation may include the small, relaxed company content with its position in the market place.

It may also include companies which are well on the way to becoming ascendant. Such companies which combine control and commitment can also be good and friendly places to work.

Ardent

The ardent organisation has high levels of individual commitment with a high degree of acceptance of the corporate goals. Such organisations are eager, zealous and fervent and like to see themselves as highly flexible and not restricted by top-down controls and rules.

Some such organisations have charismatic founder/leaders such as Richard Branson of Virgin or Anita Roddick of The Body Shop, and many, encouraged by the advocacy of popular writers, would like to see themselves in this category – but few attain this goal. It is easy to drift into anarchy, and as such organisations grow they find they need controls to prevent this happening. The big question is whether they become ascendant (and many ascendant organisations achieve a high score on this axis) or autocratic. If they fail they can also fall into apathy. Such organisations may also include the creative boutiques, niche companies and the inspirational businesses dependent on keeping ahead of the game.

Anarchic

The anarchic organisation has high levels of individual commitment but virtually no control or co-operation. People do what they, individually, think is right for the organisation or themselves without much concern for any corporate objectives or for others. It is also easy for anarchic organisations to become apathetic when people realise that no one really cares, or to crash into autocracy as someone determines that the organisation needs to be shaken up and sorted out. Such organisations may include sales companies operating on the edge of the legally acceptable, brokerages working on commission, creative businesses in which it is everyone for themselves or any organisation in which management has lost control.

The ascendant organisation can display some anarchic tendencies if control and commitment are not properly balanced and it is not unusual to find this axis scoring more highly than absolute, alienated and authoritarian. A little anarchy is no bad thing but too much can be destructive.

Ascendant

The ascendant organisation combines high control of the processes and a high degree of commitment of the people. People control their own processes and are responsible for maintaining and improving them. Ascendant organisations are positively led by people who care about all the stakeholders and who seek to align the objectives of the organisation. They have an understood, shared culture which permeates all behaviour and ensures equity of treatment throughout. Responsibility is genuinely devolved, allowing individuals, within the accepted framework, to be creative and make their own inputs. Such organisations combine the best of all cultures and can appear almost anywhere. There is little overlap between the anarchic and apathetic organisations and the ascendant: but absolute, authoritarian and ardent can move 'through the globe' to the ascendant.

It is not to be supposed that becoming an ascendant organisation is the only desirable state. Apart from alienation and apathy there is something to be said in favour of all other organisation types, and in some business sectors, the ardent, authoritarian and amiable organisations can be highly desirable. At other times, absolute and autocratic may work well or be necessary transitional steps. Nor do I wish to imply that organisations cannot be successful unless they are ascendant. There will always be examples of the autocratic company, the amiable caring organisation or the ardent innovator which are extremely successful.

Similarly an organisation may comprise units of different organisational types. Whether this is good or bad depends on the overall objectives and whether it is by accident or design. For example, if marketing and product development are ardent, production is autocratic and personnel authoritarian, is the organisation as a whole anarchic or ascendant? When discussing leadership I shall show that a key responsibility of a leader is to align the organisation. Whether this is achieved by consistent or diverse behaviour is a decision for each organisation. The important point is that it must be a conscious decision and not just happen accidentally.

However, I do believe that all organisations which succeed and grow move towards the ascendant. Remember the definition of ascendant – 'rising towards the zenith'. It is about progression towards a condition, not an absolute. The most successful ardent organisations, for example, Body Shop, Virgin Atlantic and Microsoft, stay in business because they manage to introduce controls without losing the commitment of the people. In the mid-1990s Body Shop hired over seventy professional managers to bring in the controls that would balance the inspirational leadership of Anita Roddick. It worked because they selected people who combined their professionalism with the commitment to the spirit of the company. The most successful initially absolute organisations, for example, British Nuclear Fuels, Toyota and Coopers and Lybrand, stay in business because they manage to generate commitment without losing their controls.

The task of Part II, 'Know-How', will be to show how organisations can move to becoming ascendant by ensuring that they maintain the balance between control of the processes and commitment of the people.

ASSESSING YOUR OWN ORGANISATION

However, before we move on, you may wish to know your own starting-point and this leads to questions such as 'Where does my company fit?', 'What sort of organisation are we?' and so on. Following publication of the first edition of this book and numerous requests for guidance, my colleagues in Organisation Development International developed a questionnaire to help organisations discover where they are. We have found that no organisation is solely in one segment; its 'footprint' will overlap several segments and it is its overall shape and position which is important.

The importance of determining your footprint is not its precision, although your eventually agreed footprint will be very accurate. As the Japanese would say, the process is often more important than the results; and the process for discovering the footprint of your own organisation, to be meaningful, must involve a representative cross-section of people from all levels of your organisation (especially top executives) and include people from all functions and business units. In particular, if you are unionised, trade union representatives must be involved.

The process begins with a full presentation of the concept and associated behaviours by an external facilitator. Then, with a good understanding under their belts, participants first complete the questionnaire individually and prepare their own footprint. They then, in small groups of peers, seek a consensus. Following this, everyone comes together with the facilitator who compares all the results and leads an examination of the perceptions, exploring both the differences and consistencies, and seeking a consensus as to where they are now and, most important, where they wish to be. Once this is achieved it is the group's responsibility to establish its priorities and determine the way forward.

This is a demanding exercise which can take around a couple of days; but in the great scheme of things this is a comparatively short period and time well spent. In any change programme it is vital to share a perception of where you are now and to agree where you want to be, and to get there in two days is brilliant. In most such exercises I have found that there are widely differing perceptions of the current position but a high level of agreement on 'where we want to be'. When you reach this point you already have a high degree of 'ownership' and that is not a bad start to a change programme. The difficult part, implementation, then begins.

For obvious reasons this process must involve an external facilitator – you cannot achieve the proper level of debate if it is conducted by an insider, who will come with preconditioned perceptions and other baggage and will not always be trusted by all participants. The facilitator can ask the difficult questions of people from all levels which the insider would not dare broach.

I give in Appendix Two the questionnaire and assessment techniques which can be used to achieve this end (and must draw your attention to the copyright statement and restrictions on its use).

Confidentiality prevents me from giving examples from named organisations but I give below two end results, the first from a company which is well on the way to becoming ascendant and the second from the other end of the spectrum.

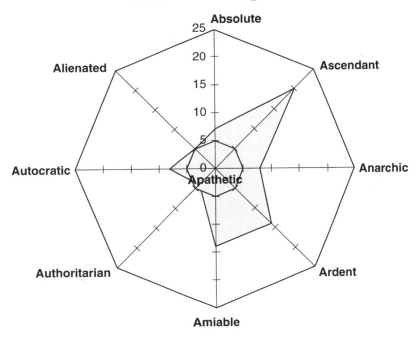

Figure 4.2(a)   An Ascendant Organisation Nine Alpha Organisation Footprint

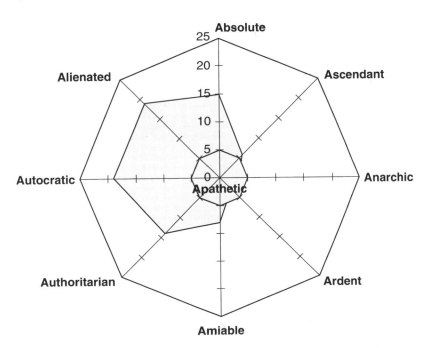

Figure 4.2(b)   An Alienated Organisation Nine Alpha Organisation Footprint

Now, if you wish to undertake a personal assessment of your own organisation, turn to Appendix Two, which gives the questionnaire and full instructions for its completion.

Please send your completed 'footprint' to me at the address given on page xiv. I will be pleased to discuss any points which arise.

PART II

'Know-How'

5 Culture, Vision, Mission – Whatever You Call It

When there is no vision the people perish.
Franklin Delano Roosevelt, Inaugural Speech, 4 March 1933
(From *Proverbs* 29:18)

When Captain Cook asked the Chiefs of Tahiti why they ate apart from women, they looked at him in wonder and disbelief at such a foolish question. They thought and thought, and finally one offered the only explanation they had: 'Because it is right.'

Anonymous

CULTURE

Every organisation has a culture – even those which have never heard the word. The chief executive or owner/manager who says 'We don't bother with culture statements in our company, we all know what we've got to do. We don't want any of that fancy consultant stuff' is directly expressing the company's culture.

In most societies the culture is instinctive, whether we speak of the chiefs of Tahiti or Wall Street financiers. It is not overtly taught or imposed; it is absorbed and constantly reinforced by our behaving in broadly the same way as our colleagues. The difference in recent years is that many organisations have consciously attempted to define their culture and write it down and, in so doing, often produced a glorious mish-mash of culture, goals, strategies, aspirations and values, with each getting in the other's way. Often, the end result is called 'Our Vision' or 'Our Mission'.

In July 1993 Lou Gerstner, the new chairman of IBM, when announcing that the company was taking an $8.9 billion charge to cover 60,000 job cuts and office and factory closures, said, 'The last thing IBM needs right now is a vision. What IBM needs now is a series of very tough-minded, market driven, highly effective strategies that deliver performance in the market place and shareholder value.' Gerstner's statement was a contradiction in terms – he was not abandoning the need for a vision; he was seeking to change both the culture and the vision of the company and in so doing spent much of his first year halving the size of the board of directors, restructuring at the top and attending meetings with tens of thousands of employees all over the world. Six months later he published his eight IBM Principles:

1. The market place is the driving force behind everything we do.
2. At our core we are a technology company with an overriding commitment to quality.
3. Our primary measures of success are customer satisfaction and shareholder value.
4. We operate as an entrepreneurial organisation with a minimum of bureaucracy and a never-ending focus on productivity.
5. We never lose sight of our strategic vision.
6. We think and act with a sense of urgency.
7. Outstanding, dedicated people make it all happen, particularly when they work together as a team.
8. We are sensitive to the needs of all employees and to the communities in which we operate.

These principles bear all the hallmarks of everything that is wrong. They were developed at the centre and handed down. They are written in the present tense as though they are already achieved. They mix up 'motherhood and apple pie' with homilies on 'strategic vision'. The chairman is speaking on behalf of all the company with everything written in terms of 'We', except that in the seventh principle '*they* work together as a team'. Perhaps the chairman is the only person who is not outstanding, dedicated and a member of the team! Some are simply not true. When IBM staff saw 'We operate . . . with a minimum of bureaucracy' a wry smile spread across not a few faces.

   However, in addressing meetings of employees, Lou Gerstner put the message more succinctly and came closer to the underlying values he was seeking to define: 'We don't move fast enough in this company. This is an industry in which success goes to the swift, more than to the smart. We've got to become more nimble, entrepreneurial, focused, customer driven. We must become a principle-based company rather than a procedural-based company (*Financial Times*, 28 March 1994). Subsequent performance indicates that IBM has made a considerable recovery.'

   Many factors affect the culture of an organisation. A local government department serving the community will have a very different culture from a private company competing vigorously in the open market or from a voluntary group. All may work hard and long but their values differ and so, therefore, will their behaviour, not only in their treatment of the customer or client but between people within the organisation. Large organisations, whether private or public, often have more in common with each other than either have with small organisations. National cultures impact on organisations. Nissan in the United States behaves very differently from its sister company in Britain. The American love of invigorating messages, coffee and donuts and the glitter of in-house celebrations would not go down well in the UK where understatement is the order of the day.

Very rarely is 'Our Culture' expressed as well as that of Sunrise Medical Inc., a California-based health care products company. It is too long and covers too many areas but clearly defines what it considers to be its seven enduring principles:

1. Product Superiority

We are a product driven company; we are only as good as the products we make. We are committed as a corporation to offering products with genuine superiority in quality, innovation and value, but the most important of these is quality. We believe that product superiority derives from paying strict attention to the details. Precision is required throughout the design and manufacturing process so that our products will operate reliably for their intended lives. Our goal is to provide defect-free products and services to our customers.

2. Service to Customers

In our company, the customer is king. Our goal is to achieve *perfection* in customer service: to leave every customer satisfied with our service every time. It is essential that we live up to whatever commitments we make. We must also outperform our competitors in demonstrating sensitivity and responsiveness to our customers' individual needs.

3. Individualism

We believe in the dignity and worth of every individual. We will treat our Associates with fairness and respect, while encouraging them to think independently. Every job is important and must be performed well if we are to succeed. A career with our company must permit our Associates to achieve personal satisfaction while leading balanced lives.

4. Teamwork

All of us together are stronger and wiser than any of us is individually. We will foster an attitude of teamwork and a spirit of enthusiasm within our company. Success within our company will come to people who are dedicated and resourceful, to people who assume responsibility, to people who care.

5. Productivity and Performance

We must earn an attractive return for our shareholders, which in turn ensures our corporate future and permits us to reinvest in growth. The key to corporate performance is achieving steady improvement in the productivity of all Associates. To do this we must harness our collective creativity and operate with the latest methods and technologies.

6. Citizenship

Through our commitment to corporate excellence we will improve the welfare of those who use our products and advance the progress of society. We will also be good citizens of every community and every country in which we operate, thereby contributing to global prosperity and harmony.

7. Corporate Character

We believe that great corporations, like great individuals, always act with integrity and character. When faced with moral choices, they do the right thing. They also bring a level of professionalism to everything they do. Above all, we are dedicated to being a company with character.

Although written from a 'We' viewpoint, this statement, by referring to the way Associates will be treated, does not make the mistake of assuming that it is initially owned by everyone. It fosters a positive approach to teamworking rather than stating 'We are a team'. It is clearly a statement which, the Executive Board hopes, people will come to share. They recognise that the commitment has to be earned but they set the tone by which behaviour will be judged.

I have met with the Sunrise executives and have given presentations at their seminars. In appreciation they donated an advanced wheelchair to a local disabled person. From my experience Sunrise executives seek to *live* their values, not just talk about them, and in so doing they have reached all levels of the company.

Another example of an expression of culture is that of Honda Motor Company's Management Policy, written in a blend of Japanese and English:

- Proceed always with ambition and youthfulness.
- Respect sound theory, develop fresh ideas and make the most effective use of time.
- Enjoy your work, and always brighten your working atmosphere.
- Strive constantly for a harmonious flow of work.
- Be mindful of the value of research and endeavour.

The important point about Sunrise and Honda is that these statements are about the 'how' as well as about the 'what'. They are concerned with the behaviour and attitudes to people. For the individual that is what matters – how he or she is treated and how they are expected to behave towards others, both within and outside the organisation. Writing it down does not, of course, achieve anything. A chain is as strong as its weakest link, and as soon as one person in the chain does not behave in the way the written statement suggests then no one below that person will believe that the organisation really means what it says. A culture statement which is not followed is the worst of all worlds.

We must not suppose, though, that having a written corporate culture is a recipe for success, however much latter-day evangelists may seek to persuade gullible executives that it will bring about the desired miracle cure. John Kotter and James Heskett in their study of over 200 leading US companies found a weak relationship between strong cultures and long-term business performance. Companies which had done well in the past such as Citicorp, Procter and Gamble, Sears, and J. C. Penney, 'had become characterised by arrogance, complacency, inward lookingness, bureaucracy and politicking' (Kotter and Heskett, 1992). Strong cultures can actually contribute to decline because that very strength makes if difficult to change direction when needed.

Kotter and Heskett found that only cultures which encourage flexibility and adaptive behaviour can achieve long-term success. Such cultures placed a high value on leadership at the top and on meeting the needs and expectations of all stakeholders – shareholders, customers, suppliers and staff. They found 22 companies which scored highly on these criteria. Over an eleven-year period those companies with the highest rating increased turnover by 682 per cent against 166 per cent for the lowest, and profits by 756 per cent compared with 1 per cent for the lowest.

MISSION

An organisation's culture is deep within it. It cannot be changed
overnight. In this it is unlike a mission. (It is possible to distinguish
between mission, vision, goals, challenges, and so on, but for simplicity I
will stick to this one word, except when using an individual company's
terminology.) A mission can be – and often is – changed overnight,
although the way that change is achieved will be affected by the culture.
    Sunrise Medical's corporate mission is:

> To build a leadership health care company, worldwide in scope, with a
> commitment to high-quality products which use innovative engineering
> solutions to improve people's lives. Our products increase patient
> mobility and independence, speed rehabilitation and recovery, and
> promote fitness and health. They focus on the needs of three special
> groups: the geriatric, the disabled and the health-conscious consumer.
> It is also our goal to provide for our Associates a positive, rewarding
> work environment which stimulates personal growth and fulfilment.

Even in its mission statement, Sunrise is concerned with the people in its
business, but unfortunately the quality of this statement does not equal
that of its culture statement. It is too long. The first sentence is all that is
needed.
    The mission of Citibank is:

> To be recognised by customers worldwide as a team of professionals
> who create and deliver financial solutions
> 1. Create a customer-keeping vision
> 2. Saturate your company with the voice of the customer
> 3. Go to school on the winners
> 4. Liberate your customer champions
> 5. Smash the barriers to customer winning performance
> 6. Measure, measure, measure
> 7. Walk the talk

All good stuff, but one can imagine a group of executives sitting around a
room with flip-charts on the wall aided by a consultant with all the latest
management books, and ending up with a handful of the latest
managerial fads. Who on earth is going to be inspired by 'Liberate your
customer champions'?

The first of Mars' five principles is:

The consumer is our boss, quality is our work and value for money is our goal.

3M's UK group mission is:

To provide and deliver on time, products and services that conform to agreed specifications in line with customer requirements. In line with the corporate quality policy these products and services must be useful, safe, reliable, environmentally acceptable and be truthfully represented in their packaging. All operations will be managed with the total quality emphasis philosophy focusing on optimised operations principles, unit cost control and the maintenance of a safe working environment.

All employees will be responsible for the quality of their own work and will be encouraged to exercise their initiative in search of continuous improvement.

Dewhirst Toiletries, a major supplier of toiletry products to companies such as Marks and Spencer, states that its mission is:

To be our customers' first choice by providing differentiation and excellence throughout our products and organisation.

Most of these mission statements are highly laudable in themselves but there is an air of sameness hanging over them and it seems as though everyone is pitching at the same level. Compare that of Federal Express:

Absolutely, Positively, Overnight

While this is as much of an advertising slogan as a mission, provided the management of the company demonstrates the continuing inspiration and control, people will sweat blood for that! It is the business equivalent of 'We will overcome!' or 'Liberty, Equality, Fraternity!' In three words it defines the business, emphasises its competitive edge, provides the basis for all decisions, focuses on the task, establishes the measure of success, and, most important of all, it inspires. Whoever thought of it had a flash of genius. Compare it with the original, 'We will deliver the package by 10.30 the next morning.' There's no contest!

HOW TO ESTABLISH A CULTURE STATEMENT

What all of this demonstrates, apart from lack of imagination, is that there is no single pattern, and all any company can do is what is right for it in its circumstances. The best are inspirational, but make it too trite and it easily turns into a short-lived advertising slogan. Make it too long and it becomes a great turn-off. Not every organisation can find three words which achieve all the objectives, but for the ascendant organisation it is possible to develop an effective culture statement provided it is recognised that the statement by itself changes very little, although the process of getting there can be helpful.

The process begins by recognising that no organisation has a right to expect its staff to share its values or cultures and the executive group should not presume to speak about 'We' unless there is a genuine basis for it. A 1991 survey by Ingersoll Engineers of 150 companies found that 80 per cent had mission statements but in 89 per cent of cases they were written either by the chief executive personally or by senior management (Ingersoll, 1991).

The actual written statement, if there is to be one, can best be shaped if a wide range of people are able to participate in the process. There is no magic formula for this. Sometimes, someone may prepare an initial draft which is then shared with a small group. Or you might begin with a totally open-ended free-ranging discussion. The structure of the group can vary. It may comprise people at the top, representatives from all business units or functions, a diagonal slice, the trade unions, or any combination. If you have 'non-core' staff, bring them into the process, for they will certainly have a different focus. The important point is that many heads are better than one and, by sharing, the ownership process begins. Some organisations may wish to take the sharing process even further and include a wider and deeper representative sample. Depending on size some may be able to involve the whole organisation. The incredible thing is that the senior executives, who probably thought they could do a good job by themselves, will find that the eventual document is better than anything they could have produced in isolation and they will also find that the broad principles they hold dear are shared by the vast majority of people. The ownership process will have taken a further step.

Do not aim for a lowest common denominator statement on which everyone can readily agree, because it does not really require anything of them. A mission is not 'motherhood and apple pie'. It must inspire, challenge and motivate. It must require effort to achieve successfully so that people know something is demanded of them and it is worth striving for.

Keep it short. It is easy to write long statements in which people subsequently get lost. It is incredibly difficult to be short, concise, meaningful and inspirational but the effort is worth it. But writing it down achieves very little, especially if it is imposed from the top.

True success comes with ownership by all. The ascendant culture cannot be imposed, unlike the culture of the autocrat. A culture in which 'Everyone is committed to the success of the enterprise and which recognises and values the contribution of all' is not achieved by decree. To some, such a culture can only result from indoctrination and is seen pejoratively. To others it is the highest objective than can possibly be attained. But in either case, ownership comes slowly as a result of the actions and behaviour of people, especially those in senior positions.

To a great extent, then, the culture of an organisation depends on its leadership and management. To this we now turn and later in Chapter 14 will consider the whole culture change process.

6 Leadership in the Ascendant Organisation

A leader is best when people barely know that he exists.
Not so good when people obey, and acclaim him,
Worst when they despise him.
'Fail to honour people,
They fail to honour you.'

But of a good leader, who talks little,
When his work is done, his aim fulfilled,
They will all say,
'We did this ourselves.'

Lao-Tzu, 6th century BC

LEADERSHIP AT THE TOP

Most writing on business leadership concentrates on the inspirers and transformers. Books are written by or about Lee Iacocca, Jack Welch, Ricardo Semler, Anita Roddick, Richard Branson, Percy Barnevik, and so on, and often seem to suggest that leadership exists only at the very top and that it is only colourful personalities who make good copy. However, most such leaders are creatures of their time and place and while they may build (Roddick, Branson, Semler) or transform (Welch, Iaccocca, Barnevik) there are few transferable lessons. Such leaders are exceptional in both senses of the word and sometimes can end up by doing harm as well as good. Although the top leader is often vital to the success of the organisation, can set its tone and sometimes transform its values, such leaders, working alone, achieve nothing. *Leaders achieve results by working with and through people and can and should be present at all levels of the organisation.*

As soon as you have one person to supervise, one process to influence, one facility to control, you can exercise leadership. Most people are not able to rise to become the transforming chief executive of a major corporation, but that does not mean that they cannot exercise leadership

80

in the jobs they do. The greatest risk for top leaders is to be surrounded by mediocrity and the greatest responsibility is to appoint good people.

Most current definitions of leadership are about creating the vision or setting the direction. The definition which best fits the ascendant organisation has been given by Murray Steele and Ann Brown.

> Leadership is about creating the conditions where people can perform to their potential in a fashion with which both they and their organisation are comfortable. It is about creating a vision of the organisation then articulating it so that others believe in the vision and successfully implement it.
>
> (Steele and Brown, 1990, p. 12)

It suggests a constructive, forward-thinking approach. But consider an alternative. Sir Neville Bowman-Shaw, chairman and joint owner with his brother of Lancer Boss, a forklift-truck manufacturer, tells the story of his 1987 meeting with the workers of a recently purchased Spanish company in the grip of the unions and losing money. Addressing the 400 employees he said, 'If you're going to bugger around I'll close the fucking factory! Follow me, and we'll be able to take the company out of the trouble. Screw it up, and we'll close it down. Make up your bloody minds!' (*Works Management*, January 1992) The Bowman-Shaws were autocratic leaders and did not disguise their them-and-us management style. In their British factory, works managers changed about once every six months because they were not allowed to run the job, and labour turnover reached 30 per cent in 1989 (*Works Management*, September 1994). As one manager said, 'There was so much fear in the place. Everyone had a plan but not necessarily the same plan!' In 1993 the German banks withdrew financial support and in April 1994 Jungheinrich of Germany acquired the British company. Six months later every possible performance indicator had improved dramatically, including labour turnover down to 8 per cent and absenteeism down to 3 per cent.

In Spain, Sir Neville acted both as an autocratic and a transformational leader, and often in such situations it is a question of 'change or die'. There have been numerous such examples and in a certain way it makes life easier. At least the alternatives are clear. But such a confrontation style can only last for a short time. Sir Michael Edwardes at British Leyland from 1977 to 1982 was able to confront the extremists and win, and in so doing cleared the ground on which others were subsequently able to build. Now, in the 1990s, his successors have constructed a successful company, The Rover Group. In 1974 I was put into the Ford Dagenham Metal Stamping and Body plant with the clear brief, 'Get back management control!' These simple messages focus one's activities and can be great fun, but it is no way to run a company!

Bill Hewlett, founder of Hewlett-Packard, had a better approach and would, I am sure, echo Lao-Tzu:

> What is the Hewlett-Packard way? I feel that in general terms it is the policies and actions that flow from the belief that men and women want to do a good job, a creative job, and that if they are provided with the proper environment, they will do so.

Speaking to a group of Nissan managers in August 1990, Jan Carlzon, President of Scandinavian Airlines, said:

> The role of the leader will be that of a visionary, a strategic leader, who gives the objectives, who guides the way to reach those objectives. The formal organisation then educates and communicates and informs the people about what is the objective and what is the strategy so that people can take responsibilitythe person who has total information cannot escape responsibility.

There is no single pattern of leadership, although numerous researchers have sought to develop models, and the fact that there are so many confirms that life is not simple. However, it is not unreasonable to seek to point to some behaviours and characteristics that can make for success in an ascendant organisation (recognising of course that someone will come along who will break all the rules and be totally successful). The following is based on observation and experience.

HOW TO LEAD THE ASCENDANT ORGANISATION

The leader who achieves long-term success in the ascendant organisation is likely to possess many characteristics which I divide into personal attributes, strategic perspective, communication and achievement.

Personal attributes

- Possesses a good level of general intelligence and a good breadth of knowledge which can be applied in specific situations
- Has an empathy with people at all levels

- Focuses on those aspects of the business which are critical for success
- Analyses logically, thinks rationally
- Acts intuitively – and is right (most of the time)
- Has uncompromising, high levels of personal integrity, honesty and ethical standards and ensures that anything less is unacceptable throughout the organisation
- Has the wisdom to know when to do nothing
- Incorporates high energy, self-motivation, determination, courage and enthusiasm – in short, passion
- Has the drive to achieve.

All of these characteristics could be said to be innate and I do not wish to enter into the nature versus nurture debate. We all start with a certain level of capability and whereas I could never be an Olympic downhill ski champion, my own basic ability has, with practice and enthusiasm, helped me to conquer runs that I once believed impossible. Virtually all studies show that mental capabilities can similarly be developed, and with use comes confidence.

What matters is not simply having high levels of intelligence and knowledge but the ability to cut through the undergrowth and apply those talents to specific situations. Applied intelligence and knowledge are what matter. Equally if not more important is instinct – the gut feel to *know* what is right or to weigh up the odds, take a risk, and be right! Some may have this capability from an early age and they become the successful entrepreneurs. Others take years to acquire it. Once when asked by a Japanese, Masaharu Futami, how I knew the appropriate response to a difficult situation, my reply was, '25 years of experience'. Intuition, for most of us, comes with experience and allows us to go from A to Z in almost one leap, automatically analysing the potential problems and alternative solutions found in steps B to Y. Another Japanese, Hideaki Hirano, on ending his assignment in the UK, explained that a British trait he had learned to value was 'Wait and see what happens.' Faced with a complex negotiation or problem, his upbringing had taught him to spend hours analysing numerous alternatives, preparing vast amounts of documentation. It was important to be seen to be doing something. 'But,' he said, 'your approach of sometimes deliberately doing nothing, sitting back waiting, perhaps, for the problem to go away or for your opponent's move and then reacting instinctively is something we Japanese should learn.' We decided to call it positive non-action.

Empathy with people at all levels is not usually on lists of leadership qualities but in the ascendant organisation it is critical. It means that leaders have a real understanding of the problems affecting others, how they feel and how they see the issues affecting them. Above all it means caring, not in a superficial, 'people are our greatest asset' way, nor in believing they can do no wrong, but just because it is right. Empathy results in leaders understanding the impact of their decisions on people and taking actions which support constructive relationships, whether it is the elimination of illogical differences in treatment or simply talking with people at the grass-roots level in a way which reinforces their importance.

In May 1994 we experienced a classic example of empathy within Nissan. Our Executive Committee discussed a proposal for 1995 vacations. The Engineering Department planned a one-week shutdown in Easter 1995, necessary in their view to undertake major facility changes. Managing Director Ian Gibson and I knew this would be unpopular with the staff who had co-operated fully in changed vacation dates in 1994 due to the recession. Ian made it clear that whereas staff did not like but understood why, in 1994, their vacation arrangements had been changed, in 1995 they would not like and would not understand. 'We had,' he said, 'tremendous co-operation in 1994, and we cannot abuse that co-operation in 1995.' This was not a cynical, hard-bitten view but a genuine belief that we had to do the right thing by the staff. The Engineering Department found a way.

Strategic perspective

The leader of the ascendant organisation:

- Develops a vision based on a strategic perspective rising above immediate problems
- Creates the right organisation structure
- Aligns the organisation
- Has a concern for all stakeholders
- Relates goals and actions to that vision and strategy
- Instinctively feels for the impact of that vision on people
- Constantly challenges the status quo.

The leader of an organisation has to be able to project several years ahead, to determine where it is going, how it will get there and the type of organisation it should be. At all times the short-term goals and actions need to be clearly related to the long term. But the vision is no good without the determination. In the tough times it will be the leader's responsibility to watch for the long-term goal, and while there may be detours, and the goal may well have to be modified, the leader remains responsible.

An important responsibility of a leader, which is often alluded to but not specifically stated, is the requirement to align the organisation, to ensure that all its components are pointing in the same direction. The effective team leader begins with the individual and seeks to ensure that all are working together to achieve the same objectives. The leader of the whole organisation not only has to pull together his or her immediate team but also, by working through others and by direct intervention when necessary, has to ensure that all the organisational units are working together to achieve the shared objectives.

[handwritten margin note: aligned to customer demand.]

No doubt we have all seen and been part of organisations in which the left hand does not know what the right hand is doing or, if it does, either ignores it or seeks to go in a totally different direction. Often there is virtual warfare between different parts of an organisation. Organisations with multiple objectives allow individual units to concentrate on those aspects they consider important, and if they achieve their priorities at the expense of others, so be it. It is not their fault that others have failed.

That is why Federal Express's 'Absolutely, Positively, Overnight' is so good. It provides a focus with which all can identify. Many functions erect Chinese walls, barely speaking to each other. That is why the concepts of process re-engineering are valuable. They force the organisation to concentrate on the essential flows and break down the functional chimneys. Whatever the organisational structure, it is the responsibility of the leader to break down the divisions, share objectives, get everyone working together; in short, to align the organisation. *[handwritten margin note: —To what.]*

In addition, the leader has continually to be challenging the organisation to improve. New ways to exploit technology, new approaches to the market and product development, new ways of motivating staff. Is the organisation right for tomorrow's environment? Few would go as far as Tom Peters' hyperbole, 'If you aren't reorganising pretty substantially once every six to twelve months, you're probably out of step with the times', but when he adds, 'The most efficient and effective route to bold change is the participation of everyone, every day, in incremental change' (Peters, 1988), I applaud him.

The leader of the ascendant organisation is also receptive to new ideas. However much I denigrate the 'instant experts', there is always value in going to the original source, whether it is a book or an organisation. Often they simply re-package things we are already doing. Rarely is there anything which is totally new but a new perspective on an old concept can spark ideas which generate change. Hammer and Champy's *Re-engineer-*

ing the Corporation (1993) presents little that is really new, based as it is on what many are already doing, but it causes people to think. It is not about new applications for information technology or 'downsizing' but about changing your mindset. Shortly, I shall describe giving back to the first-line supervisor many of the processes that over the years the functional specialists have taken to themselves. That requires a mindset change.

Communication

The leader in the ascendant organisation:

- Inspires, enthuses and motivates others
- Communicates the vision and strategy and creates the conditions which enable everyone to share it, primarily by asking them to contribute to it
- Is a member of the team as well as leader of it
- Recognises and responds to the needs and feelings of others
- Relaxes and make others feel relaxed
- Has respect for others, values their contribution and listens to and learns from them
- Communicates in the appropriate way at all levels
- Explicitly recognises the achievement of others, helps them through their shortcomings but takes decisive action when necessary.

None of this is about the techniques of communication. Techniques are not difficult to learn. Real communication is about relating to people, respecting them for what they are and enabling them to develop into what they might become. The gift of feeling comfortable with people and making them feel at ease with you can be developed but some never achieve it. It is communication of this type, more than anything else, that results in true leadership in the ascendant organisation – people doing things for you and the organisation because they want to. People have to feel that their leader cares, not simply about the bottom-line results but about them as individuals.

Being accepted as a member of the team is of vital importance. If people at all levels in the organisation do not feel that the leader is on the same side as them, that they are not all working to the same objectives, the critical trust and empathy will never develop. The transformational or inspirational leader may stand outside the team and may get things done but without making friends. Often such a person will get rid of those who do not agree. Margaret Thatcher was a transformational leader but no one ever suggested she was a member of the team. When she ran into difficulties, few were willing to forgive her excesses.

But it does not mean being soft: in fact it is often easier to take the hard line and get rid of problem people than to spend long periods seeking to correct and improve. However, if there is no improvement, then, after due process, the required action has to be taken. I once explained to a bishop who was concerned about the performance of a parish priest, that he was doing no one any favours, least of all the parishioners, if he did not tackle the problem. Often, poor performers know they are failing and it comes as a relief when their boss finally communicates the concerns.

Achievement

The leader:

- Sets high performance and behavioural standards and objectives and leads by example
- Is committed to growth
- Is not satisfied with existing high standards, seeks improvements and better ways of doing things
- Calculates risks and takes decisive action when required
- Genuinely devolves responsibility, authority and accountability throughout the organisation
- Assesses and measures achievement levels, sometimes objectively, sometimes intuitively
- Is concerned with the 'how'.

The leader of the ascendant organisation is results-oriented and is never satisfied with today's standards. Personal effort is high and seen to be so, but these leaders recognise that it is only through others that sustainable achievement is developed. Teamworking is paramount.

The leader of the ascendant organisation must also be concerned with the processes, attitudes and relationships within the organisation – the 'how'. It is the easiest thing in the world for people at the lower levels, where the task is often paramount, to become so narrowly focused that they forget about the culture of the organisation. And it is the leader who has to pull them back. It is easy for the tools of management to become the ends of management but part of being an ascendant organisation is to care about the way you do things.

Perhaps the most important ability a leader can possess is:

> Have the wisdom and judgement to employ good people and give them headroom.

Richard Branson, Chairman of Virgin Atlantic Airways, recognises this. Speaking at the annual convention of the Institute of Directors in 1993, he said of his recipe for business success:

> The basic principles are that people matter and that small is beautiful shape the enterprise around the people . . . plan and operate the enterprise so as to enable its key assets, its people, to work at their very best. This governs the priorities of the business, its size and style. Our priorities in managing the business do not appear in most management textbooks or most British companies. We give top priority to the interests of our staff; we give second priority to the interests of our customers; and third priority to the interests of our shareholders. Working backwards, the interests of our shareholders depend upon high levels of customer satisfaction, which enable us to attract and retain passengers in the face of intense competition. We know that the customer's satisfaction which generates all-important word-of-mouth recommendations and fosters repeat purchase, depends in particular upon high standards of service [and this] depends upon happy staff, who are proud of the company they work for. That is why the interests of our people must come first.

no recir

Many will disagree with the way Richard Branson puts his argument, and it is somewhat circular, but the essential point is that a good leader creates good followers. There are no bad soldiers, only bad generals. The leader does not actually have to have a precise vision from the beginning. The leader's responsibility is to provide the spark which defines the broad direction and creates the environment in which all the people in the organisation can put flesh on to the bones, and often make fundamental contributions to the direction of the organisation and the detail of needed change.

But the most difficult task for an executive is genuinely to devolve responsibility. The worst thing that can happen is for the boss to say something like, 'Right, this is now your ship, get on with it . . . but could you just let me know on a weekly/monthly basis what you are up to; maybe we can have lunch together a couple of times a month.' That is sending out mixed messages. It confuses responsibility and authority and tells the subordinate that he or she is not really trusted. It is important to remember, however, that even if the leadership role changes from 'controller' to 'facilitator', the leader remains accountable for the performance of subordinates. The alternative is abdication of responsibility, and it is so easy for the lazy manager to drift from control to abdication.

The serious point is that it takes great confidence in one's own abilities and in the abilities of one's staff not to want to know what is going on all the time and not to feel threatened if your boss has to go to a subordinate to find the answer to a question. I like to think I am a genuine devolver. My philosophy is to appoint good people and let them get on and run their part of the organisation within the shared values. I do not require detailed reports on every aspect of their business, only on the key performance indicators, and rely on the judgement of the managers to let me know whatever else they consider important for me to know. But I am available for consultation when needed and will choose to become involved in any area which needs a prod. At the same time a golden rule is 'No nasty surprises'. If there is bad news coming, let me know early so that I can decide if I wish to become involved. I will talk to anyone without feeling that I have to go through the directors or managers, and am sure that no one feels threatened by this.

Such an approach can lead to the occasional difficulty: 'You should have told me earlier', or 'You should have known that.' However, the benefits of genuinely devolving responsibility – allowing people to develop and grow as individuals – far outweigh the occasional embarrassment and allows the leader to concentrate on those aspects of the business he or she judges to be important. That, hopefully, is the difference between being a leader and being a boss.

In the ascendant organisation, leaders at all levels are made; in fact the very style of the organisation makes such development inevitable. There is not one of these characteristics that does not rub off on to everyone in the organisation and, apart from those few mavericks who succeed by being totally different, most of us learn from the behaviour and example of people we admire. When that behaviour devolves responsibility and authority, genuinely communicates, values the contribution of everyone and encourages continuous improvement, it becomes self-reinforcing and allows everyone the room and opportunity to grow. Douglas McGregor and Fred Herzberg would be proud!

MANAGING

One definition of management, comparing it with leadership, is that management is about doing things right whereas leadership is about doing the right things. Alternatively, management is about the organisation and development of resources, whereas leadership is about getting people to do what you want them to do because they want to do it for you. Research by Henry Mintzberg led him to the conclusion that managers' activities are characterised by 'brevity, variety and discontinuity and that they are strongly oriented towards action and dislike reflective activities'. They prefer the verbal media, that is, telephone calls and meetings, to any other, and much of their accumulated programmes – to schedule time, process information, make decisions and so on – 'remains locked deep inside their brains' (Mintzberg, 1975).

There are dozens of models of management but the truth is that, to be successful, managers must both manage and lead. Leaders, also, must be able to manage, or at least be surrounded by people who can. A manager who cannot lead is a waste of space and money!

Managers and supervisors must be accountable for what they do and for what happens in their part of the organisation. Businesses are not democracies. While considerable responsibility and authority can be devolved, accountability must be clearly defined. The first-line supervisor may assign an individual to be responsible for a manufacturing task and give considerable authority to that person to allow the job to be properly performed, but accountability cannot be devolved. If it goes wrong, it is the supervisor who is to blame, not the individual. The managerial role is therefore performed when an individual is held accountable for his or her own actions and for the actions of others. In seeking to determine if there are any managerial characteristics specific to the ascendant organisation the critical issue to consider is how far down the line accountability is passed. The ascendant organisation has positive leadership and devolved accountability at all levels.

The Japanese, while having much in common with the West, do have some different perspectives on the philosophy and practice of management. Many of these differences are illustrated throughout this book, but some others do sit most comfortably at this point.

A Japanese manager regards himself as a stage in a time continuum. When assigned to a new position he must finish what his predecessor left unfinished, take initiatives of his own and then lay the foundations for his successor. Yoshio Hatakeyama, President of the Japan Management Association, writing for Japanese managers, said of the middle stage:

He must gather data and figures and learn the opinions of his staff, the desires of his superiors. He must weigh the entire situation of the organisation, decide what there is to be done, win the approval of all involved and strike while the iron is hot – that is, within his first three months in the new position. (Hatakeyama, 1985, p.11)

On laying the groundwork for the successor he says:

Laying strategic groundwork for one's successors entails spotting potential problems in their early stages and taking whatever action is necessary, either to begin solving them or to prepare for their eventual solution. In neither case will a manager see the results of these efforts during his own time on the job. Nevertheless it is the duty of every manager to effect a chronological division of labour – that is leave his successor an environment in which he can work efficiently. (p. 11)

All Western managers, whatever their organisation type, should take on board Hatakeyama's teaching. How many Western managers do we know who have built their career on the basis of 'Get out before found out?' The Japanese, because they anticipate being with the company throughout their working life, know that they will almost certainly work with their successor again. They cannot be seen to have left the job in a poor condition. But they do wish to be seen to have made a contribution, so their objective is always to make at least one significant and lasting contribution in each position; a contribution that will be recognised by their peers as having added to the well-being of the organisation.

The leadership attributes described in this chapter permeate all levels in the ascendant organisation. Rather than describe minute differences at each level of the hierarchy, I now turn to the group who leads and manages at the sharp end of the business, the first-line supervisors.

LEADERSHIP IN THE FRONT LINE

Whatever the attributes of the top leadership, it is the people at the first level of management who really make things happen. Top managers can pontificate and inspire all they want but unless they get the supervisors on their side they will fail. (Note: I use the term 'supervisor' as a generic title for the first level of management. Often, in traditional companies, such people are not even regarded as part of management. In other companies this person may be called a team leader, unit manager, section head and so on and can have anything from five to 100 direct reporting to him or her.)

> Supervisors, if carefully selected, well-trained, highly motivated and given the status and pay appropriate to being, 'the professional at managing the processes and the people' can make more difference to the long-term success of the organisation than any group other than top management. And even here it is the supervisor who delivers top management's strategy and goals in the workplace.

In the Anglo-Saxon world of Britain and the USA the role of the supervisor has always been uneasy. Located in the centre of an adversarial relationship, he or she is 'the pig in the middle'. Talk to any group of supervisors and you will hear a predictable tale of woe. 'One day I was supervised, the next day I was a supervisor. I've never been trained for the job.' 'Nobody tells me anything, the unions know first.' 'I get kicked around by management, by the unions, and if the staff are having an off day they take it out on me.' 'The management makes decisions without consulting me and I'm left to carry them out.' 'If I try to discipline someone, the personnel department doesn't support me.' 'Those 25-year-olds from the Finance Department keep coming down and make me justify every minor overrun against a budget which I had no say in fixing.' 'If I want to change something, the management doesn't listen because it costs too much and the staff don't listen because they won't change anyway.' This list could go on and on, and while it may seem exaggerated I have heard such a litany so often that there is no doubt that these views are commonplace and justified. Many companies are in a vicious downward spiral of low responsibility, low authority, low accountability and low pay. Good people avoid the job.

The Supervisor in the Ascendant Organisation

Contrast this with best practice in the ascendant organisation where appointment to the position of supervisor is seen as the beginning of a career, not the end of it.

An unpublished paper prepared in 1990 for the National Economic Development Office (NEDO) studied five companies considered to exhibit best practice in engineering organisations. These companies were Acco Cable Controls, British Aerospace, TG Brooks, X Ltd (an engine systems and components company) and Nissan. At British Aerospace, supervisors were appointed to replace four previous grades (senior supervisor, supervisor, senior foreman and foreman) and were expected to take on managerial responsibility for motivating employees to achieve the required standards of quality, timeliness and cost. This involved them in the recruitment, development and training of staff, communications, leadership, and resource management, and required of them the qualities of judgement, interpersonal skills, decisiveness, crisis management and critical awareness. Such a listing would more likely qualify someone for the chairman's role – if such attributes were a common requirement for such a position!

The NEDO study found that best-practice companies sought to improve performance by combining advanced manufacturing technology with a desire to improve the competence and status of supervision. Within these companies they found that supervisors fulfilled a number of similar roles:

- Technical leadership, quality and continuous improvement responsibilities
- Work allocation, standard operations and supply/delivery of materials
- Housekeeping, maintenance and health and safety
- Recruiting, developing, appraising and training staff
- Communication, motivating and team building
- Personnel, disciplinary and industrial relations duties

In short, gaining the commitment of the workforce and control of the processes which is necessary to secure long-term success.

The Nissan supervisor's job is probably bigger than any similar job anywhere else in the world. The overall company objective is 'To build profitably the highest quality car sold in Europe', and to achieve this the supervisor has to meet strict quality and production objectives. Everything else contributes to these ends. Responsibilities include those shown in the box overleaf.

Much of this is discussed elsewhere, but some aspects are worthy of expansion at this time.

Selecting the team

While the complex recruitment process is administered by the personnel department, the supervisor plays a vital and continuing role. They are present at every stage – the aptitude tests; the practical skill tests; they take the candidates into the working environment allowing them to assess the candidate in both the physical task and with the rest of the team (this also allows the candidate to assess the job and possible future colleagues);

Achieving schedule	Operator care
Achieving the required quality	Materials management
Setting budgets	Cleaning and organising
Leading the team	Team building/motivation
Controlling costs	Preventive maintenance
Selecting the team	Health and safety
Measuring skills/developing staff	Abnormality control
	Employee counselling
Performance appraisal	Problem solving
Communication	Employee relations
Visual management	Input into new
Balancing the work	products/facilities
Preparing standard operations	Discipline
Continuous improvement	Acquiring technical knowledge
Administration	

they conduct the final interviews, make the final decision and, wherever possible, make the final job offer, face to face. While the personnel department follows up with the written job offer, what really counts is the personal, mutual commitment of the supervisor and the candidate.

The supervisor can blame no one else for the selection decision and the candidate has a good feeling towards the person who made the job offer. That is not a bad start to the team-building process and it can only be done when there is a genuine shared culture. The supervisor is then able to select people who have an empathy with that culture. This does not mean selecting clones, but people who want to be treated as individuals and who are able to make individual contributions within a team environment.

Being the leader and a member of the team

You cannot be seen as a leader of the team unless you are first accepted as a member of it. Most of this depends on the supervisor's capabilities and approach but you can do things to make it easier. The supervisor's desk is in the team meeting area (usually a clearly defined area about 8 × 4 metres) not somewhere separate. In this area there is a large blue table surrounded by benches, individual lockers, a sink, tea/coffee-making facilities and often a microwave cooker and refrigerator. Some have managed to acquire easy chairs, others are attractively decorated. These areas belong to the team; they have their morning meetings, tea breaks and, if they wish, their lunch breaks in them. All documents are kept in these areas and the vast majority of one-to-one meetings take place there. The supervisor eats and drinks with the team and they often socialise together.

Communication

All communication goes through the supervisor. If something is worth telling, it is worth telling quickly and the only way to do that is every day face to face. Thus Nissan established the five-minute meeting that takes place every day at the start of shift. At these meetings the supervisor talks with the team about matters of the moment affecting that group. If there is no business to discuss, they talk about the local soccer team; it does not matter. The important thing is that the team is together, talking together.

It also means that if there is occasionally the great message from on high, the mechanism is in place to handle it and can be initiated within minutes if needed. The team becomes used to hearing things from the supervisor and the grapevine has less credence. I hold no truck with those who say everyone must get exactly the same message at exactly the same time. It really does not matter if different groups get slightly different versions of a message. But it does matter that they are told what is important to them in a way that is appropriate for them. While occasionally this may lead to inconsistencies, this is a minor problem which can easily be corrected, compared with the major problem of delaying communication because the written word has to be precisely correct!

Skill measurement and staff training

One of the most difficult questions ever asked was Toshiaki Tsuchiya's question to John Cushnaghan, then Nissan's Production Director. 'How do you *know* the operators have the right skill level?' After several attempts to come up with an acceptable response John realised that while we trained and assumed we knew, we did not truly *know*. From small acorns grow great oaks!

The great oak was the skill matrix and what we came to call the ILU system. See Figure 6.1.

This matrix is visually displayed in the meeting room; all team members knows their own assessed capabilities and the capabilities of others. It is a simple but extremely powerful tool which the supervisor is

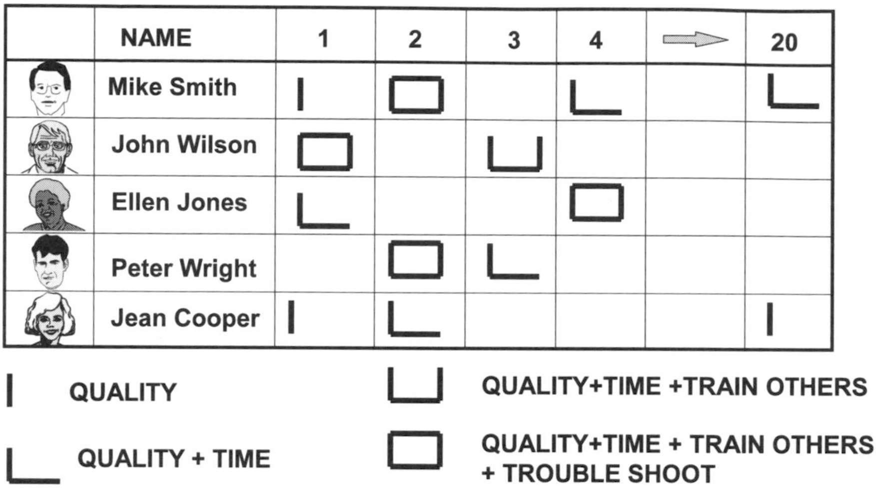

NAME	1	2	3	4	⟹	20
Mike Smith	I	□		L		L
John Wilson	□		⊔			
Ellen Jones	L			□		
Peter Wright		□	L			
Jean Cooper	I	L				I

I QUALITY ⊔ QUALITY+TIME +TRAIN OTHERS

L QUALITY + TIME □ QUALITY+TIME + TRAIN OTHERS + TROUBLE SHOOT

Figure 6.1 Skills Matrix

responsible for maintaining. Every section will have its own optimum mix. Where jobs are all very different it may be 'Every job to have three people capable of doing it and every person to know three jobs.' Where jobs are only slightly different the mix may be much richer; where training takes a long time and familiarity is needed to maintain capability the mix may be thinner; where tasks are physically demanding and frequent rotation is necessary the mix may be rich. The listing can be extended beyond the immediate physical tasks and include capabilities in maintenance, continuous improvement, problem solving and so on. It is also applicable in indirect areas. The optimum mix for a section can only be determined by that section. The supervisor is responsible and accountable for determining that mix and for ensuring that the team as a whole achieves the required level. The supervisor will also undertake much of the instruction, although on-the-job training is the responsibility of everyone.

Standard operations and line balancing

The preparation of standard operations (the defined best method of performing a task) and line balancing are intellectually demanding tasks and in most organisations are the responsibility of industrial engineers. It requires preparing the standard operation as the basis for all line balancing, training and improvement activities. Then, ensuring that for a given volume, production rate and staffing level, the work of everyone within the section is evenly spread, build constraints are properly accounted for and everything is done in the optimum order. In order to achieve these objectives, work has to be moved between operators and sections and both shifts have to be in full agreement – otherwise the standard operation is not common. The responsibility requires a deep understanding both of the tasks and the psychology of work.

Cost control

Supervisors are fully involved in developing their controllable costs budgets. This includes direct costs, for example materials used in actually building the car; indirect costs, such as gloves, tools, disposable material and so on; scrap costs and control over time. They are responsible for achieving improvements in all areas of cost, including productivity.

Quality and delivery

It is the responsibility of the supervisors to ensure the required quality and production levels are achieved. If the schedule is, say, 220 cars per shift then that is the number to be produced – no more, no less. If, because of a major breakdown, there is a shortfall on one shift a plan will be put into place to recover; but the company does not want more than 220 because (a) quality will suffer and (b) the stock is of some components is so tight that it is simply not possible.

Quality is not a voluntary activity and supervisors are expected to motivate their staff so that everyone becomes committed to achieving the required quality level and also to have in place the mechanisms and procedures for so doing. In the event of problems, supervisors need to understand the true cause, whether it be faulty parts, technical issues or operator or process error. They are expected to respond quickly to feedback from audit studies and implement an abnormality control process leading to countermeasures. It is their responsibility to decide whether or not to pull in other departments. They feed back concerns to the operators both as and when they arise and in relation to problems experienced on the other shift.

The supervisor is the 'professional at managing the processes and the people' and as such is at exactly the same level in the hierarchy as the other professionals, the engineers, financial analysts, buyers, personnel officers and so on. What you cannot do is to emphasise the importance of the role and then pay them £5,000 a year less than other professionals. To do so would send out all the wrong messages. In Nissan, this means that in 1998 the difference in annual salaries between production operators and their supervisors exceeds £10,000. While there is an intermediate step of Team Leader, this difference demonstrates the importance of the role; therefore the best people aim for it, they receive high responsibility, authority and accountability. You are then into a virtuous upward spiral of high-calibre people, high pay, high responsibility. This was one of the best decisions we ever made.

It must not be supposed that it is only large sophisticated companies that are able to go down this road: Tinsley Bridge Limited, a small manufacturer of truck springs, was born via a management buyout from British Steel Corporation. Following a visit to Nissan, TBL's Operations Director, David Roberts, was convinced that they needed to change their supervisors' roles if they were to survive.

They wanted to get their supervisors to become team leaders, leading and briefing their teams on each shift and taking responsibility for attendance and discipline, running each section as a business in its own right, ensuring that effective maintenance was performed and high-quality standards achieved. But to get to this point TBL's supervisors needed to make a culture change. They needed to see the logic of the proposed working method and their place in it. Primarily, they had to recognise their own importance. TBL's managing director, Michael Webber, said, 'It was vital that the supervisors saw themselves as managers and what is more as the critical point of management that makes things happen.'

With this in mind, and knowing in general terms what they wanted, Webber and David Roberts involved me in seminars which followed the classic pattern of getting people to define everything that is wrong and then come up with their own solutions. It is imperative to give ownership of change. Said Michael Webber, 'If we'd just told them what we wanted, cold, it would not have worked. They had to own that definition themselves.' But as important was the conceptual change that was taking place. Webber summed it up: 'The idea of leadership had got lost along the way. They did not see their role as leading, helping, developing and defending their people. They saw it as doing what management told them to do. We had to do something about that. They are the cornerstone to all we're trying to achieve.'

TBL *has* succeeded – it is still alive, and with the major recession in its industry that is no mean achievement. It is still trying to improve and while supervisor development is not the only answer, TBL is convinced that it has played a critical role.

HOW TO CHANGE TO TEAMBUILDING SUPERVISORS

How do you move from having 'top-down but ineffectual controllers' to genuine teambuilding supervisors?

Before you are able to commence such a process you need first to effect a change in the managerial culture, but if you do then decide to attempt to change the supervisors' role you will find two major problems. First, the current bunch have been rewarded for behaving in a totally different way, and second, following from this, they may be the greatest resisters of change. As they will be critical in delivering the change, if *they* are not convinced, it simply will not happen. In working with many companies I have generally found that around 75 per cent of the existing staff are capable of making the transition.

Therefore, in moving from the traditional role to that of supervisor in the ascendant organisation, I advocate the following process:

1. At the top, establish your vision of where you wish to be.
2. Genuinely share this vision and, if it includes a changing role at the first-line level, bring them into the process, as did Tinsley Bridge Ltd. If it is *their* idea they will own it, and it will happen.
3. Give an absolute guarantee that no one will lose their employment with the company if they are not able to make the transition – even though they may need to change their job. If they subsequently wish to leave, make generous separation payments. The small cost of this will be repaid a thousandfold!
4. Allow all those who wish to be considered for the new role to have the opportunity.
5. Ensure that your selection process assesses the skills and attributes needed for the new way, not the old.
6. Appoint some incumbents, promote from the shop floor and bring in people from outside. Make sure that they all are carefully selected using the same standards for all. Do not appoint second best simply because you need the numbers.
7. Provide comprehensive training and on-the-job experience to ensure they are fully equipped to handle the job in the new way and provide subsequent opportunities for continuous development.
8. Provide continuing management support. Behave in the way you talk. If you want your supervisors to involve their people make sure *you* involve *them*.
9. Genuinely treat your supervisors as professionals. Continue to expect high capability and high performance and pay them as you do other professionals.

Once the first-line supervisors are convinced, and are thinking and behaving in the new way, then you begin to expect changes in behaviour.

I referred in Chapter 2 to the work of Tannenbaum and his teaching that influence is not a zero-sum game. The traditional authoritarian supervisor relies on the exercise of control, and believes that by giving more responsibility to a subordinate his or her own responsibility will diminish – the zero sum. But meeting with a group of resisters, drawing the 'responsibility pie' on a flip-chart and showing how it can grow as the roles change can achieve more in five minutes than hours of presentations and awareness exercises.

All of this leads to changes of behaviour and to this I now turn.

who are
1st line sup.?
in a call centre:
not just the
need to change

7 Ascendant Behaviour

If you have eleven workmen you will never win. If you have eleven artists you will never win. It is important that the team complements each other and we have that.

Eric Cantona, Soccer International
Manchester United Football Club, 1993

In modern industry the co-operation needed involves the spirit in which subordinates exercise their judgement. Beyond what commands can effect and supervision can control, beyond what incentives can induce and penalties prevent, there exists an exercise of discretion important even in relatively menial jobs, which managers of economic enterprises seek to enlist for the achievement of managerial ends.

R. Bendix, *Work and Authority in Industry,* 1956

The concepts and practices of single status, teamworking, flexibility, employee involvement and communication are inseparable. Take away one element and the whole thing falls down. However, for clarity, this chapter attempts the impossible and separates them.

EVERYONE A FIRST-CLASS CITIZEN

Karl Albrecht has said:

> The way employees feel is ultimately the way your customers feel
> . . . Many organisations turn their employees into quality terrorists
> by the way they treat them.

In the ascendant organisation there is no place for second-class citizens. This does not mean that everyone has the same status. Status is a state of mind, it is your perception of your position in relation to others. The chief executive has a different status from a manager or a shop-floor operator. Nothing is going to change that, but it *is* possible to eliminate the illogical differences in the way people are treated. In the ascendant organisation there are no reserved car parking spaces, no separate dining rooms for executives and no separate entrances (unlike Japan, where all three exist). The ascendant organisation begins to provide common terms and conditions of employment and finds that once you start down this route there is no logical stopping place. There is no case for one group of people having longer vacations than others – even if there are additional days related to length of service, the same formula should apply to all. Sickness benefits, medical insurance, pension plans, retirement age should be the same for everyone. If managers do not clock-on, no one should. It can even extend to the reward system. While salaries will be different, the actual structure should be transparent. This does not mean that it has to be exactly the same throughout the organisation but any differences must be based on logic and not unduly benefit one particular group. Exotic bonus systems based on short-term financial indicators which reward top executives generously but give nothing to anyone else have no place in the ascendant organisation. The reward system must motivate all staff, not just a few.

One of the early decisions we made in Nissan was that everyone would have the same workwear. Many organisations provide free protective clothing on the shop floor but few extend this to office-based employees. Our reason was not to impose uniformity but to avoid artificial divisions – the 'suits' in the office separate from and superior to the people on the shop floor. It was another message that we were seeking to be different. Today, a trend is to 'dressing down' days and this may be great in a predominantly office environment, but when you have a mixed manufacturing/office workplace and you provide company workwear for all people it might send out the wrong messages to the shop floor workers when on one day a week the office people come in their 'smart casual' civvies.

A similar dilemma arises with working hours. Does everyone have to be at work for exactly the same period every day? Should the organisation allow flexitime? If it believes in both common terms and conditions of employment and flexibility, which takes precedence? It is indefensible that office workers should have shorter working hours than manual workers. There is an argument, however, that office workers should be able to operate a flexitime arrangement, even if to do so on the shop floor would be more difficult. I come down on the side which says everyone should be treated the same. If in a manufacturing company, it is imperative that shop-floor workers have to be in for an 8.00 a.m. start, it is galling for them to see the office workers arriving when they choose. It can only increase the 'them and us' syndrome. If, in a totally office-based environment, it is possible to apply flexitime to everyone there are other arguments which will determine its value but, as a general principle, harmony is better than division.

When discussing common conditions the area that generates most heat is payment for absence, whether it be for sickness or lateness. Traditionally, white-collar salaried staff have been paid when they are sick or late; blue-collar hourly-paid staff have not – they are not to be trusted! 'If we pay them when they're sick our absence rates will go up.' There is no greater 'them and us' division.

Blue-collar absenteeism *is* generally higher than white-collar, but when we realise that those who are least likely to be paid when sick are those with the worst attendance record the correlation is negative, not positive. Attendance is much more determined by commitment than it is by health and control. The reason why many people come to work when they do not feel 100 per cent is because they have interesting jobs; they feel their contribution counts, they are valued and they do not want to let their team down. The reason why others do not attend in similar circumstances is because they do not have interesting jobs, their contribution does not count and they have no team to let down. The attitude develops that, 'If I am away for a day I lose a day's pay, the company loses a day's work and that's a fair trade.'

The alternative, paying for absence, generates a totally different approach. It creates commitment, a sense of responsibility and an attitude of not wanting to let down the team. It also allows control. It gives the supervisor the right to chase up people who have not telephoned in with their reasons, to follow up with questions and to pick up patterns of absence. If people abuse the trust they can be subject to disciplinary action – perhaps loss of pay or eventually dismissal. Using this approach it is not unusual to attain attendance rates in excess of 98 per cent and to eliminate all but the 'accident on the road' lateness.

The ascendant organisation creates the atmosphere in which attendance on time is regarded as the norm. It generates commitment to effective working which means that not only do people arrive on time but they work 100 per cent effectively while they are there, that is they start and finish on time (including both sides of all breaks) and work at a 100 standard throughout the day. In most organisations most people start late and finish early, often adding five or ten minutes either side of break periods, and when they do work it is certainly not at 100 per cent effectiveness – in many cases it is as low as 50 per cent. ('As high as that!' is a frequent response.) It is not difficult to calculate that 40 per cent effective working is the most many companies obtain. Effective working is achieved through a combination of commitment and control where it counts – at the interface between two people, not between the individual and some remote human resources department.

If you start paying for sickness and do nothing else, then, of course, absence rates will rise. Such changes need to be part of a total programme, but those who argue that 'We can't afford to make this step' have not fully thought through the consequences of 'second-class citizenship'.

There are few organisations that go to 'all the way' and I would not argue that anything less than total harmonisation prevents them from being ascendant. Some argue that improving benefits as people rise through the hierarchy is itself a motivator and this may well be true. The key test is one of perceived fairness. There is no case that a shop-floor worker should have a worse sickness benefit scheme than a senior executive and if people perceive that they are being treated unfairly they will react adversely. You do not get a first-class response from people who perceive they are treated as second-class citizens.

This also means that some of the perks that come the way of top executives have to be denied to them. I have lost count of the number of invitations I have received to participate in golf matches and have listened to all the usual 'reasons' about doing business on golf courses and cementing relationships. Basically they are no more than an excuse to have a pleasant day out of the office. There is nothing that can be done on a golf course that cannot be achieved elsewhere and if your relationship with a supplier or customer is such that you enjoy each other's company then do so at weekends or take a vacation day. Operational staff would be delighted to be given the opportunity, but rarely do such chances come their way. When we are looking at perceived fairness, there is no justification for such differences of treatment.

When harmonising, the pressure is always to harmonise upwards. I know of one company which gave 'personal time' to white-collar staff in a fairly uncontrolled way, and as part of its harmonisation package extended the benefit to the shop floor. They have lived to regret it for it is now regarded as a right and seems to be out of control. Everyone expects three or four days a year to go to the dentist, visit the bank, see the solicitor and so on, and while it was accepted among the white-collar group who worked independently of each other, it has created major problems on the shop floor where there is a high degree of interdependence. It would have been easy to give a couple of days' extra holiday to everyone and cut out the 'personal time'.

Some staff may need to want a weekend or should be demoted driver

Common terms and conditions are necessary but not sufficient to achieve that first-class response. They are the initial step which has to be taken by management as a symbol of the confidence in the new way. But if that is all management does, it will get all the costs and none of the potential benefits.

The way people are treated in organisations is critical to their behaviour and, referring back to Karl Albrecht, to ensure there are no quality terrorists we need to delve further into behaviour.

TEAMWORKING

According to Ingersoll Engineers, six out of ten UK manufacturing businesses have adopted an organisational structure in the past five years that reflects their product or market and involves cross-functional teamworking; and having 'teams in production' was said by three-quarters of organisations as being the factor most vital to future business success (Ingersoll, 1997). A study by Ed Lawler of the Fortune 1000 companies found that 68 per cent were using self-managing work teams in some part of their organisation (Lawler *et al.*, 1995).

Unfortunately, there is possibly more misunderstanding about the concept of teamworking than about almost any other aspect of the ascendant organisation. 'Team' has a nice cosy feel about it, and in the senior executive's lexicon has replaced 'family' as the desirable corporate glue.

Most discussion has been about the multi-level, multi-functional teams and task forces pulled together to undertake a specific task, perhaps with membership changing as the project progresses through its cycle. Tom Peters popularised the term 'skunk works' to denote a group of people who go off together to achieve wonderful things, and phrases abound such as hot groups, super teams, high performance teams, small group activities, autonomous work groups and a myriad of others. A great problem with all of these terms is that they all seem to regard teamworking as something special – groups of people selected to perform specific tasks with others left behind. The other problem is that only rarely do any of the surveys say anything about the 'depth' of teamworking – 'Using self-managing work-teams in some part of their organisation' is just one example of the loose language that is bandied about. It can mean everything or almost nothing.

Others talk of reorganising the company into teams – Pearl Assurance is a good example of this, where the previous functions in which everyone performed a small part of, for example, claims vetting have been reorganised into teams in which the group takes responsibility for the whole process – rather like re-engineering. Other companies introduce cell manufacturing and say that they have reorganised into small teams.

Many make the mistake of believing that teamworking is always in the company's interest. When in the mid-1970s I was put into the Ford Dagenham Metal Stamping and Body Plant, the most effective team was the group of militant shop stewards. They could run rings around most of the management. They were a cohesive group, positively led by Danny Connor, the Communist convenor. They had clear objectives which were to ensure that any change was solely in the interest of the workers, to defend to the end any worker subjected to the disciplinary procedure and in so doing tie up the management in lengthy procedural debates, to denigrate the authority of the first line supervisor, to create an atmosphere of continuous tension so that management was always uncertain as to what would happen next, and last but by no means least to make sure that they as individuals did as little physical work as possible. For many years they had succeeded. Teamworking can be very effective when it is focused against the company!

Others follow the work of the theorists and attempt to construct teams based, for example, on Meredith Belbin's team characteristics (plant, resource investigator, co-ordinator, shaper, monitor evaluator, teamworker, implementer, completer and specialist) (Belbin 1981). While Belbin and the plethora of others who have developed similar lists may have been able to identify some helpful characteristics, if any manager sought to build a team on the ideal mix of personality types, sanity would quickly go out of the window. All most of us can do is to select people who combine the right skills and aptitude with an empathy with our way of doing things. We then find over a period of time that particular strengths emerge and if we have a series of such teams it may become possible to choose members with reference to the optimum mix. In practice, such analysis rarely goes beyond 'Joe's a good note-taker', or 'Janet will move things along'.

The great mistake in all of this is to confuse teamworking with work groups. Work groups have always been with us – they are about structures such as manufacturing cells, airline cabin crews, military platoons and so on, but you can have a work group without teamworking. Teamworking is a culture, a pattern of behaviour. The real gains come from the permanent group working together to build a product or provide a service. Soccer star Eric Cantona, quoted at the head of this chapter, got something else right. He spoke of his love to win and added: 'For Manchester, it is the same. We have the same vision of football and victory.' We must never forget that a team begins with individuals and my definition of teamworking is, therefore:

> A team is a group of individuals who work together to achieve shared goals.

It is no more than that – even if on many occasions people try to dress it up. The key words are *together* and *shared,* for it is comparatively easy to establish 'a group of people working to achieve an objective' and totally fail to establish a real team. We have all experienced the sports team in which only one of those words is present – we may have had a shared objective but we were not working *together* to achieve it.

HOW TO INTRODUCE TEAMWORKING

How then do we develop teamworking? There is no single prescriptive answer, but it must begin with the realisation that in organisations as they have developed, teamworking is not the natural order of the day because of the way people have reached positions of authority and because of their desire to protect their status. The irony is that it often requires a strong individual who has reached the top in the traditional way to take the lead in changing the culture of the organisation, and such individuals, converted to the concept of teamworking, are the least able to behave as both a member and leader of a genuine team.

We have seen Lou Gerstner's 'when *they* work together as a team'. When an executive says, 'I'm telling you we're going to become a team' the immediate, sometimes unsaid, response is, 'Don't I get a vote ?' If we wish to develop a culture in which teamworking and involvement become the norm the prospective team members must be involved in developing the culture that they wish to be a team.

The behaviour of the leader is the key to the development of teamworking. In developing a one-off team of people who have never before been involved, the process can be as follows:

1. Depending on the type of team, for example operational, service or cross-functional, select the members of the group based on their technical competences and/or aptitudes balanced with their broad

empathy with this way of working. Ensure that together the team members have the capability to carry out the full range of the tasks and, at the same time, keep the team small – four to eight members is about right. Try to select people whom you believe can work together, but often the best you can do is to avoid the obvious misfit (remembering also that the superficial misfit may turn out to be the grit which makes the oyster produce a pearl). There is no such thing as the ideal mix. People grow with the experience. You need to decide on the team leader. Should the leader be appointed from the outset or should the leader emerge? Perhaps there is no need for a leader. There is no right answer.

2. It is not possible to teach teamworking but it is possible to put people into situations in which they come to learn of its benefits. Some form of team development activity may help and it does not really matter what form it takes, provided it has relevance to the task in hand. Physical activities may be of value as part of generally developing people, if they provide learning opportunities, but will be of little value when they are seen as a test of physical endurance and some sort of survival course. Relevance and immediacy are of far more importance for a group established to tackle a particular situation. A few days as a group, learning how to solve problems using the most relevant of the available techniques adapted to the project, is as valuable as anything. Truly successful exercises occur when participants are able to review their performance and realise, for example, that all gain by assisting each other, by bringing out strengths, by analysing mistakes and learning from them, by understanding that the process is important and by learning to plan before taking action.

3. It is during these days that the task must be fully explored. The most effective teams are given the broad goal, but participate fully in defining the precise targets and methodology. The Parkinson principle, 'Work expands to fill the time allowed to achieve it', operates at all levels, and tough but just achievable time scales will place the right level of pressure on the team. What really counts is ownership of the goal and you achieve ownership by letting the team share in its precise definition and the means by which it will be attained. The contribution of the leader is critical. A dogmatic, domineering approach at this stage will turn everyone off but abdication can lead to anarchy. The positive leader, however, is not afraid of the group making its own decisions, as long as they remain pointing in the required, broad direction or can genuinely persuade the leader that the broad direction needs changing.

4. From then on the team must develop its own way of working and in so doing will develop as a team. What matters is not that the rules or plan are the best but that they are understood, shared and owned. The team can agree on confidentiality or openness, deputies allowed or not allowed, on-site or off-site meetings, regular meetings with joint activities or infrequent meetings with individual activities, roles assigned from the start or roles allowed to emerge; the initial leader remains throughout, another is appointed or the leadership changes as the project progresses. The permutations are endless and those that initially seem the most conducive to success may end up being of little significance. Ownership leads to self-accountability which in turn makes for success.

5. Establish intermediate goals and measure progress. The goals can be time-based, using a master schedule to determine the dates by which key stages of the programme have to be achieved, or they may be qualitative or quantitative. 'What gets measured properly gets done properly.' It is a measurable task based on fact, not opinion, that makes the group function as a team, not some abstract call to work together. However, the team has to decide if those objectives which are really important are measurable and if those objectives which are measurable are really important. To distinguish one from the other is crucial and if not properly done will reduce the chances of success. Do not underestimate the power of positive feedback. Whatever the tangible results might show, a word from the team leader, 'You did a great job getting the programme back on time', is worth a hundred symbols on a master schedule.

A most vital lesson is, do not spend vast amounts of time learning the theory of teams or participating in team-building techniques introduced by expensive consultants. Just get on and do it. If you have the will, a good leavening of common sense and have spent a few minutes reading the preceding five points you will be amazed at what you will achieve. Make mistakes. Do not worry about getting everything right before you begin, because you cannot and will not. Next time you will do better!

But this is about teams that form, do their job, and end. In the ascendant organisation, most teams will be continuous – they will comprise people working together every day in their normal task. They will develop over a long period of time as trust builds up between the members. In such an organisation it may barely be necessary to go through the team development process that is needed when *ad hoc* work groups or task forces are established. The continuous team has positive leadership and shared goals. As we saw when discussing front-line leadership, the leader has responsibility for selecting the members of the team. As a result he or she feels a commitment to the chosen people and the individual has a good feeling towards the person who has offered the job, and that is not a bad start for a relationship. Real teamworking, however, results from the total behaviour of the group – starting with communication.

COMMUNICATION

There is rarely an analysis of organisational difficulties that does not conclude, 'We need to improve our communications.' Most such analyses fail to distinguish between information and communication, and fail to take account of the fact that we communicate all the time, whether we like it or not.

Information is a one-way process, usually from the topdown. It relies on the internal newspaper, the corporate video (a 1997 survey by Vista Communications showed that in 1989, 90 per cent of respondents used video but by 1997 the proportion had dropped to 50 per cent – still too high but a welcome reduction; usually, they are no more than an ego trip for the chief executive!), the notice board or, in some companies, the formal brief, which is based on the mistaken concept that everyone should get the same message at the same time. Such methods take days or weeks to put together and usually the grapevine is there first. This confusion between information and communication was well illustrated in the *Wall Street Journal* (I found it in a 1994 diary). 'What do you mean we don't communicate? Just yesterday I faxed you a reply to the recorded message you left on your answering machine.' Today, an e-mail to your colleague along the corridor is rapidly overtaking the short walk for a chat. Jack Welch gave an admirable definition of communication:

> We've learned a bit about what communication is not. It's not a speech like this, or a videotape. It's not a plant newspaper. Real communication is an attitude, an environment. It's the most interactive of all processes. It requires countless hours of eyeball to eyeball back and forth. It involves more listening than talking. It is a constant, interactive process aimed at [creating] consensus. (Tichy and Sherman, 1993, p. 62)

One of my first lessons when visiting Japan resulted from my participating in the morning exercise period which, I felt, was of virtually no benefit, but it was followed by the supervisor talking with his team for a couple of minutes about matters that were directly relevant to that team. *That* was what mattered! I learned that if something is worth telling it is worth telling quickly and the only way to do that is face-to-face every day! Most people are interested primarily in what is happening in their immediate environment but as the subject becomes increasingly distant from their direct experience their interest decreases. The beer-delivery men of Scottish and Newcastle Breweries had no interest whatsoever in what is happening in their company's newly acquired holiday group, Center Parcs, and made sure their management knew it!

The focus must therefore be a group of people and their immediate leader, talking with each other on a daily basis on matters which affect them in a way which is appropriate for them. In 99 per cent of cases it simply does not matter if one leader gives a slightly different version of the same story or chooses to highlight different aspects of a common message. What is important is that the team together communicates in a way that is right for them and that the team looks for information to its leader, who is able to respond quickly. It must be a genuine two-way process, for if there is no subsequent feedback on comments raised, then employees will regard the exercise for what it is, a cynical exercise in deception.

Of course, it is not always possible to get a group together every day. Salesmen out on the road, service engineers operating from home, and so on, all pose problems and there is no single solution. Vista Communications found that about 60 per cent of briefings are held monthly – but that is not frequently enough, for the grapevine will always get there within a month. There is always a way if you are determined to beat the grapevine. One company uses e-mail, another uses cascade telephoning, another makes a point of bringing people together once every two weeks. If you find any of these difficult, ask, 'What route does the grapevine take?' Then build on that. Unless there is an accepted structure in place, Jack Welch's attitude and environment will achieve nothing. You need, not surprisingly, commitment and control.

When such a structure is in place it can readily be used on those few occasions when there is the need for the 'great message from on high' to be communicated accurately to all the people at the same time. One such example in Nissan was in November 1993 when a formal staff briefing was issued about the plans that had been worked out by the Company Council to deal with the 1994 recession in the European car market. In order to avoid press leaks (it is a great crime for employees to hear from the media before they hear from their own management), preparation of the document was kept within a very tight circle. It was briefed formally down the management chain with the clear objective that the supervisor should be the person to give the message at the operating level. When it has become natural that the first-line leader is the person who communicates about small matters it is also natural that this is the route for the big issues.

Similarly, during formal negotiations it is the supervisor who informs staff about the progress of discussions. It then becomes the representatives' role to seek the individual and collective views of their constituents and report these back to management. Of course, management will also use the supervisory network to get a feeling of their teams' attitudes. Usually, if supervisors are fully in touch with their teams, their initial reports and the subsequent reports from representatives will not be a million miles apart.

People should not feel that they can get something done by by-passing their own management and going directly to the top. Whether it is IBM's 'Speak Up' programme or Body Shop's (literally) red letters (whereby employees can write directly to the top), or an approach to my desk, the end result could be that people lose confidence in their supervisor's ability to solve the problem. It is a delicate balance. Nissan in Tennessee has a policy of rotating people every two to three hours. If this is not done, the individual can take it to the top by phoning a hot-line in the Vice-president, Human Resource's office. Questions are asked and, whatever the reason or result, the supervisor's authority is unacceptably undermined.

We all communicate all the time. As we walk through the door everyone immediately knows our mood. The manager who says a cheerful and genuine 'Good morning' is constantly reinforcing the message. The manager who ignores most people most of the time is perceived as only going through the motions when he or she does attempt to communicate formally. Much communication is non-verbal. Whether or not the organisation has a separate executive floor or genuinely open-plan offices with no one having a separate office sends out a message. As does the whole employment package as previously discussed.

Managers being seen to be on the shop floor, not to ask stupid questions about an employee's background but to be genuinely involved in the process, is vital; showing respect at all levels is fundamental, not by talking down to junior staff but by listening and talking at the correct level. The phrase 'Management by walking around' has achieved considerable popularity but like all such phrases it simplifies a complex situation. Toshiaki Tsuchiya walked around a great deal but 'with purpose'. He spoke very little English but when he was on the shop floor he was the most effective of communicators, for he understood what he saw, and through an interpreter was able to converse with operators about their job, its difficulties and potential solutions. They knew that he cared, and while neither directly understood what the other was *saying* they both understood what the other *meant*.

Top executives cannot manage a company by walking around it but they can get a feel of it by being frequently at the front line – provided the intermediate managers do not create a sanitised version of the real thing. Many top executives actually feel uncomfortable on the shop floor. They lack empathy. They are unable to bridge the perceived gap, and if they cannot, the shop floor worker will also feel uncomfortable, the contact will be artificial and they will end up doing more harm than good. Much better in these circumstances, after a few efforts, to retire to what they do well – which is certainly not managing an ascendant organisation! However if they are able to get close to the people, then, through honest and open communication, they will begin to earn the trust which is essential to long-term sustainable success.

This does not mean that top executives should not communicate directly to the whole organisation. One of the most effective processes if handled well and one of the most self-defeating if handled badly, is the chief executive meeting face to face with all staff to talk about those issues that need that level of authority. The bad are impersonal and highly structured, with beautiful visual aids but with information pitched at the wrong level. They inhibit questions but if someone does raise a hand the question is invariably something like, 'That's all very well, but we've been trying to get the washroom cleaned up for weeks. What are you going to do about that?' Or the trade union activists seek to score debating points. Good presentations are informal and relaxed; they may still use beautiful slides but they are pitched at the right level and the questions are related to the subject – because the washroom issues will have been sorted at the point at which they occur. That is the job of the immediate management.

Ian Gibson, Nissan's second managing director and I have stood up in front of all employees and said, 'We do not offer life-time employment. None of us has a guarantee against a collapse in the market but we do guarantee that none of you will lose your employment because of productivity improvements. It is not contractual – it is written in our blood!' That is how people at the top earn credibility and trust, and if they do not deliver that is how they lose it!

Real communication must start in the good times, for if you begin in the bad times you will hear, 'They only talk to us when there are problems!' If you communicate effectively and truthfully in the good times you can hope to build up the credibility which will see you through the bad. The worst thing that can happen is for employees not to appreciate that a company is in difficulty. They will know it anyway, but being told the truth by people they trust is what really counts. And that trust does not build up overnight. If the first time you genuinely communicate with people is in the bad times, you have lost before you have begun. A good leader spends more time communicating than almost anything else, but we know that leadership exists not only at the very top.

The good and the bad messages are most effectively conveyed by the immediate leader with the occasional direct injection from the very top. The ascendant organisation creates the atmosphere in which, within the team, communication is natural, spontaneous and genuinely two-way. The immediate leader is always walking around and is not by-passed. The chief executive communicates the vision and sets an example but not by usurping the responsibilities of the immediate leader.

INVOLVING PEOPLE

Teamworking and communication are both sub-sets of involvement. There is a spectrum of involvement which includes performance reviews, attitude surveys, project groups, teamworking and so on. Also, we need to distinguish between Employee Involvement and involving people. The first, with initial capital letters, is about formal structures, often negotiated with trade unions and involves the *representatives* of employees. The second is about genuinely involving all people in the organisation in those areas they can directly affect and ensuring they are fully informed about those areas they cannot directly affect.

The Germans have taken the *structure* of involvement as far as anyone. Their Works Constitution Act provides for the establishment of Works Councils in workplaces with more than five workers and requires that, 'The employer and the works council shall work together in a spirit of mutual trust' and provides a clear statement of the issues which are the subject of co-determination, separating out those areas which are subject to agreement from those which are subject to consultation and information.

Although this system is credited with the harmonious relations of German industry many German industrialists see it as a weight around their neck. Heinrich Weiss, President of the Federation of German Industries, said in 1992 that the process led to good industrial relations but slow decision-making. 'The process of seemingly endless discussions is becoming an increasingly great disadvantage in our industrial system' particularly when the market is demanding rapid change. Increasingly, German industrialists are trying to find a way round the system and a study by Industrial Democracy in Europe found that although the formal and actual rights of German workers representatives are among the highest in Europe, formal and actual management control is also among the highest (cited by Lane, 1989, p. 232). Perhaps this is why they resist real involvement.

The Confederation of British Industry (CBI) takes a non-structuralist view:

Nobody can compel enthusiasm. It tends to develop where jobs are satisfying; where opportunities exist for employees to contribute to workplace decision-making; where managers are readily accessible; where respect for the individual is shown; where information is shared and where everybody has a clear idea of their own and their company's objectives. This is employee involvement. (1988)

Central to successful involvement is not the structure but the range of subjects and the style, but at its simplest, and perhaps most profound, involving people is no more than seeking their views on how best to do something or how to resolve a problem. Generally, it is most successful when it relates to his or her job, which is the essence of *kaizen* – that the person doing a job knows more about that job than anyone else and that people have brains as well as hands.

The impact is well illustrated by the comments of Janet Jeffries, a Section Team Leader and Senior Shop Steward at car component supplier Marley near Bristol. After working with Nissan's Supplier Development Team she said:

For years it was taken for granted that shop floor workers left their brains with their clock cards . . . Supplier development training has changed all that and brought us out of the dark ages and into the 20th century . . . I was probably the most sceptical member of the first SD team. I thought, 'Here we go, another way to increase production – but giving nothing in return!' How wrong can you be? From being a sceptic I soon became totally committed. I have now been part of three SD teams and have watched the massive changes taking place. Cycle times, methods and layouts are studied by these teams and with the involvement of all the team, lots of changes are made. The environment is cleaner and brighter and layout changes have cut down on walking. Easy working has resulted in increased production without the need to work harder.

The whole concept is based upon involving people in contributing to improvements as a normal part of everyday life. Many companies will point to the enormous benefits they have gained from suggestions schemes, especially new style schemes in which the old bureaucracy is eliminated and the implementation and award decisions are made by the immediate supervisor.

These are a great improvement but, however effectively administered, they all reinforce the view that most people are not paid to think and that if they do they should be paid something extra. The ascendant organisation pays people to do *and* think. We really do have to get to the point where improving the way the job is done is a normal part of everyone's daily life. This does not mean that success should not be recognised somehow, but 'payment for suggestions' sits uneasily with genuine team-based *kaizen* activities and while I appreciate the practical difficulties in getting rid of an existing suggestions scheme there is considerable merit in putting it on hold (by agreement) while you are beginning to go down the *kaizen* route.

In Nissan we estimate that about 90 per cent of the changes made to current processes come from the people doing the job. In 1993, Neil Mackenzie of the QA Vehicle Test team proposed the deletion of a redundant pulley on Micras built without air-conditioning. This was accepted and saved the company £1.5 million. It was the largest identifiable saving and he received a plaque and the team a refrigerator for the meeting room. There was also a report in the internal company newspaper. This was picked up by the local and national media and Nissan was castigated for its meanness, with comparisons being with other more generous companies. They entirely missed the point. *Everybody* contributes to product improvement. Neil Mackenzie considered it a normal part of his job and said so in subsequent media interviews. When you are motivated to work for the success of the enterprise, are given responsibility, are trusted and your contribution is valued and recognised, the extraordinary becomes the norm.

Using *kaizen* all people in the ascendant organisation are involved in continuously seeking to improve the current best method. In most Western organisations the best method, the standard operation, if it exists, is the property of the engineering department; they prepare it, issue it and, with varying degrees of enthusiasm, police it. Consequently it is adhered to with varying degrees of enthusiasm and certainly no operator ever tries to improve it.

In the ascendant organisation the standard operation is the property of the people doing the job. They prepare it and adhere to it because it is theirs, and continuously seek to improve it. When an individual gets an idea, he or she shares it with the supervisor who, if happy with it, gives the go-ahead. The individual liaises with the people on the opposite shift, ensures that making life easier in one section does not cause problems in another and if everything is OK the individual, if he or she has the technical capability, physically makes the change. Of course, there are a few rules. Nothing can prejudice the safety of the product in use, reduce quality or safety, but within these rules it is the decision of the responsible production people as to whether or not to proceed.

Once the change is implemented, the standard operation is rewritten and the revised method then becomes the new 'one best way' which must be followed until the next change comes along.

The ascendant organisation does not negotiate technological change but has far more genuine involvement of employees in the change process than traditional organisations. If you genuinely believe that employees know more about the job than anyone else it makes sense to seek their views on whether and how changes are needed, but the process goes a lot further.

In all such situations what happens is that control *of* the process is given to those who are normally regarded as being controlled *by* the process, and it is this as much as anything, when combined with all other concepts and practices, that marries together control of the processes and commitment of the people leading to the ascendant organisation.

A clear example of involving employees in the bigger decisions was Nissan's response to the 1993/4 recession in the European car market mentioned in the previous section. We had taken all possible action to protect the core workforce. Temporary workers' contracts were not renewed; some work previously contracted out was brought in-house; employees were found temporary assignments elsewhere in Nissan in Europe; overtime was cut; hiring was stopped and towards the end of the year we cut out the night shift without reducing basic pay. But by October it was obvious that the European car industry recession would be continuing for at least the next year and possibly beyond that. As a result we had an imbalance between our projected volumes and the number of employees, a not uncommon experience in the car industry. Most manufacturers, particularly in Germany, announced redundancies and lay-offs. Instead, Operations Director, John Cushnaghan and I met with the Company Council, fully explained the position and set in train a company-wide consultation as to how we might handle the imbalance. We genuinely wanted to involve everyone in the company in the biggest downside decision we had had to make and which would be the true test of whether our philosophy worked in the bad times as well as the good. The elected members of the Company Council accepted this task and said that we should not be surprised if they came up with a different solution from anything we had thought of. In turn I told them that they were taking on a tough job – and they were.

They spent two weeks talking with virtually every employee. Often, people were surprised. No one had ever been involved in anything like this and could not conceive that they would be genuinely consulted on such a matter. Many had come from traditional companies and had experienced redundancies, often simply by being called together and told that they were going. When the representatives reported back they amazed us.

They said that there was a clear recognition that there were too many people for 1994 volumes; however, they wished to avoid short-time working and get back to full work patterns as quickly as possible. They recognised that to achieve this we would need to accelerate our natural wastage rate and to do this there would have to be some sort of encouragement payment. If this were to be done it should be done quickly, it should be generous and there should be no compulsion. They also recognised that the company might have to refuse some requests in order to maintain its operational integrity.

The incredible thing was, that given the full business information, the workforce came up with the optimum business solution. They had got there in one go. Perhaps it was not so incredible – just that we underrate people's maturity.

We subsequently agreed a package – separation by agreement – which provided that within a specified period anyone could apply to leave and, if agreed, a payment of six months' salary would be made. There would be no compulsion and no target numbers. We agreed that we would adjust the shift patterns, line speeds and the balance of work done in-house or externally to meet the available workforce.

The company's response was greeted enthusiastically by the workforce. It was felt that the Company Council had done an excellent job and proved that sensible people, given full information and asked for their views, can come up with sensible answers. We had involved all the people in the company in the big issue, not just in the small ones – but the fact that they were used to being involved in the small issues in the good times, meant that they were quite capable of being involved in the big issues when times were not so good. There is a fundamental lesson lying in there. As with communication, do not start the involvement process when times are tough – you will not be believed. Begin in the good times and build up the credibility which will hold you in good stead when you really need it.

Teamworking may be regarded as one of the higher forms of involving employees and seems to be one of the most widely used concepts. A 1996 study by Ingersoll Engineers is one of many which emphasise the growth of teamworking. Ingersoll stated that six out of ten UK manufacturing businesses have adopted cross-functional teamworking. The trouble with most such surveys is that they rarely say very much about the intensity and depth of the practices they measure nor do they indicate their longevity. This was partially corrected in 1997 when the European Foundation published the results of a survey of 5,786 establishments across all sectors of the economy in ten European countries. The study examined six types of participation as follows:

Form of participation	*Examples*
1. Individual face-to-face consultation:	Performance reviews, 360° appraisal, development reviews
2. Arm's length consultation:	Attitude surveys
3. Group consultation – temporary:	Project groups, task forces
4. Group consultation – permanent groups	Quality circles
5. Individual delegation	Job enrichment
6. Group delegation	Group work, teamwork

The results of the survey are shown in Table 7.1.

Except for 'Individual delegation' around one-third of workplaces reported each form of participation, but of the three examples centring on what would be generally termed 'Teamworking' only about one-sixth of workplaces claimed to have more than 50 per cent of their workforce involved and these forms were not generally seen as being the most important!

Table 7.1   Extent and Depth of Participation in Teamworking (per cent)

| | Individual consultation | | Group consultation | | | |
	Face-to-face	Arm's length	Temporary group	Permanent group	Individual delegation	Group delegation
Workplaces using	35	40	31	30	55	36
Workplaces involving 50% + of employees	Not covered	Not covered	15	14	Not covered	17
Workplaces judging given form as the most important	10	22	13	27	10	17

Source: European Foundation, 1997 (From Paul Edwards, University of Warwick to author).

The study goes on to examine the scope of participation and the degree of autonomy granted under group delegation. Respondents were asked how often employees were consulted about issues such as quality and whether they were able to make their decisions on matters such as work scheduling, dealing with internal and external customers and selecting their own team members. Limited delegation was found. Of those respondents practising individual delegation, only one-fifth were given a high score on intensity and only 19 per cent of those with group delegation achieved a high score.

The conclusion is that that when real power over work is measured, the number of organisations practising advanced forms is low. Involvement and participation is still much more talked about than practised.

KAIZEN IN PRACTICE

I described the broad principles of *kaizen* in Chapter 4 and also referred to it when discussing involvement – the elements are inextricably linked. By definition *kaizen* changes are rarely large. The vast majority of people are not mavericks coming up with crazy ideas, but when their mental juices are stimulated they will frequently come up with simple, low-cost solutions, often missed by the professionals who usually find the complex and expensive solution. Wolfgang Strinz, then the Chief Executive of Opel's Bochum plant in Germany, discussed with a supervisor a device he saw in Nissan for lifting petrol tanks to the underside of the car:

'Who developed that?'

'The operators – it took them about three months.'

'Did it work first time?'

'No, but they kept at it until they got it right. It may not look a masterpiece of engineering but it does the job and saves a lot of time and effort.'

'We've been trying to do something like that for three years but every time the engineers come up with a new solution the operators don't like it, they can't work with it – and it's cost us thousands of Deutschmarks!'

That is the difference between *kaizen* and *kaikaku* (radical improvements), between involvement and imposition and between ownership and external control.

Many of the *kaizen* activities relate to material delivery systems. Tremendous effort goes into reducing lineside stock and ensuring that it is delivered to the operator in the correct mode. For example, the large rear axles were delivered lineside in pallets which needed the operator to lift them out by bending, increasingly acutely as the pallet was emptied. After considerable experimentation, including assistance from engineers, the operators developed a gravity-fed roller system which delivered the axles lineside at the right height on small platforms ready for placing into position. The platforms, when cleared, dropped down and were gravity-fed back to the aisleway to restart the cycle.

My favourite *kaizen* of all time is . . . drainpipes! In any form of manufacturing one of the most difficult material supply tasks is the delivery of small parts – nuts, bolts, grommets, and so on. They usually arrive in cardboard boxes and end up either in an untidy mess or, in decanting the parts half of them finish on the floor. The brilliant solution was to use small lengths of drainpipe attached to the pallets and angled down towards the operator. The two ends were half cut away so that the parts could be poured in from the rear and then drop down to the operator (with of course the front end stopped, to prevent them falling on the floor!). So successful has this been that banks of a dozen can now be seen. Such an idea could only come from the person doing the job. The professionals would come up with the £5,000 solution; the operator's idea cost a few pounds!

The history of *kaizen* within Nissan illustrates a number of points about both the company's culture and how *kaizen* can develop. After a considerable debate, and not having got the culture firmly embedded, we decided to try what we called *kaizen* teams and planned an extensive training programme throughout 1987. From January to May the steering committee was trained. The first teams formed and trained and Kaizen (with a big K) was formally launched in May 1987. The aim was that everyone at all levels should be involved, with managers and engineers providing support, encouragement and facilities and then participate in or lead teams.

The first teams were from Body Construction and Personnel – the 'Diamonds' and the 'Pioneers'. The 'Diamonds' looked at the use of safety equipment in the Body Shop and how higher levels of production could be achieved at lower cost, and the 'Pioneers' at the recruitment management system. We went through all the usual paraphernalia including the big presentation of the results to a wide spectrum of people within the company.

The results were, in themselves, good but the process was uniformly criticised, including by those who had been advocates of what we had come to call 'Big K', compared with 'little k' which was the informal bottom-up approach. When reviewed, the main comments were:

- 'Big K' is too formal and structured – too much paperwork causes a reluctance to become involved.
- Groups do not like making presentations to large meetings.
- 'Little k' is more important than 'Big K'.
- The steering committee is too remote. The commitment has to be felt at the personal day-to-day interface.

As a result 'Big K' was dropped.

We concluded that *kaizen* does not have to be carried out in formal teams meeting out of hours and that often an individual or small informal group can think of a better way in a very short time. *Kaizen* means thinking about what you do, how you do it and then finding a better way. It does not have to be big to be impressive. The essential points must be that:

- The search for improvement is continuous
- No improvement is too small
- Once implemented, improvements must be maintained to ensure a steady progress
- Any aspect of work performance and the working environment can be improved
- Everyone can participate, not just experts.

Also, it is not restricted to the shop-floor activities. *Kaizen* can work anywhere, in any function at any time.

However, over time *kaizen* became more systematic. We introduced *kaizen* workshops, in which a small permanent staff work on some of the more complex improvement tasks. At all times the safety of the workplace is paramount and we were finding that individuals, with the best will in the world, did not always have the ability to fabricate the devices they had conceived, or that they could not always appreciate the effect of such devices on adjacent sections of the workplace. Using welding torches, for example, is potentially dangerous and if the integrity of the weld is not right the device can be dangerous in use. Thus, we had to introduce some formality, and while 90 per cent of the ideas still originate from the production staff, the actual fabrication is now more frequently undertaken by those with professional skills. The commitment of the people is now balanced with control of the processes.

This is almost inevitable in any organisation which develops the concept to a great extent. Individuals' enthusiasm may exceed their capability, and while much remains with the originator, a responsible management must ensure a safe working place. The great thing, however, is that while one would expect this to dampen enthusiasm, the general reaction is that when people see their original concept being developed and made to look and perform better than they had originally conceived, it fires enthusiasm rather than dampens it. Many of us were worried about the potential for losing the spark. We need not have been.

Kaizen virtually institutionalises improvement – it builds it into the fabric of the organisation. And when it is in the fabric it results not just in small improvements but in the radical changes – *kaikaku*. A company which is constantly seeking to do things better will quickly get round to asking if it needs to do certain things at all and will find that often it does not. It will also breed a culture which welcomes the big change when it comes. Innovate and then improve. I refer you back to the example of 3M. Not all contributions can be major innovations, but when you have a spirit which is dedicated to improvement in all things, then somehow the big ones emerge. And you do not achieve continuous success by sending small groups away to work in isolation – you achieve by creating the environment in which all can contribute.

HOW TO INVOLVE PEOPLE

Stop talking about it and

> ### JUST DO IT

It does not have to be initiated at the top of the organisation – although that might help; involving people can start anywhere.

Define a very specific practical issue that needs to be tackled. It really does not matter very much what it is, except that it should be achievable – it doesn't help to start with a failure. Then let them get on with it. They will quickly find out if they need assistance in one form or other – training in problem-solving techniques, assistance from someone outside the group, and so on – so be ready and prepared to give it. There is nothing better than just-in-time training related to a known need.

Once the problem is solved, do not necessarily seek the big presentation to senior management for there is nothing worse than seeing a group spending more time preparing a presentation on what they have achieved than they spent on the achievement itself. Often, such presentations seem condescending – 'Look boss, haven't we done a good job?' and then getting a pat on the head! This does not mean that management should not take an interest, but if involving people is to be the norm then you cannot have a continuous series of presentations which makes it abnormal and which, if successful, would tie up management for most of its time. If it is felt that something is particularly worthwhile, an expression of interest and a word of thanks by top managers on their normal walkabouts is worth a hundred formal presentations.

This does not totally preclude the presentation. Many organisations swear by them, and find that people enjoy making them; indeed, speaking in front of an audience can bring out hidden talents in some and develop confidence in others. They may be a necessary stage but if responsibility really lies where it should and involving people is the norm they could be become self-defeating. Maybe real success comes when involvement is so ingrained that top management makes presentations to the front liners to explain what the top has done to help the front line!

Genuinely involving people can open Pandora's box. Management will have to give up some of its perceived control without necessarily knowing what the outcome will be. It may have to change its support structures – the job of the finance department may have to become one of providing information to help the direct departments do their job better rather than continuously asking those who add value why they have overspent their budget or exhorting them to reduce their costs even further. The payment system may have to change from rewarding service to rewarding initiative. The permutations are endless, but the important point is that such changes must follow and not precede. In the ascendant organisation the indirect departments provide a service to the direct. They do not control. Remember the teachings of the behavioural scientists in Chapter 2.

To be truly successful, involving people must then be an integral part of everyday life, not something special. It must be integrated with the overall business objectives and strategy, not stand alone. Success is determined not by the structure but by the process, not by the short-term results but by the trust which is built, not by participation by representatives but by the involvement of everybody, not by a formal determination of prerogatives but by an expansion of contributions, not by only involving people in the good times but also by valuing their contribution in the bad. Maybe, just doing it is not as simple as it seems but, tomorrow, ask someone what he or she thinks or if they can come up with a better way. You'll be amazed at the results!

FLEXIBILITY

When we speak of single status, teamworking, communication and involvement, we have in the same breath to include flexibility.

Flexibility comes in many guises and with an increasingly diffuse terminology. We distinguish, for example, between functional flexibility, numerical flexibility, organisational flexibility, financial flexibility, structural flexibility. Part-time working, job sharing, flexible hours, zero-based contracts, fixed-term contracts, casual work and home-working all come within the flexibility framework. However, in this section I am concerned with flexibility of working practices.

One of the real causes of inflexibility within organisations is the job evaluation system. For more than twenty years I have argued against job evaluation, job descriptions and their associated paraphernalia. Job evaluation is the managerial equivalent of the trade union restrictive practice, but it is widely used. A 1996 survey of 530 companies by the Industrial Society found that 281 (53 per cent) operated a job evaluation scheme

In two companies, Continental Can Company and Nissan, I have been able to develop organisations which had none of these, and the process was fully described in *The Road to Nissan* (Wickens, 1987). In summary, however, if you aim for total flexibility, a flat organisation, teamworking, devolved responsibility and continuous improvement with change being the only constant, then any process which analyses in detail what people do at any point in time, writes it up in immense detail, assigns a grade and a specific job title, allows grading grievances and so on, ends up by restricting rather than expanding what people do. I often use a slide which shows a cartoon of a tombstone on which is written

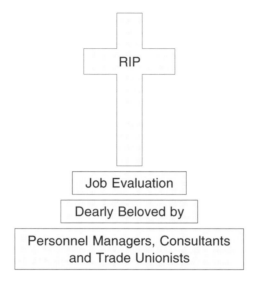

RIP

Job Evaluation

Dearly Beloved by

Personnel Managers, Consultants and Trade Unionists

Job evaluation creates vast amounts of work for people in personnel departments and a good living for those purporting to provide objective measures of relative job values. But what added value does it bring to the enterprise? None! All it does is add cost and restrict flexibility.

I know why organisations have job evaluation – an attempt to achieve an objective measure of comparative worth and a defence against the comparability arguments put forward by trade unions; but the ascendant organisation does not require precisely analysed jobs, described in minute detail and fixed at a point in time. Of course, no organisation can simply abandon its system overnight, but in many organisations the tail is wagging the dog. The tail of maintaining the purity of the internal relativities and job descriptions is wagging the dog of flexibility, teamworking, continuous improvement and rapid response to changing circumstances.

Further, job evaluation systems only works if the results are perceived as being fair, so when raw scores fail to give the 'right' relativities, the weightings of the factors are 'balanced' so as to achieve an acceptable result. Of course, there will always be disagreements at the margins, but in any organisation a small group of people who know the organisation well can, within a day, come up with a broad ranking order of jobs, fully integrating the manual and non-manual. While it may be argued that this in itself is a form of non-analytical whole job evaluation (and I would concede the point) it is so far removed from the vast majority of analytical systems as to be something genuinely different. Job evaluation should be laid to Rest in Peace.

The ascendant organisation, in order to maximise flexibility, minimises the number the job titles. For example, in Nissan we established a fully integrated occupational classification which includes the generic job titles Engineer and Senior Engineer. We deliberately avoided the '57 varieties' of engineer common in most large companies. The only job description, and this is not written down, is, 'An engineer will do everything an engineer is required to do.' The Senior Engineer is in charge of half a dozen Engineers, but at any time may be doing work that is less complex, as complex, or more complex than an Engineer. Engineering, or any other work, does not come in discrete levels of complexity nor is it precisely divided into electrical, electronics, mechanical, pneumatic, layout, process, facility and so on. An engineer is restricted only by capability, not by narrow job descriptions. This does not mean that everybody does everything. Were that to be the case we would spend all our time training and no time working, but there are no artificial constraints on what people do.

Real flexibility of working practices does not need to be spelled out in detail. The Nissan agreement with the Amalgamated Engineering and Electrical Union (AEEU) says:

- To ensure the fullest use of plant, equipment and staff . . . there will be complete flexibility and mobility of employees.
- It is agreed that changes in technology, processes and practices will be introduced and that such changes will affect both productivity and manning levels. To ensure such flexibility and change, employees will undertake and/or undertake training for all work as required by the Company. All employees will train other employees as required.

Once you have that, anything additional will restrict.

Very similar words have since been used in many companies, including Coca Cola and Rover. But you must use this flexibility. People easily revert to type. If a company establishes a multi-skilled maintenance technician position which provides that an individual can be trained to work in electronics, mechanics, hydraulics, pneumatics or electrics and then does not use the new flexibility, it has only itself to blame.

Multi-skilling in the ascendant organisation is not just about expanding the range of physical tasks for which a person is responsible. New technology means that the amalgamation of traditional work practices is only the beginning. Operators learning to programme CNC machinery or robots is a classic example of technology-driven flexibility. But true flexibility is concerned with expanding the role and responsibilities of every individual. It encompasses teamworking, small group activities, continuous improvement; taking on responsibility for quality and housekeeping, working with suppliers and internal and external customers; training others and becoming involved in multi-disciplinary teams. It means accepting responsibilities that once belonged to more senior, or more junior, people. Thousands of organisations can now point to a reduction in their number of job titles. Few have fully understood the implications of true flexibility.

PERFORMANCE APPRAISAL

Quality guru W. Edwards Deming was totally opposed to performance appraisal, citing the evaluation of performance, merit-rating and annual reviews as one of his 'deadly diseases' (Deming, 1982, p. 101). Peter Scholtes, a disciple of Deming, writes that for Deming, 'Merit rating rewards people that do well in the system. It does not reward attempts to improve the system' (Scholtes, 1987). Deming and Scholtes stylise evaluation systems as being based on establishing measurements of standards against which performance is judged – units per day, calls per week, timely completion of a project, and so on. They relate it to past performance. But, they argue, an employee's work is tied to many systems and processes – individuals cannot be appraised apart from the systems in which they work, nor from their group. Says Scholtes, 'Performance evaluation encourages "lone rangers" . . . [It] will force workers to choose between individual reward and recognition of teamwork. Such a choice will seldom reinforce teamwork.' It encourages mediocrity and safe goals, it encourages employees to work around the systems, not improve them; it will, over time, become top heavy as ratings drift upwards, and will always create losers. Or so the argument goes.

If such a stylisation were right, Deming and his disciples would be right, but in their universal condemnation they are wrong. Performance evaluation is not irredeemable if it is part of an overall performance management process which supports the culture of the organisation, values all the elements the organisation values and assists in driving it in the direction it wishes to go.

Deming nt against Dev.

Any appraisal system must satisfy the fundament principles of being objective, consistent, open, motivating and be fair and be seen to be fair. In addition it should:

- Reflect the culture of the company, valuing all those element the company values
- Compare actual against expected performance using assessments that are clear and understandable
- Improve the performance of the individual in his/her present job
- Help identify potential, development needs and opportunities
- Identify problems and/or weaknesses and plan improvement activities
- Provide the opportunity for the individual to express openly his/her views and aspirations and for the appraiser to listen*
- Allow the individual to give feedback to the appraiser on the support or otherwise he/she has provided*
- Provide the opportunity to agree objectives and goals
- Ensure proper follow-up and implementation of any actions and development activities
- If the company has any form of pay progression based on performance, provide the link between performance and pay.

The two asterisked objectives might be considered to be 360-degree appraisal, a business fad which is more discussed than performed. However, I refer to a relaxed and non-threatening two-way discussion from which all parties can learn, not a formal system which may end up being referred to the 'boss's boss' and which creates a wholly artificial relationship. For example, Mike Thatcher reports that Federal Express gives a questionnaire to every employee asking them to assess the performance of their line manager (*People Management*, March 1996). Around 112,000 forms are sent to world headquarters in Memphis where they are analysed and returned to the managers concerned. Good and average performers then discuss with their staff how they can further improve, and those said to have a 'critical concern score' meet with the personnel department to discuss improvement actions and they are reassessed six months later. If there are employee relations problems the personnel department investigates and the results can determine pay increases and bonuses. Alan Rankine, vice-president for personnel in Europe, said that some managers cannot cope with this. 'I guess we would say that it is best that those particular individuals not be in management at Federal Express.' Does this faintly suggest a slightly arrogant view?

A 1996 survey by Ashridge Research of *The Times* Top 1000 UK companies found 45 which had introduced 360-degree appraisal. Although 'generally thought of as successful' 50 per cent said it was time-consuming and expensive, 36 per cent said it is threatening to participants receiving feedback and 45 per cent believed that subordinates who reported felt threatened and unable to be honest.

In preparing an appraisal the views of a variety of people with whom the individual is in contact should be taken into account, and some companies such as NSK, one of the top two bearing manufacturers in the world, have developed a system of team evaluation in which the assessment is prepared jointly by three or four people who work with the individual. WH Smith trialled a system in which thirteen people were involved in assessing one individual – no wonder the company is in difficulty!

This is a lot to ask of any system. A 1990 survey by the Wyatt Company found that only 20 per cent of 600 personnel professionals described their performance management process as 'effective' and only 11 per cent said they had systems which delivered performance pay effectively (Wyatt, 1990). But success is possible.

Perhaps the most critical point is that the appraisal system should assess those elements of performance that the company considers important. It is no good valuing teamworking, quality of work, flexibility, innovation and so on, if they are not assessed. And this is where current thinking on the value of competences comes in. Competences are, broadly:

Qualities and behaviours an individual needs in order to perform effectively.

They are what people bring to the job, and can include reasoning, creativity, leadership, communication, teamworking, and so on. They contribute to the achievement of results. Reigate and Banstead Borough Council has made tremendous efforts to combine task specific skills with fourteen competences which are used in different degrees across the full range of jobs from the chief executive to car park attendant. Divided into four categories, their competences are:

Understanding what needs to be done   Strategic thinking
                                             Decision making
                                             Problem solving
                                             Know-how/experience

Managing relationships	Communication skills
	Inter-personal skills
	Influencing and negotiation
	Building relationships
	Customer care
	Teamwork
Active management	Planning
	Achieving through others
Achieving results	Self-motivating
	Adaptability

Introduced in 1997, that is a pretty good list.

One of the most difficult areas is how to bring teamworking into the equation. No team is totally self-sufficient; its success depends on the previous learning experiences of its members, the framework within which it operates and the support it receives from those less directly involved. Some team members make an outstanding contribution to a team that does not succeed; others may make a poor contribution to a successful team. Others question if assessing teamworking and valuing individual contributions are compatible.

One company which has successfully incorporated 'teamworking' into its performance management process is Sun Life Assurance. It describes teamworking and gives negative and positive examples before asking for an overall rating:

Teamworking
Valuing teamwork and the desire to co-operate and take an active part within the team and to align own behaviour with the needs, priorities and goals of the team:

Negative examples

- Show reluctance to help others in team
- Keep self to self, fail to participate
- Be insensitive to others in the team

Positive examples

- Build on suggestions of others
- Show understanding of colleagues' difficulties
- Volunteer to help other with exceptional workloads

It is always possible to quibble with the detail of such descriptions, but Sun Life has shown that it is possible.

Within the ascendant organisation the rules of transparency and common terms and conditions mean that if *some* are to have performance appraisal, *all* are to have performance appraisal. However, in view of the very different types of work and responsibility, it may not be possible to develop a single performance appraisal system that applies to everyone. The important points are that the system(s) should be fair, that a 'blue-eyed boy' syndrome is prevented from developing and costs should be controlled. There is no magic formula for this but I favour a forced choice approach in which the appraiser has to rate an individual against specific statements. Examples of this are shown in Figure 7.1. Such a system should not be restricted to a top-down box-ticking exercise. It must include space for written expansion and at all levels it must be part of a two-way discussion of corporate and individual objectives and individual development needs.

The critical point in any performance evaluation system, but particularly for those which relate to salary progression, is the overall

---

Quality of work
Consistently excels in all aspects
High standard in all aspects
Acceptable quality
Of varying quality; sometimes below
  minimum
Unacceptable quality

Flexibility
Constantly increasing personal
  flexibility
Welcomes new methods and tasks
Shows expected flexibility
Needs encouragement
Accepts change reluctantly
Rigid and inflexible

Performance against objectives
Consistently exceeds all objectives
Consistently achieves all objectives
Achieves some but no others
Does not achieve most objectives
Unacceptable: does not achieve
  objectives

Teamworking
Always recognises and respects
  needs of the team
Works well as a team member
Becomes involved when encouraged
Not supportive of team
Prefers own company – a loner

Safety and Housekeeping
Always attains highest possible
  standard
Regularly achieves a high standard
Tries hard but needs reminding
Unacceptable standard; a danger to
  others

Attitude/motivation
Exceptional commitment and
  determination
Genuine interest and positive
  attitude
Displays a positive approach
Shows little commitment
Negative motivation and attitude

Figure 7.1 Performance Evaluation Elements

performance rating. Appraisers like to be liked and can easily over-rate their staff; the phenomenon of rating drift occurs; 'Average' becomes unacceptable, 'Above average' is the norm (and 'Above average' then becomes the average!) and salary costs creep upwards. Further, as you move up the hierarchy, the more likely you are to receive high assessment, for you are judged not against your peers but against those at a lower level. Chris Bottomley, HR Director of Nat West Bank, told the 1995 conference of the Institute of Personnel and Development, 'Those who are management seem to have got a higher level of performance rise than the staff.' In an attempt to avoid this, the rating into which the majority of people will fall has to be defined in a way which will be regarded as acceptable. While a slight positive skew in the rating distribution curve is acceptable if by design, it is unacceptable if it happens by accident.

One way of overcoming this is by giving clear guidelines as to the proportion of the population which should fall into each rating level. Nissan's ratings, their description and guideline percentages of the population falling into each level are shown in Figure 7.2.

Rating	Description	Guideline
Outstanding	Leaves little to be desired. Consistently make exceptional contributions, both individually and to the company. Consistently exceeds objectives.	Less than 3%
Highly commendable	Tasks and assignments particularly well handled and regularly makes significant contributions. Often exceeds some objectives.	20–25%
Fully proficient	Fully acceptable performance. Normal tasks and assignments, and individual and/or team objectives carried out effectively.	70–75%
Requires improvement	Most tasks, assignments and objectives carried out acceptably but displays inconsistencies that require improvement.	Less than 3%
Below expected performance	Below minimum requirements. Tasks and assignments not usually properly completed. Objectives not usually met. Requires a high level of supervision.	Less than 2%

Figure 7.2 Performance Rating Distribution Guidelines

The real trick lies in controlling the distribution of ratings, and the responsibility for achieving this lies with managers. Each year every manager, after consultation within the section, has to predict the distribution of ratings within his/her area of responsibility. This information is passed to the personnel manager who collates it, produce pretty graphs showing the prediction against the guideline and, at a meeting of all managers, the predictions are shared. If a manager significantly deviates from the guidelines, he/she has to justify to all the others why their section has, say, twice as many people rated 'Outstanding' as any other section. If they can succeed in convincing their peers, who usually will know the individuals concerned, they have probably got it right. There is no tougher jury! Because the system has gone through nine or ten cycles they are now able to track the trend through the year, and measure the year-end actual against both the guidelines and the predictions.

This may seem mechanistic, and to a certain extent it is. It is a controlled process and while it may seem less *avant-garde* than those in the forefront of thinking would wish, it provides for consistency, equity and a high quality of assessment. It would be somewhat difficult to implement performance contracts for 2,000 direct production staff! And if it is difficult, it will not be properly implemented and will then fall into disrepute. It is just one method, among many, but the important point is that it works in its environment, and when in 1996 people at all levels and in all functions were involved in a root-and-branch review, nobody sought to make fundamental changes.

It has been argued that such a system requires a sophisticated workforce, that people like clarity, that they need increases of 10 to 15 per cent if they are to be meaningful. The ascendant organisation *has* a sophisticated workforce; it is able to absorb and fully understand such an approach and it does not require 10 to 15 per cent pay increases to secure commitment!

8 The Processes and Practicalities

The continuing increases in purchasing power and leisure time that have made many Americans the envy of working people everywhere have not come from working ever harder – but from working ever smarter.

William C. Freund

One trouble with Americans is that we're fixers rather than preventers.

General James Doolittle

For years the aim of many manufacturers was to achieve full automation with centralised planning and control of the production process. The unmanned factory was the ultimate goal, achieving high levels of quality and efficiency at low cost. However, automation as an end in itself failed to take into account the fact that the contribution of the people doing the job could be a major source of improvement in quality and productivity. But technology can begin to provide at least some of the answers. This chapter looks at what people actually do in this new environment which seeks to pull together control of the processes and commitment of the people. (Two other key elements, the elimination of waste and the standard operation, have already been discussed in Chapter 3.)

However, let us never forget that the systems we will discuss are devised by people and are implemented by people. They are as good or as bad as the people make them.

CELL MANUFACTURING

Manufacturing cells were first introduced in the early 1970s when it was recognised that, for example, having all the lathes together, all the welding machines together, all the assembly operations together was wasteful – and waste has to be eliminated! Engineers began to realise that grouping a lathe, a welder and an assembly operation together could dramatically reduce the transfer distance and time between the various stages. Further, they recognised that groupings could lead to reduced set-

135

up times and allow one person to control the whole of the manufacturing process for a particular product. Previously, machines were grouped by process: under cell manufacturing, they are grouped by product.

Manufacturing cells can be highly sophisticated, using CNC machine tools and flexible manufacturing systems, or simple assembly processes entailing little more than a reorganisation of existing equipment. Final assembly cells may even be fed by their own sub-assembly cells, their own sole supplier of components.

The actual work organisation within a cell can vary considerably, depending on how much authority the management wishes to devolve, but usually the operators will take on broader responsibilities. At a minimum, responsibility for quality and material movement are added to the production tasks but responsibilities can extend to routine preventive maintenance activities, problem-solving, improvement, material ordering, scheduling, and so on. Some may even become virtually self-contained business units responsible for their own cost and performance monitoring, relationship with suppliers, and the selection and training of their team members.

Ingersoll Engineers describes the trend to manufacturing cells as the 'quiet revolution' and has plotted its growth for several years. In 1990, 51 per cent of UK manufacturers employed cell manufacturing techniques and by 1993 this had risen to 73 per cent. By 1993 nearly a third of those with cells already had fully cellular operations and half were planning additional cells (Ingersoll Engineers, 1991 and 1993).

One of the most successful users of manufacturing cells is Rearsby Automotive, a long-established mechanical components manufacturer based in Leicester. Rearsby's Chairman, Ivor Vaughan, led a management buy-out and set about trying to change both the culture of the company and its manufacturing processes. Rearsby was a typical metal basher with a complex process, top-down management by control approach, an order to delivery time measured in months, high inventory, obsolete stock, too much scrap, high rework levels and no teamworking. Said Ivor Vaughan, 'We thought we were laid out well but we were totally higgledy-piggledy with vast storage areas and the manufacturing areas divided into specialities with no relationship to product flow.' In fact everything that could be wrong was wrong at Rearsby except that Ivor Vaughan realised that, 'The only difference between us and the competition is us' and was determined to do something about 'us'.

Ivor Vaughan also passionately believed in simplification. 'Look at a task see if you can stop doing it, do less of it or let someone else do it.' Only when you have simplified it as much as you know how, put it in a cell with low-tech automation and then only use the cell when it is needed, otherwise leave it unused. Do not manufacture for stock but aim for such a quick response time that you do not need stock.

Simplification is Ivor Vaughan's vision, his stand. To him a stand is made by one person, not a group. It is saying, 'I declare. . . do it now. . . there is no evidence that it will work; if you wait for evidence it is not a stand. Our stand in Rearsby was simplification.'

Other factors are, however, essential for successful cell manufacturing. Prime among these is the need to train the supervisors and the operators and to involve the people who will be working in the new system in its planning, layout, systems and tooling. As always, achieving ownership and commitment is critical for success.

The key to success in Rearsby was that Ivor Vaughan realised he did not have a monopoly of wisdom. It was only through the people that he achieved success and, in particular, the operators were the greatest untapped source of knowledge. One operator took over the redesign of a section, she put different processes together, changed the method to group work, simplified everything as much as possible and took on additional work. She said, 'Under this system you're your own boss, its more varied, more interesting.'

The benefits were considerable; stock fell, lead times shortened and responsiveness rose, expertise became higher, productivity increased dramatically and, above all, employee ownership became real. One dramatic example is that of a product which spent ten days travelling 2.5 times the length of the plant, involving 21 people to undergo 99 seconds of processing time. At the cost of £2,000 all the required equipment was brought into a cell, with the result that one person now controls the whole process and the cycle time has been reduced to 43 seconds!

MAINTENANCE

In the traditional company, workers and management rarely have enough time to look after their equipment or undertake routine maintenance. They enter into a vicious spiral of running the equipment until it breaks down, calling for the maintenance staff who are not available because of all the other demands on their time; as a result they lose production which has to be caught up so they have even less time to maintain the equipment . . . and down they spin, out of control.

At its simplest, involving production operators in routine maintenance is based on the concept, 'If you use it, you should keep it from breaking', and this means, at the minimum, cleaning, lubricating, replacing consumable materials, and undertaking routine maintenance. But this is the minimum.

Total productive maintenance (TPM) means something different in virtually every company. For the Japanese it has to be part of *genba kanri*, workshop management. The Japanese Institute of Plant Maintenance says, 'TPM aims at maximising equipment effectiveness with a total system of preventive maintenance covering the entire life of the equipment. It involves everyone in all departments and at all levels; it motivates people for plant maintenance through small groups and voluntary activities.' It requires everyone to be developed to their full potential and requires a high degree of professionalism among the production workers.

The concept of the professional production worker is important in the ascendant organisation. Such people are not craft workers in the traditional sense; they do not engage in the complex maintenance work that requires a specialist, although they will undertake first-line maintenance and will help the specialist as required. This entails not simply routine preventative maintenance work to prevent breakdowns, for breakdowns are the tip of the iceberg. TPM requires attention to be paid to set-up times, minor stoppages, and problems with speed, defects and yield. Maintenance is everyone's responsibility. TPM recognises that if the equipment is not right then quality will suffer. Its goal is to replace a part *just before* failure and achieve zero breakdowns. But modern analytical techniques such as Reliability Centred Maintenance seek to analyse the potential incidence, impact and cost of breakdowns if you do *not* maintain, for TPM is costly in terms of both time and materials. Therefore, in circumstances in which a machine is costly to maintain but quick and easy to repair and the consequences of failure are minimal, then, provided performance does not deteriorate to the unacceptable, it may be better to extend the maintenance cycle or not maintain it at all. 'If it ain't broke, don't fix it.'

At the other extreme, critical equipment with high impact may need to be maintained more frequently. There are many examples of maintenance actually inducing problems; often the cost–benefit decision is complex, and the decision process must involve the production people.

TPM recognises that the person doing a job knows more about the feel or sound of the equipment than anyone else, and can often predict a problem before it occurs and take the necessary action. Where limited technical expertise is required, the operator will carry out all the planned maintenance, rectifying any faults that are found, eliminating the 'three evils' – mishandling, poor lubrication and poor clean-up.

The role of the professional maintenance staff changes dramatically. They become responsible for the complex planned maintenance programmes where specialised technical knowledge and judgement are required and attend to major breakdowns which the operators are unable to fix. They are responsible for analysing problems and undertaking *kaizen* activities. They may undertake equipment performance analysis aimed at, for example, reducing maintenance frequency, improving maintenance instructions, adjusting spare parts stock levels, improving quality or reducing scrap.

TPM, however, goes further – for the goal must be not just to keep equipment working but to improve its performance and ensure it is regularly upgraded. Very rarely is equipment delivered and installed in a perfect condition. Because of the partnership between operators and maintenance staff they can work together from the very beginning to improve its condition, often very significantly, particularly in reducing cycle time, increasing efficiency or in making it more ergonomically acceptable.

TPM is, perhaps, more accurately defined as *total partnership maintenance*.

CHANGEOVER TIMES

John Scott of the Strathclyde Institute has calculated that around 40 per cent of production time does not add value, even in the best organised plants. Half of that non-adding-value time is due to changing over from one product to another and adjusting tools. The problem is that most improvement activities have focused on making the value-adding part of the operations more effective, not on reducing the non-value-adding activities. If we are also to concentrate on the latter we need to pay particular attention to reducing the time taken between completing one run and starting the next, so that we minimise the 'OK part to OK part' time. Reducing changeover times can dramatically reduce the necessary length of the subsequent production run.

For example, the automobile industry used to take four hours or more to change the dies in the giant body panel presses. Consequently, when the presses were running they wanted to keep them producing for as long as possible, often stamping two weeks' supply of a single panel, and would live with the inventory costs, slow response time, undetected quality problems, and obsolete stock. It made managers lazy and the workforce careless. Today they can change the dies in less than ten minutes. In machining operations highly skilled technicians used to take an hour to change the tools but now a combination of operators and automation can do the job in seconds.

Taiichi Ohno and Shigeo Shingo developed the concept of 'single minute exchange of dies' (SMED) in which they aimed to achieve die and tool changes in less than ten minutes. Under this system the aim is to maximise the amount of work which is done outside the machine while it is still running, first by distinguishing internal from external work and then seeking to convert internal setting work to external. Having done this, the next step is to eliminate work that needs to be done while the tool is actually being fitted into the machine. Finally, the amount of external work is reduced. Once this is achieved, and changeover times are measured in minutes not hours, machines need not be run for hours – they can be run for minutes. Stock is reduced, less storage capacity is needed, quality problems are minimised and the operators are fully engaged virtually all the time. They can be trained in all tasks – setting, operating, quality checking, material delivery and removal. The old job of machine-minder disappears, so also does the specialised setter who used to receive a four-year training programme, achieving a high status but in a very restricted area of skill.

This means that operating and technological advances allow us to manufacture in small batches while retaining the advantages of mass production. We can thus respond more rapidly to the changes in market place demand. Said Ohno, 'Procure only what is needed when it is needed and in the amount needed' (Ohno, 1988b, p. 15). He did not believe in demand forecasting: it's better 'going to the racetrack and betting on horses' (ibid, p. 126). And Shingo wrote that, 'The root of all evil is planning for demand on the basis of speculation' (Shingo, 1988, p. 49).

INVENTORY REDUCTION

While component inventory is only part of the JIT system, it is an important part. Richard Schonberger says that it originated almost by accident in the Japanese steel industry in the late 1950s at a time when the steel-makers' over-expansion had led to very high stock levels. Consequently, the shipbuilders could get very fast delivery and because of this they dropped their safety stocks from one month to three days and received their new orders just in time (Schonberger, 1982, p. 17). Taiichi

Ohno, on the other hand, visited the USA in 1951 and 1952 and, inspired by the 'customer pull' system of the American supermarkets (whereby the customer 'pulls' the product from the shelves and it is then replaced), developed the first *kanban* system in 1955 in Nagoya (now renamed Toyota City). The significance of Toyota City is that the supplier plants are mainly located within a very short distance of their only customer, Toyota, thus reducing the risk from traffic delays and making possible the low stock system.

JIT is very much a philosophy, not just a manufacturing practice. In Japan the emphasis of JIT is on the 'J' – Just. Deliver *just* what is necessary, build *just* what is needed, use *just* the required amount of effort, have *just* the right amount of stock in the system. It is about the elimination of waste. In the West we have tended to concentrate on the 'IT' – In Time – and build up our stocks to give us the protection we feel we need to ensure on-time delivery, 'just in case' our suppliers run into difficulties or our machines break down or our workers go on strike!

Concentrating on the 'in time' element actually achieves little and can be positively harmful. It gives the impression of efficiency when all that has happened is that the inventory holding is passed from the customer to the supplier, or that a huge warehouse is built, space is rented by the supplier and the inventory holding is relocated.

JIT does not totally eliminate stock and to attempt to do so will result in disaster. No manufacturer can accept a system which is so fragile that a traffic accident can cause major disruption to its manufacturing processes. But again, new technology is enabling manufacturers to get close to the ideal. First, the risks must be reduced and then the safety cover can be minimised. The risks can be reduced by suppliers locating close to the customer and by working towards mutual commitment. Synchronous supply can then become the step beyond just-in-time. Synchronous supply is the system in which, through electronic data interchange (EDI), the computer of the customer 'talks' to the computer of the supplier. As the customer's computer schedules the product build sequence it links with the supplier's computer and says, 'Start building a component to this specification.' The supplier follows this instruction, places the components in pallets suitable for direct lineside delivery, puts the pallets in a small truck, delivers to the customer's plant, hitches the pallets to a small tractor and delivers direct to lineside. The component has gone from production line to production line with no intermediate storage and arrives genuinely just in time. Some may arrive just a few minutes before needed and at the most there will be an hour's stock at the point of production. Demand has truly pulled supply.

Such a system is highly efficient, very fragile and relies heavily on the skill and commitment of all people at every stage of the process. It places a responsibility on the supplier's staff, far greater than anything under the traditional systems, and depends on high levels of attendance. When staffing levels are reduced to eliminate waste it becomes critical that those people who are employed have high attendance rates. There is no fat to cover absenteeism. Many doubted if such commitment could be achieved in the West, where individualism and competitiveness are the order of the day. Some companies have succeeded surprisingly well. Nissan, at the extreme, is down to door pads arriving at lineside ten minutes before they are needed!

MATERIAL SUPPLY

JIT is as much a philosophy as it is a practice but the hard edge of the process is control of the logistics. In fact, in a complex manufacturing process it is logistics management that makes JIT work. Materials managers are fond of saying, much to the annoyance of production people, that production is easy; the difficult part is getting the right components to the right place at the right time in the right quantity. If you can achieve that with virtually no stock in the system you have cracked the production problem. The aim is to minimise inventory without increasing risks.

Of course, they are wrong in underestimating the complexity of the production process – but when you consider the fact that a car can have about 3,300 parts with ten or more colours and that there are around 7,000 variants, the difficulty of achieving the delivery objectives 100 per cent of the time is immense. Very few succeed.

Richard Lamming, in an attempt to provide hard evidence of delivery performance, studied the actual experience of 47 companies receiving 4,600 deliveries over a two-week period in 1993. He found that only 14.7 per cent of deliveries were made on time, on the day or within the week specified. He also found that 62 per cent of items delivered for use in production have a specified delivery tolerance of a week or more. Only 6 per cent of customers specified a tolerance of plus or minus one hour and only 26 per cent a tolerance of within a specified day (Lamming, 1993). This means that the vast majority of deliveries have a tolerance level far greater than that acceptable for JIT processes and that, in any case, only a small proportion actually achieve even these slack tolerances. So, however much companies may profess to be operating a JIT system, the only hard evidence shows that the real world has barely scratched the surface.

Against this overall performance level of 14.7 per cent ontime achievement within a one-week window, Nissan in the UK is achieving 98 per cent ontime deliveries within a two-hour window! In Japan the figure exceeds 99 per cent. If we are to talk of really moving towards JIT, that is the level that has to be attained!

To reduce inventory significantly it is necessary to go further and examine the total logistics of the supply chain. The companies that really have the answer are the fast-moving supermarket groups. Manufacturing needs such a supply system in which there is minimal stock in the store, virtually nothing at the supplier and the only stock on the road is in the trucks which are moving, not standing in a lay-by waiting to be called in.

Nissan, after an extensive study of road hauliers, chose Ryder Distribution to develop its delivery network. Under the eventual arrangement Nissan, through electronic data interchange, advises the supplier what and when to build, and Ryder, the precise time at which to collect. On a round-robin basis the truck calls at about six suppliers on an optimised route picking up a part load from each. Each truck travels to a central cross-docking facility where the mixed loads are transferred on to large final delivery trucks in the optimum sequence for delivery to the manufacturing plant. Nissan calculates that with 86 of its UK suppliers on this system, if each were to deliver individually twice per shift they would cover an additional 31.4 million miles per year with an additional fuel cost of £7.6 million and the plant would be so congested that it would grind to a halt! As it is, the system allows an average inventory holding of less than one day, with no warehousing, no stock at the suppliers and the trucks are moving all the time. Components are presented in the optimum way for the end-user, and the quick return of reusable packaging to the supplier is assured. It sounds complicated and technologically took a huge amount of development. But it works. Stock turns exceed 200 per year!

This again returns us to commitment and control. JIT provides the commitment and logistics management the control.

LEVEL SCHEDULING AND DISTRIBUTION

The JIT system and the elimination of waste require a high degree of predictability. If a manufacturer of complex consumer durable products relies on confirmed end-customer orders before commencing the build of the product, the orders will be irregular, production staff will be standing around much of the time and the customer will have to wait for delivery. But most customers, when we have made up our minds to purchase a new dishwasher or motor car, do not want to wait. We want it now, not in two months' time when the order has creaked through the system with only a few hours spent actually building it. The problem is that manufacturers like low inventories which depend upon predictable volumes and predictable volumes result in building for stock. Demand pull exists to the point of manufacture. Thereafter it changes to supply push. Car companies are superb at reducing inventory up to the point of production, while the fields of Europe and the United States have been full of cars for which there are no customers. Paradoxically, only 25 per cent of British customers get the exact specification of car they originally wanted, 55 per cent accept different specifications and 20 per cent do not buy (Harbour and Brown, 1993, p.12). There is a loss of profit from lost sales, wrong stock in the system and substantial carrying costs. Dealers often have to offer heavy discounts to dispose of wrong stock, particularly when there is a market slump or when new models are about to be introduced.

The objective of a distribution system must be to get the right product to the right place just in time, with the minimum of stock in the system and at the lowest cost. But if such a system creates major inefficiencies for the manufacturer and therefore adds to costs, there must be a balance. Achieving that balance has in the past been an art. Fortunately, technology is beginning to turn it into a science – but there is a long way to go.

Technologically, a customer could go into a showroom, virtually design a car on a terminal, adding or deleting options to the price limit, and finally press a button which instructs the manufacturing plant to build the car of the customer's choice. From just in time to real time! The problem is not the ordering. It is having to stock the components necessary to meet all possible options. To make such a system fully operational there will need to be a dramatic commonisation of non-visual and performance parts plus a range of customised options. But to avoid high inventories of the customised options the JIT systems will have to link electronically with key suppliers who will be directly instructed to produce and deliver the components. The logical conclusion is a production run of one; the end customer pulls final production! Anything else produces waste.

Unfortunately such an approach, because of the irregular nature of customer demand, will lead to major manufacturing inefficiencies. The compromise solution comes from the fast-moving consumer goods industries and begins with accurate sales forecasting. Most manufacturers of consumer durables maintain twelve to eighteen months' rolling monthly forecasts and become more precise as production dates get closer. Often this final schedule is frozen two weeks to a month before actual production, allowing ample time for most suppliers to deliver. In practice most organisations can predict that 80 per cent of orders will come from about 20 per cent of the range, and this allows the development of regional or national distribution centres from which the 80 per cent of predictable orders can be distributed without requiring dealer swaps. Such centres allow for a lower stock base, reduced carrying costs and quicker service.

With such systems it should not be impossible for a customer to receive a car within a week of ordering it from stock and within three weeks if it is a special build.

'FIVE S'

To achieve such efficiency requires, however, much more than a highly skilled group of operators. It requires high levels of housekeeping, a task which is much maligned because of inadequate understanding of its value. Western managers pay lip-service to housekeeping. While visiting a medium-size enterprise in Japan I noticed sets of small scales at various points.

'What are they for?'
'Twice a shift we sweep the floor and weigh the amount of waste we collect, usually a few grammes per operator!'

The largest weight used on these scales was 100 grammes!

To the Japanese, housekeeping is much more than sweeping up. They have introduced 'Five S':

Seiri (consolidation)	Separate the necessary from the unnecessary and dispose of the latter (for example, tools, machinery, defective products, documents).
Seiton (orderliness)	Put the necessary objects in a safe place, convenient for use. Arrange in rows. 'A place for everything, everything in its place.'

Seiso (clean up)	Maintain a clean and safe condition, and while cleaning, check for deterioration and change.
Seiketsu (cleanliness)	Routinely maintain cleanliness and order to prevent deterioration.
Shitsuke (discipline)	Train everyone to systematise the discipline. Follow the procedures (standard operation, safety procedures, start and finish times, keeping appointments, and so on).

While 'Five S' goes significantly further than simple 'housekeeping', it achieves nothing if not implemented and assessed. Not just by a walkabout but in a systematic way – that which is properly measured is properly done! Nissan has consolidated 'Five S' into 'Three S' for practical day-to-day purposes – *seiri, seiton* and *seiso* (this variation of the system is quite common) and the senior supervisors regularly measure achievement. Points are awarded and when the points from all other elements are added, an overall rating is achieved. Depending on that score is the timing of the next inspection. The worse the score, the sooner the next visit!

The responsibility for achieving the required level lies with the operators. There is not an army of cleaners to do this work for them. Involving the people doing the job means that they find the true cause of any problems that exist and can then deal with the problem at source.

VISIBLE MANAGEMENT

The Japanese practised 'Management by walking around' long before it became fashionable in the West.

Visible management, however, goes further than managers being seen in the workplace. To the Japanese it is a pictorial display of the performance of the section but it is used also to highlight potential problems. Using diagrams and graphs, performance achievements against quality, cost, volume and people (QCVP) are displayed on boards adjacent to the workplace; they are maintained by the team and require the performance to be readily known to everyone – the team, the managers and casual visitors. But, as with most things Japanese, there is a philosophy behind it. A visiting Japanese, Hideo Kakimoto, said:

> To use visual management to our advantage we must have the courage
> to make the problem clear to all of the people by means of words and

graphics . . . To help you learn and achieve your targets you must have a person who has a strong character who can find potential concern before they happen and graphically display the potential fault . . . *Solutions are easy to find, anticipating the concern is much more difficult.*

Performance measures which are displayed can include:

- The zone objectives and achievements to date, including productivity and quality improvements
- Current volume and quality achievement
- Energy costs
- Use of direct and indirect material
- Scrap costs
- Staff training/skill level
- Attendance
- Safety record
- Facility utilisation rates, and so on

The format is standard but the measures may vary and a high degree of individuality in the presentation develops. Some are so artistically produced they are a delight to study; others are very basic. They visibly indicate to the individual the way his or her efforts contribute to improved performance; they can give a broader understanding of the business and provide a simple and accessible format for introducing people to basic graphical and statistical concepts. While some of the information may originate from outside the group – for example, the actual cost of non-production material – most originates from within and often an individual operator will be responsible for completing and maintaining a specific chart as part of the 'discretionary' work. They bring home to people those elements which are controllable. 'Scrap', for example, will be shown as 'The cost per car of the scrap created in this section' and similarly with energy costs and the use of material. Individuals cannot always appreciate that they can have an impact on the company's total costs but they can see it as a meaningful objective to reduce the use of indirect materials in their section from eleven pence per car to nine. This is cost control where it really matters!

Whereas such an approach is easier in manufacturing areas where results are easily measured, it should not be supposed that it cannot be as effective in an office environment. For example, in Nissan all indirect departments have their own visible management boards. Performance indicators in purchasing include localised parts reject ratios, warranty claims, design initiated cost reductions, annual settlement levels, training, travel and overtime. In the training section, performance indicators include training days delivered, non-attendance on scheduled programmes, progress on developing new programmes, external qualifications achieved, flexible learning centre usage; all measured against previously determined targets. Many organisations measure performance. How many display it for all to see?

OPERATOR CARE

As we have seen, *The Machine that Changed the World* (Womack *et al.*, 1990) barely mentioned the impact of lean production on the people in the organisation, and people like David Robertson have stepped into the breach maintaining that it is the logic of the system that leads inevitably to both physical and mental problems. The constructive critic, however, seeks to avoid such situations arising.

Often, manufacturing processes *are* demanding, both physically and mentally, and it is a managerial responsibility to minimise their impact on the people and to plan production so that staffing levels are always right for the product mix, not fixed at the lowest level. One of the key objectives of *kaizen* must be to make work easier and I refer back to Chapter 3 and the discussion on operator care to illustrate the lengths to which an ascendant organisation will go to achieve this goal.

There are literally hundreds of minor improvements that can be made once operators and their supervisors have real responsibility and the resources to implement change. Often, descriptions of such improvements are meaningless unless you can actively see the operation, but in March 1993, in order to promote these initiatives, the Nissan production department began to produce its own, very simple *Genba Kanri News*. Hand-written, photocopied and with simple line drawings, the publication served to illustrate small but significant achievements. The very first example in the very first issue showed this simplicity.

The objective was to alleviate bending and stretching over an assembly jig and prevent the potential for back and arm strain. The jig was at an angle of 45 degrees and fairly deep, and the operator – using power tools – had to bend over to reach the rear, resulting in considerable strain. To correct this, the jig height was raised, relaid in the horizontal plane and a central section cut away, thus allowing the operator to work closer to the component. Although simple, this study resulted in four improvements:

- Improved conditions – no bending or stretching
- Improved quality – spot-weld positions more accurate with no edge-welds or burrs
- Cycle time reduced by twenty seconds
- Improved safety

Operator care does not just make the job easier!

9 Beyond TQM – Integrating Quality

If our factories, through careful work, assure the quality of our products, it will be to the foreigners' interest to get supplies from us, and their money will flow into the kingdom.

(Jean-Baptiste Colbert, Finance Minister to Louis XIV, 1664)

THE CHANGING NATURE OF QUALITY

The quality revolution has long been with us. Despite Jean-Baptiste Colbert's seventeenth-century recognition of its importance, it was not until the 1950s that the work of people like W. Edwards Deming, Joseph Juran and Armand Feigenbaum started to become influential, first in Japan, then in the USA, and later in other parts of Western industrial society.

Since the 1950s the attitude towards quality has rapidly changed. Though not absolutely precise, the progression has been something like:

1950s What's this about quality?
1960s Nice to have good quality but we can sell all we produce so it's not critical.
1970s Japanese quality is good and we need to match their levels but it will add to our costs to get there.
1980s Crosby tell us that 'Quality is free'. If we get it right first time, that actually saves us money.
1990s Achieving high levels of quality, consistently, gives us a competitive edge.

But today, in many businesses, and by the twenty-first century in most, consistent high quality will be the norm. It will give no competitive advantage. It will not win the race. It will be the entry price to get to the starting gate. If you do not have a high level of quality, and are not continuously improving it, you may as well not bother.

150

The simplest and best description of Total Quality Management (TQM) was given by Professor John Oakland:

Go to a company that sports posters instead of beliefs and the falseness is rapidly apparent. TQM moves the focus of control from outside the individual to within; the objective is to make everyone accountable for their own performance and to get them committed to attaining quality in a highly motivated fashion . . . Consistency can only be achieved if we ensure that for every product or each time a service is performed the same materials, the same equipment, the same methods or procedures are used in exactly the same way every time. The process will then be under control . . . Control by itself is not sufficient. TQM requires that the process should be improved continually by reducing its variability. (1990)

John Oakland is not a million miles from the synthesis between motivation and control.

Evidence of the success of formal TQM programmes is patchy and contradictory. A survey by Arthur D. Little of 500 US companies found that only one-third felt their programmes were having a significant effect, and A. T. Kearney (management consultants) found that 'About 80 per cent of all TQM initiatives fail to produce tangible results. A significant proportion flounder after the initial period of enthusiasm, training and team formation. Some lack the unrelenting sustained commitment of senior management; some stall in spite of the commitment'.

Two UK surveys presented conflicting views. Coming out of the University of Bradford, 'Does TQM Impact on Bottom Line Results?' reported on a study of 29 companies over five years of audited results and showed that around 22 of the TQM companies outperformed their industry averages in profit margins, return on total assets, turnover per employee, profit per employee, total assets per employee, fixed asset trends and average remuneration. Although not proving direct causation, the authors believe that the results point towards a strong association between the introduction of TQM and bottom-line results. 'TQM merely offers companies the opportunity to carry out improvements and focuses on getting closer to customers. It is only a licence to practise. Companies must still have the right strategies in place, the right products and services, the right commitment and the right investment strategies to be successful' (Zairi, Letza and Oakland, 1994).

On the other hand, a research report by the Institute of Management of 880 responding companies found only 8 per cent rated their quality initiatives as 'totally successful' with the majority claiming 'a moderate degree of success' or neutrality. Fewer than half of those surveyed said that the initiatives had led to an improvement in sales or profitability. One respondent said, 'The worst problem for those of us who believe in quality excellence is the tenuous link between our success in the commercial environment and the quality of service. Most of our customers buy on price as long as there is an acceptable level of service.'

As I said, high quality is the entry price.

CUSTOMER FOCUS

What is quality? Armand Feigenbaum defined it as 'The total composite product and service characteristics of marketing, engineering, manufacture and maintenance through which the product and service in use will meet the expectations of the customer' (Feigenbaum, 1983). This definition, though complex, requires all key functions to work together to satisfy the customer. Definitions which speak of 'zero defects', 'right first time' and 'fitness for purpose' are OK, but in a limited way. They seem to restrict quality to the manufacturing process. In one of his typically provocative statements Tom Peters said, 'Phil Crosby's "Get it right first time" is the single sickest statement I have ever seen' (Peters, 1992).

However, most final customers do not choose to use such definitions. They might ask questions relating to the product's reliability, features, durability, performance, safety, ease of use, ease of maintenance, environmental friendliness, after-sales service, newness or uniqueness. They are concerned with point of sale service, resale values, price and value for money. For many products the issues may be of status, appearance, aesthetics and perception: the intangibles which may be the deciding factor. The customer's definition is often irrational, illogical and always changing. Rover's marketing director, Rod Ramsay, said of his company's marketing strategy, 'The bottom line principle is simple. We want people to think "I'd look good in a car like that" – because in reality that's what people buy cars for these days.' *Perception is reality.*

Most writers on quality ascribe to the customer their own beliefs on what quality issues are important. However, Mintel, the market survey organisation, undertook a comprehensive survey of what customers actually valued (Mintel, 1993). Under separate lists for products and services the top five attributes were:

Products	*Services*
Well made	Helpful staff
Safe to use	Efficient service
Value for money	Knowledgeable staff
Reliable	Clear pricing
Durable	Guarantees

It is interesting that Rod Ramsay's 'looking good' does not come into it. Perhaps it applies only to cars; or maybe people will not admit to buying things for what it says about them. More likely the latter!

Following Mintel and accepting irrationality, quality must never be determined by the provider of the product or service but in terms of customers' needs. Therefore, in relation to the final customer, I offer the following definition:

> The quality of a product or service is the customers' perception of it taking into account their total experience of those features they consider important.

These features might include price, sales experience, specification, performance, reliability, durability, ease of use, after-sales service, disposal and image. Not all customers will regard every element as important and most will have different priorities. Some may include elements I have omitted. 'Value for money' is often mentioned, but I regard that as a conclusion arising from the sum total of the elements.

A few years ago I purchased a new briefcase from the Salisbury chain store, at what I thought was a good price. The sales staff were helpful and knowledgeable. It had the right specification and looked good. However, I quickly found that the locks did not operate well and after two months one lock catch broke off. I had not kept the receipt, but the staff could not have been more helpful. They immediately changed the briefcase without question. Unfortunately, the lock catch of the second briefcase broke in exactly the same way. Again the staff were helpful and explained that they had received several complaints, the manager had tested the catches herself and found that it was a problem with the batch received at her shop. She had returned all unsold stock, had been assured that no other store had experienced problems and now had a new batch. But then I had the same problem with the third, and again with the fourth, until I asked for my money back.

I then went to the Argos catalogue store and ended up buying a very similar briefcase at half the price – which I still use. I have not shopped at Salisbury since that experience. No amount of smiling and understanding outweighs poor-quality products!

The beginning of the road of integrating quality into the culture must be to get close to your customers to understand what quality really means for them, and then move from simply meeting the customers' needs to working with them to understand their demands and develop your capability to meet them. The most successful companies have the most demanding customers but it requires both of you to develop the relationship so that it becomes a partnership. This means ensuring that your staff meet with your customers to ensure that you have a precise understanding of their needs and the use of your product; that you obtain detailed feedback on your product's performance; that you know the quality of service provided by your representatives and how they perceive your product in relation to your competitors.

But staff can be wrong. Barrie Hopson and Mike Scally (1989) tell the story of British Airways, when in 1993 staff were asked what they thought their customers wanted. They responded with requirements such as safety, good time-keeping, baggage arriving safely, good food, friendly service. True, but this is what the customers *expect*. When it comes to gaining positive goodwill customers want to be made to feel special, to be welcomed, to see staff demonstrating care and concern for the more vulnerable passengers, to see mistakes and difficulties dealt with well, with sensitivity and concern. It is these things that make for a real high-quality service. But not for everyone. The regular business traveller may not want smiles and assistance but simply to be left alone to get through the journey with the minimum of hassle. The real trick is to recognise that different people have different needs and treat them appropriately.

This personal service can only be given by a motivated, dedicated front-liner – in the 50 million moments of truth of Jan Carlzon's (1989) SAS staff, or when the check-out assistant thanks the customer, not when 'Thank you for your custom' is printed on the receipt!

Awareness of customer care is not new but the crucial contribution of the front-line employee to the achievement of genuine and sustainable improvements in meeting customer needs is less well integrated in corporate goals and strategies. For that, you need employee ownership, which is not achieved by sending people on customer care courses. Smiling is not enough: you must have the systems and procedures in place to support that smile, otherwise it is seen for what it is – superficial gloss. However well the customer is treated by Carlzon's front-liners, if the planes do not run on time or are not clean, no amount of smiling will compensate for a poor service.

The internal quality objective of a business must then be to ensure that it is managed so as to meet its external customers' definitions of quality. As John Oakland (1990) implied, you do not do this by sticking up posters. Nor do you achieve success by the grand single programme. It is achieved by combining motivation and control, and we begin our examination at the beginning – designing for quality.

DESIGN FOR QUALITY

Depending on the product, some 70–85 per cent of its lifetime costs are determined at the design stage. Once it is accepted for production, a company will be lucky if, over the life of the product, it is able to reduce total costs by more than 10 per cent. Similarly with quality. The product which is difficult to build at its production launch is likely to remain difficult for years to come. Marginal improvements may be made to the product, facility and task, but rarely will the 'pig' ever become a 'pussycat' (with apologies to pigs).

This is not the book to go into immense detail about the practice of simultaneous engineering, but in pursuing the synthesis between commitment of the people and control of the processes we cannot neglect this concept which, if properly managed, can have a fundamental effect not only on the quality of life of the people but also on the quality of the product and subsequent customer satisfaction. The quality of the final product, however defined, is in great part dependent on the quality of the parts that go into making it and the quality of the final assembly process. I offer therefore what I hope is a reasonably non-technical explanation.

Before the era of simultaneous engineering, the product design process was something of an ivory tower activity paying little attention to the demands of the market place, and no attention to the needs of suppliers or production. Suppliers were given a detailed component specification and asked to quote a price – and usually the business was split between the two cheapest who could then be played off against each other at the next tendering round. As a result they had no incentive to undertake long-term investment in their own design capability or in facility investment or in the training and development of their staff. If they might not have the business next year, why bother? Manufacturing engineers who had to design the facility were able to see the product but, inevitably, late design changes and delays meant that their time was squeezed. Production management barely got a look in, and were unable to contribute suggestions, or request features that might assist the build of the product. The results were that the design and development process took a very long time as each stage had to be completed before the next began, and quality was a major casualty. No one really owned the product.

Simultaneous engineering seeks to integrate all stages of the process from market research and product planning through styling, design, engineering, prototype build and test, facility design, production, marketing and sales. It involves multi-disciplinary teams, including people from the component suppliers, who have to be involved at a very early stage of the project. Some of the key elements include:

- The product being defined in terms of the customers' needs
- Design for ease of assembly
- Simultaneous development of the product and process
- High level of component integration
- Clear project leadership with a team authorised to make decisions
- Strong support from non-involved functions
- Early definition of much of the specification
- Team members co-located in open areas
- Few top management reviews

Simultaneous engineering requires not only considerable overlaps between the product development stages but also early involvement of suppliers. When suppliers were regarded almost as the enemy, to be screwed into the ground on price and beaten over the head on quality, this was clearly not possible – but with the development of partnership sourcing it becomes a practical reality. Under this concept the customer enters into a long-term relationship with a single source supplier. They are committed to work together in many areas but, in particular, suppliers are assisted in developing their design engineering capabilities. It is ridiculous, for example, that in the past suppliers have employed specialist external companies to produce prototype parts. They learn nothing by giving this responsibility to someone else. More can be achieved by high levels of pre-production quality assurance than by all the post-production fixes. It allows companies to aim for reject rates of parts per million instead of parts per thousand.

One result of simultaneous engineering is that design problems come to the fore much earlier in the process. These problems are registered as design changes and the later a change the more difficult and expensive it is to introduce. This process, however, not only shortens the total product development time, it also pulls forward design changes. The Japanese have been at this much longer than Western manufacturers and the typical number of design changes in the period prior to start of production is illustrated in Figure 9.1. The exact pattern will differ according to the product, but the principle is to maximise the number of changes before start of production and then, after the immediate post-production hump, reduce them as quickly as possible.

The traditional pattern leaves much of the product design to the customer – either the internal customer, that is the production people who have difficulty in building the product, or the external customer who finds that the product does not perform. But simultaneous engineering, in shortening the total process, allows the latest technology to be introduced and, for fashion-related features, allows the most up-to-date to be added. Customer needs can be accommodated in the design stage. As new, lower-cost products are developed they can be introduced more quickly. Together, these elements can add up to a higher quality, more advanced but cheaper products hitting the market quicker. Some manufacturers may even be able to charge a premium price. Whatever the pricing strategy, at a time when product life cycles have dramatically shortened, six months earlier to market can make the difference between profit and loss.

Team Taurus was Ford's first attempt at developing a product through the multi-disciplinary approach. Led by Lew Veraldi, my old boss from

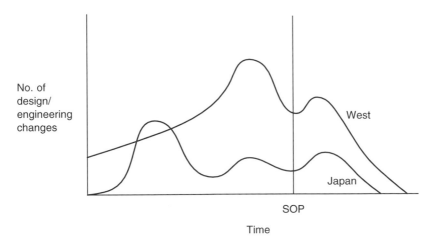

Figure 9.1 Design Changes Over Time

Ford's European Product Development Centre, the team sought to bring in everybody, including the shop-floor operators. Said Veraldi:

> Involving all groups in the process actually lowered costs . . . It was much easier to get people to talk about and come up with constructive changes when they couldn't pass off responsibility by saying 'That's really a manufacturing problem, not a design one.' There were no specific incentives set up for this project other than pride of workmanship . . . We motivated people by making sure they had an equity in the product and then listened to them carefully. (Quinn, 1990)

It is clear, then, that successful simultaneous engineering requires teamworking and involvement of the highest order throughout the organisation. The contribution of everyone is valued but they work together for the shared goal. Sometimes, referring back to teamworking, people in modern product development groups can seem to be only in the multi-functional, multi-level teams, but usually they have a home base to which they can return, although sometimes they may see that home base as the whole of their department!

INTEGRATING QUALITY

Several years ago I gave a presentation, 'The people side of quality', to the directors of ICI Chemicals and Polymers Division. In preparation, they gave me copies of their documentation on Total Quality Management, beautifully produced, saying all the right things, quoting all the right people, setting up systems with facilitators, co-ordinators and change agents and presenting all the right training programmes. But after several years 'at it' they still had problems. Although quality had improved, they had not made a major breakthrough; there was no real commitment throughout the organisation. Their problem was contained in their stated 'at it'. They still thought of TQM as something slightly separate from the normal day-to-day business. It caused me to reflect that when quality is properly integrated into an organisation it does not need glossy publications, facilitators or change agents. There need be no training courses specifically dedicated to quality and no TQM programme. We must achieve a company in which the commitment to quality is absolute at every level, permeates everything and is organic, and although none of the training programmes is about quality, all of them are.

The ascendant organisation moves beyond seeing TQM as something separate needing initial capital letters, to a state in which the achievement of existing high levels of quality and progression to ever higher levels is the normal way of life of everyone. Real success comes when there are no quality programmes as such, but when quality is an integral part of the business.

That is very easy to say and very difficult to achieve. First we must examine in a little more detail what it means and, as with all concepts, it depends on the right balance between control of the processes and commitment of the people.

The control of the processes begins with our old friend, the standard operation. By definition, any deviation from the standard operation will result in a worsening of quality. It establishes the standard to be achieved and the method of achieving it. It defines the material to be used and the equipment – every time in the same way. If there is no standard operation, quality will be determined by the experience of the operators and in a volume manufacturer or service organisation this will lead to an unstable process and unstable results. There will be no base from which change can be determined or improvements measured. In a craft-based organisation such differences may, of course, be desirable.

The standard operation, applied properly, assigns responsibility for quality to the operator and the team. If responsibility is passed to an inspector, the attitude develops that, 'If I don't do it right it will be picked up.' To counteract this the Japanese developed the concept of the internal customer – meaning that you do not pass faulty goods to your neighbour or to the next section. But if you do not have time to complete a job or a fault occurs, you may either stop the process and seek assistance or flag up the fault so that it may be corrected. 'Neighbour checks' mean that within a zone each person is responsible for checking someone else's work. To do this effectively, operators need to learn at least the jobs before and after them. One of the myths about Japanese management practices is that they do not inspect. They recognise that people will make mistakes and regard statistical methods of measuring quality as a mathematical compromise which attempts to achieve a balance between minimum inspection and maximum confidence. Not only do they inspect but they also build in *poka yoke* (mistake avoidance or fool-proofing) devices into their systems which are aimed at preventing mistakes from happening or, if they do, to automatically reject the faulty product. For bought-out parts the ideal is to achieve such confidence in the supplier that there is no goods inward inspection (although it takes years to achieve) but throughout the manufacturing process there is virtual 100

problem?' or, 'Do you think you could find a better way of doing this?', that for a period *is* their job. It is vital that the supervisor creates the climate in which such an approach is natural and that those involved are properly trained in the best methods of achieving results.

INVOLVING EVERYONE

Quality is not just about the manufacturing process or the face-to-face provision of a service, although both are of critical importance. Ethicon Limited, the Edinburgh-based subsidiary of health care company Johnson and Johnson, has recognised this more clearly than most. Writing in the company paper *Quality First*, Operations Director, Gerry Fagan said:

> There is no area of our business which is less important than any other in making sure that quality happens and that the final product meets customer requirements to specification, on time and at the right price. No matter which department an employee works in they, as an individual and as part of a team, have a bearing on one or several of these three essential ingredients.

For example, an individual's first introduction to a company is usually an advertisement or a casual application. How well is the advertisement worded? Does it tell the applicants what they need to know? If they telephone are they answered promptly and courteously by people who know to whom they should be referred? If they write, do they receive an immediate acknowledgement instead of either being ignored totally or having to wait weeks? If they enquire about progress, are they answered quickly and correctly, or are they told, 'We've had hundreds of applications. Yours is somewhere in the pile and I'll get round to it eventually!'?

CLUB MED

There are many well-told stories of quality success. Instead of repeating the usual Milliken or Xerox stories, I shall turn to Club Med and thank George Binney for this example.

Club Med, the French holiday company, established in 1950, quickly built an image of sun, sea, sand, sex and sangria. It has since expanded to become an organisation employing some 24,000 people in holiday villages and hotels around the world. In 1985 it began its own TQM programme – seeking first to define what quality meant to its *gentils membres* (customers) and, at the same time, to understand the approach developed by companies regarded as quality leaders. It then established a group of six people to work on the project and each developed a network of fifteen others representing a cross-section of staff. Together they prepared a Quality Charter containing ten dimensions of quality as perceived by the customer (see box).

Club Med Quality Charter

- To arrive and live at the village without worry and risk
- An attractive location
- To be paid attention, receive generosity and imagination
- To be able to use the village's facilities easily
- Everything works and is clean
- Freedom of choice
- To eat and drink, what, when and as much as the customer wants
- To meet people easily
- To learn new skills
- For the contract to be honestly respected

The Chairman, Gilbert Trigano, met with the group of six on a weekly basis and the next step was to develop standards for each activity, using a three-part framework:

- What is the standard (expressed from the customer's viewpoint)?
- What task must the *gentil organisateur* (GO – nice organiser) undertake to deliver this standard?
- How is this task to be carried out?

The standards applied to tangible measures – cleanliness, appearance, availability; and to the intangible – problem solving, quality of attention, and so on. Several hundred were developed and in the process many GOs were involved, so that while the company benefited from their input the ownership process had also begun.

The next step was to bring together the village managers at a week-long seminar presided over by Trigano, to share with them the rationale and the way the standards should be used. Critically, the managers saw the standards not as a straitjacket but a formalisation of much of what they were already doing. They could be used to good purpose for training and benchmarking, and for achieving consistency. Especially, they would have flexibility in applying them to their own specific situation. The seminars were then cascaded throughout the organisation.

Having set the standards, Club Med wanted to learn about their impact. About 250,000 questionnaires are returned by GMs every year. A computer system analyses the results, allowing corrective action to be taken, trends analysed and team performance evaluated. Letters are separately analysed to follow up issues raised on a personal basis. The commercial director for each market also solicits information from Club Med's own distribution network, from travel agents and through GM focus groups. Even while on holiday, GMs' views are formally solicited by the manager via a Round Table and, informally, GOs pick up comments and are encouraged to act on them.

(As a postscript to the Club Med story, in February 1997 the chief executive, Serge Trigano, was replaced by Philippe Bourguignon from Disney Paris. Club Med reported a loss of £83 million, mainly due to a one-off restructuring charge, but it had not closed loss-making villages quickly enough, had suffered disappointing diversification, dropping occupancy rates and cash-flow problems. Quality, alone, is not enough!)

The Club Med experience demonstrates not only the importance of ownership but also of feedback from the customer. Van den Bergh Foods, manufacturers of Flora vegetable fat spreads, include their company phone number on every pack. 'Monday to Friday 0800 44 64 64 Call the Flora Careline Free.' About half the 500 calls a week are resolved immediately. In the USA nearly 90 per cent of branded goods carry a telephone number. In France the figure is 30 per cent, in Germany 15 per cent and in the UK just 8 per cent (*Financial Times*, 13 January 1994). Burger King displays its phone number prominently in its restaurants and on take-away bags. Coca Cola has been printing a careline number on its products since 1992, and receives some 150,000 calls a year. Coca Cola has seen the number of calls rising, but says, 'We are making it easier for consumers to tell us if they are dissatisfied.' On the positive side, such calls can provide early warnings of quality problems and can be used to track customer satisfaction.

HOW *NOT* TO INTRODUCE AN INTEGRATED QUALITY CULTURE

Jonathan Smilansky, HR Director of Méridien Hotels and Resorts, has shrewdly determined how *not* to introduce TQM. His recipe for failure is:

1. Get the senior management team to agree – with someone at the top being 'sold' TQM, consultants involved, top team workshop, and so on.
2. Tell everyone that 'we are doing it' with conferences, newsletters and briefings prophesying that all will become clear when they are trained.
3. Train, top to bottom, about customers and suppliers, and measurement and service-level agreements and empowerment and the upside-down organisation and cross-functional teams and the basic tools and the gurus.
4. Start to improve everything. Tell everyone to go back and improve quality, one step at a time, maybe set up cross-functional teams and talk about internal customers
5. Give out the hats. Recognise and reward with hats and pens and shirts and competitions and lunches with the boss and maybe even a 'trip to Disney'. (Smilansky, 1992)

What is wrong with that? As Smilansky says, 'TQM is not a religion, it's a tool.' Remember that a realistic definition of quality must be written in the terms of the customer. TQM is only an internal process aimed at achieving an objective. It is not an end in itself. If we are to integrate quality into the whole company, there are essentially three main elements which must be firmly embedded: strategy, the planning and the process. The trouble with most recipes is that they forget some of these ingredients or demand a precision that is not possible. The following is therefore presented as a guideline but, as will quickly be seen, it returns to a main theme of this book – control of the processes and commitment of the people.

HOW TO INTRODUCE AN INTEGRATED QUALITY CULTURE

I divide this into strategy, planning and the process.

Strategy

In seeking to integrate quality into the whole organisation, the task of top management is to determine that the quality of its products or service will be defined in customers' terms and that standards will continuously improve. It then has to create the environment within the organisation which enables this objective to be achieved, recognising that it will not know the 'how' in detail. Top management must recognise that there will be many surprises along the way and have the courage to accept that if the direction taken is broadly consistent with the long-term objective, it is better than one which is imposed. It is therefore critical that top management is both consistent and persistent, that it does not interfere nor keeps seeking the quick bottom-line result, and recognises that absolute integration will take many years – although specific practical success can come very quickly.

There is not one way of developing this strategy. There is usually an initial inspiration that comes, perhaps, from someone reading a book, attending a seminar or being beaten over the head by a market place failure. It may come from the chief executive or from someone else in the organisation. It does not always have to start at the very top. Much is said about gaining commitment from the very top and, if quality is to be fully integrated, then at some stage the CEO will have to be convinced, but, as we know, leadership can exist at all levels. We all have part of our organisation that we can influence and success anywhere can be a catalyst both laterally and vertically. Indeed there may be advantages in this route, for the worst thing that can happen is for an initiative to be seen as 'Another bright idea thought up in the ivory tower and imposed on us.'

Planning

At whatever level the initiative begins, the first stage must be to understand what quality means for your customers, for it is only when proper understanding is achieved that the benchmark by which future results are to be assessed can be established. For many, this may be uncomfortable. It is much easier to jump in as an act of faith and subsequently applaud success based on some after-the-event criteria.

The great thing is that the medium can easily become the message. Following top management's definition of the broad strategy, the first task is to select a group of experienced people who will seek to understand what quality really means – not an overseeing 'steering group' but people who will actually do it. It may comprise a mixture of line managers and service departments from all locations, a horizontal slice or a lateral slice; it may include trade union representatives. Only the organisation can determine the right mix, but there are three golden rules:

- Each member must have high personal credibility within the organisation.
- Each member must be an innovator and achiever.
- Each member must retain his or her normal responsibilities.

The first two rules are obvious but the third is not. As soon as people are moved from their normal job, the group becomes a little more isolated, something special, and resources disappear. The group will wish to call on others, but if they no longer have line responsibilities their ability to do so may be reduced. This does not mean that they will have double the work (although they will certainly have more). They may depute some of their normal work – and this is no bad thing – but not their assignment.

The corollary is, do not appoint as the facilitator or co-ordinator someone who can be spared from their normal job. If top management is not prepared to give the time and authority of people who have real responsibility and credibility they should not start the process. Equally, do not give the responsibility to a consultant. There is little that cannot be done by a capable group of managers who understand the business; but the value of someone from outside is that he or she can ask the difficult questions, can challenge and prod in a way that even the most capable insider cannot, and the outsider can sometimes help by cutting through the organisation's politics – as long as the consultant does not bring a precise formula and is a servant of the process not the master.

Within the overall strategy it is this group who will undertake the studies, calling on others when needed, determining their own broad targets for the organisation. But they must remember at all times that, just as with themselves, commitment follows involvement. They must walk like they talk and not live in isolation from the rest of the organisation for several months and suddenly produce words of wisdom and precisely determined targets. They may believe they have a monopoly of wisdom but they will be amazed at the contribution others can make. Again there is no prescription for how this is done – small departmental groups, multi-site, multi-functional, horizontal, vertical, lateral, customers, suppliers, trade unions, and so on. All can contribute, and being given the opportunity is just as important as the value of that contribution.

The group itself may need some training or team-building activity but this should not be overstated. A group of people selected in line with three criteria will probably know each other and will previously have proved their problem-solving capabilities. In any case, they will have the ability to determine their own strengths and weaknesses and know when to seek advice and assistance. Any development or training must be done just in time. There simply is no point in bringing in an outsider to train or build a team in advance. Again, it makes something special of a process which must become integral, but lower in the organisation it may become clear that such a need exists. If so, let it grow out of the process, not be a precondition.

The process

The steps in the process which leads to integrating quality are then as follows.

Step 1

Determine your customers' views, requirements and critical success factors. Ask them what they want, how they judge you, assess past problems and future needs. Club Med did a superb job. Listen to the views of your own front-line staff, listen to their complaints, know why they receive or fail to receive repeat business, understand the problems caused by failure to deliver on time. But front-line staff will not always tell of their own failings, perhaps their rudeness to a customer, their own inability to arrive on time, their lack of knowledge of their product or service or their ignorance of customers' real needs.

Step 2

Compare yourself with the best. Companies have always done this, whether it is 'tearing down' a rival company's new products, or the small local store checking out its competitor's prices.

The most sophisticated comparisons are now termed 'benchmarking', defined by Rank Xerox as 'A continuous, systematic process of evaluating companies recognised as industry leaders, to determine business and work processes that represent best practices.' Benchmarking is more than just making performance comparisons within your own industry, for if you stay within your own industry you will be stuck with the standards of your industry. ICL had a concern about its technical manuals. Customers had difficulty finding their way around them. It looked at its competitors' manuals and found little to learn. The breakthrough came when it examined railway timetables and cookery books. In particular, the team found that Marks and Spencer's cookery books were masterpieces of clarity – with outstanding illustrations, precisely defined ingredients and clear instructions. If ICL's technical manuals now look like cookery books, it is no accident.

Looking at the best, wherever it occurs, helps raise expectations of what it is possible to achieve. The highest standards of cleanliness and hygiene are in hospital operating theatres, the fastest changers of car components are motor racing's Formula One pit crews, the most efficient distribution systems are in the perishable goods sectors. Studying the very best generates ideas about different ways of doing things. But it is no guarantee of success

However, benchmarking can also be defined as 'institutionalised copying' and when you copy you do not know if the standard you are emulating really is the best possible. You are considering *relative* positions when you should be defining the *absolute best* – which no one may yet have achieved. The greatest difficulty for those who are not 'there' is gaining an appreciation of what is possible. In my consulting work on 'Leadership and Management of People' I have developed some 75 areas of performance all of which include a definition of the highest possible level, and the response, particularly among those who have already benchmarked against the perceived best, is always something like, 'We just didn't realise what is possible!'

Step 3

Position yourself in relation to your competitors and determine where you want to be. You may not want to be the number one innovator or the most aggressively profitable – or even of the highest quality. It is no good aiming for high quality if quality, in the narrow sense of the word, is not a factor in your market, and at least you will save yourself a lot of time, money and effort. There will be products and markets in which, provided the product does its job for a short period and is of low price, it is better for the customer than a long-lasting, higher-priced item, whether it be cars or kettles.

I saw in a London underground train an advertisement for the Kwik Save discount store: 'Remember when they used to pile it high and sell it cheap – we still do.' If that is what your customers want and that is the business you are in, there is absolutely no problem. You are meeting your customers' perception of quality. Unfortunately for Kwik Save, customers' requirements moved on. They were attracted to the balance of quality, service and price offered by Sainsbury, Tesco and other mainstream supermarkets which continue to expand while Kwik Save in

1996 announced the closure of 107 of its 977 UK stores with the loss of 1,900 jobs. Seeking to break the mould can go disastrously wrong!

Step 4

Prioritise your key measures of externally assessed quality success. Whatever part of the market you wish to be in, you must know which are the most important measures. In the automobile industry the J. D. Powers international measurement of customer satisfaction is now *the* criteria. In the service sector, particularly within the media, awards are the benchmark. Other companies are interested solely in the bottom line. But when you do not have independently assessed criteria it is always possible to define your own particularly in relation to your competitors' performance. If you know that they have high customer satisfaction reflected in repeat orders, what target will you set for yourself?

Step 5

Determine internal measures of quality which correlate with external success. You may not get it right first time. In Nissan, after many years, we settled on 'straight through ratio' as being the measure which has highest correlation with independent surveys of customer satisfaction. The 'straight through ratio' is the proportion of cars which go through the entire assembly process without having to undergo any rectification work at any stage. In the early days we concentrated more on 'end of line' quality but this additional measure is based on the concept that any rectification anywhere in the process must have an adverse effect on delivered quality. Anything which has to be fixed is not going to have the same integrity as something which never needs fixing.

However, recognise that a universal standard may not always be appropriate. Much will depend on the local circumstances and standards must accommodate what is realistically achievable. For a job placement service the number of people successfully appointed may be very different in a high unemployment area from those appointed in a high employment area. If, however, they were to choose 'Those still employed after one year' the league table of success might well be reversed. Some organisations may choose to use both measures or to assess the rate of improvement as being a better indicator than absolute achievement. Such decisions can only be made within the organisation after extensive analysis and discussion.

Within the overall target there are advantages in allowing the detailed measures to be developed at the operational level. If everyone is to buy-in to the targets then, as far as possible, they must be their own targets. In a multi-site company, with some old and some new facilities, it may not make sense to impose a company-wide standard of, say, rejects per million when rejects per thousand is the maximum that can be achieved without significant capital investment. If the job placement service has a run-down facility with a poor ambience, it begins with a major handicap if 'Customer Satisfaction' is determined from above to be the key performance indicator; nothing could do more to demotivate. 'We can never do well so it's not worth bothering' can easily become the pervading atmosphere. But if this is a key measure established *by the staff* nothing could do more to stimulate efforts to improve that ambience.

Step 6

So far, no name has been given to this process, nor has there been any great announcement, but certainly it is no secret (secrecy is the kiss of death). It is just happening. You must decide if you wish to focus attention by giving it a name or if you just want to get on and do it. There are benefits and dangers in both directions. Focusing can concentrate attention but lead to a 'flavour of the month' response. 'Getting on and doing it' can cause some confusion as to what is happening but lead to a greater chance of it becoming integrated into the organisation. 'We're integrating quality' by itself says very little, but maybe, 'We're starting a process which we hope will involve everyone in the company in ensuring we all get much better at understanding and meeting our customers' needs' will provide the starting point. Whether or not a name is needed will emerge. The danger is to develop an acronym too early, thereby fixing the concept and raising hopes which can easily be dashed. The whole organisation will be learning, and from learning comes change.

Step 7

There comes a point when progress and achievement are necessary. If people have contributed to defining the targets many will have been working towards them long before any corporate targets are published. If managers, supervisors or operators say, 'Let's not wait, let's just get on and do it' then, provided they have not omitted their own analysis and planning, that is great. Indeed, the lead group should encourage such gun jumping. Leadership exists where you find it and there is nothing like solid achievement to motivate and nothing like learning from the odd failure, provided it is constructive. There is no need to wait for the major training programme to be completed, for in large organisations it will take years and small organisations may not be able to afford one. Problem-solving techniques can be built into the supervisor and management training programmes and they can then teach those who report to them.

The projects or tasks do not even have to be about specific quality issues. If the job is made safer or the ambience more pleasant, quality will improve, and the next project may be about quality. The need for multi-functional teams will also emerge. The production group will realise that it cannot improve a process without involving people from engineering, safety, finance and so on. Multi-functional teams in such an organisation are constantly forming, achieving and disbanding. They are the way of life.

Step 8

You may find that such an approach will render your recognition systems obsolete. You may no longer need a bureaucratic suggestions scheme but if it is to be retained make sure that the decision process is close to the operator, preferably with the immediate boss having the authority to make decisions. Alternatively, you may already believe that that everyone is paid to think and contribute and that recognition means the boss taking out the team for an after-hours drink. You may opt for the formal presentation and lunch with the chief executive, although such an event can be another kiss of death if the chief executive or individual is uncomfortable with it.

Even deeper, it may turn out that your whole reward structure built up over the years will need to be revised. Individual piece-rates or bonus payments are often incompatible with such an approach, but do not rush it. The need for change, if need there be, will emerge. No one can get it right in advance.

Deeper still, the need for a total restructuring of the organisation may be an outcome. Organisation structures which have developed over the years without being fundamentally challenged are often an impediment to achieving the new goals. But I criticise those who present instant off-the-shelf solutions. It's rather like going to a doctor who, immediately you walk in the door, says, 'I've got just the thing to cure you, here it is. Now, what's your problem?' If you believe the analogy represents an unfair criticism of the approach of the instant experts, I suggest you sit through one or two presentations!

Step 9

It is critical that everyone knows how they are performing against the targets and it is here that the visual management systems and daily communications processes come into their own. It may be necessary to make an initial 'song and dance' but, unless your company's normal style is to celebrate achievement, aim to accept high quality as a fact of life as quickly as possible. If quality is to become the norm it is simply not possible to make a big noise about it all the time.

Step 10

The final stage comes when quality is fully integrated into your normal way of life and permeates every level in the organisation. None of your training programmes is specifically about quality but all of them contribute to your quality performance. The commitment encompasses everything you do, from the recruitment process, employee involvement and control of the processes to termination procedures, relationships with trade unions and new product development. Measurement of quality is the norm and all employees seek continuously to improve on their previous achievements. All elements of the business are aligned.

However, even when you reach this happy state, you will not be able to relax. Without continuing top management interest and attention, standards can easily decline you will not be able to sustain the gain.

Top management attention has to be maintained for ever!

Finally, and optionally, you may decide to go for accreditation under ISO 9000, the international standard which assesses whether your procedures and practices enable you consistently to achieve your desired quality level. I end with ISO 9000, not begin with it, for it is a bureaucratic process and unless there is already a deep commitment to high quality it could be a great turn-off.

ISO 9000 does not define your quality level. That remains your responsibility. But the disciplines are important and the ISO 9000 requirements will expose weaknesses in your systems. The continuing audits will ensure that you are kept on your toes.

ISO 9000 will add more control to your commitment, but if you do not already have commitment it will be putting the cart before the horse.

10   Customer–Supplier Partnerships

When capacity permits, manufacturers are better off with single source suppliers. A carefully selected and managed supplier offers the greatest guarantee of consistently high quality, namely commitment to the product.

(David N. Burt, *Harvard Business Review*, 1989)

There is a Japanese word, 'karanage', which means simply asking your suppliers to cut prices without doing anything on our part. This does not work any more.

(Yoshifumi Tsuji, President, Nissan Motor Company, 1993)

ADVERSARIAL RELATIONSHIPS

Central to the quality of a finished product is the quality of its components and materials, but whereas most organisations profess concern about the quality of their bought-out parts, the ascendant organisation is also concerned about the quality of the actual relationship with its suppliers.

In the past, customers have sought to keep their suppliers at arm's length, many preferring the tension of an adversarial relationship. In the automobile industry, the major assemblers each had several thousand suppliers, most with short-term contracts based on price. At the end of the product development process a number of suppliers were called in, given the detailed specification, and asked to submit competitive bids, often with little information about the customer's cost, delivery and quality targets and with unrealistic volume information. The buyers enjoyed playing suppliers off against each other and ended up by selecting at least two for every component with the decision based primarily on price. The customer had little or no interest in what happened inside the suppliers' plants and discouraged suppliers from visiting its own operations. The relationship was restricted to those directly involved in buying and selling.

174

Suppliers, because they had no guarantee of a long-term relationship, did not seek a true understanding of their customers' needs. Knowing that they were going to be screwed on price, they kept their costs secret. They had little incentive to invest in their design and development capability because it was not required of them. Consequently, they learned little and were able to contribute nothing to ongoing improvements except always to complain that their task was impossible. Often, they were not even able to accommodate their customers' requirements because of their capacity limitations. With no certainty of a future relationship, capital investment to meet uncertain demands was a low priority.

The result was a relationship in which neither party had much understanding of the other's needs. The supplier had often acquired the business on the basis of artificially low prices and constantly sought price increases for every subsequent modification. The customer tolerated high reject levels as the price to be paid for this relationship but screamed all the time at the suppliers for their inadequate performance, and threatened them continuously with losing the business. The financial equation was (is) based on 'cost plus', i.e.

$$\text{COST} + \text{PROFIT} = \text{PRICE}$$

This means that a predetermined profit margin is added to the cost, so that if costs rise, profits follow. There is no incentive to reduce costs.

THE JAPANESE WAY

In 1993, Anderson Consulting published the results of an investigation into the productivity and quality performance of 18 matched automotive components companies, nine in Japan and nine in the UK. The key comparators are shown in Table 10.1.

The study found that the 'high productivity and high quality' plants were all Japanese and that not one British plant ranked 'high' on both scales. The world-class plants had an almost 2:1 productivity differential and a quality superiority of 100:1, achieved despite a higher number of live parts and a significantly higher rate of new product introduction. The world class plants had one-seventh the inventory and delivered to customers six times more frequently.

Table 10.1   Automotive Suppliers' Performance

Factor	Measure	World-class plants	Other plants
Units per hour	100 = best	95	54
Throughput time	100 = best	59	32
Quality	% defects	0.025	2.5
Rework/rectification	% labour time	1.5	4.1
Stock turnover	Times per annum	94	32
Inventory	Hours	11	75
Delivery frequency to customers	Hours	3	18
Number of live parts		188	161
Parts introduced in last year	%	44	17

Source: Anderson Consulting (1993).

In looking for explanations the survey found that, statistically, automation counted for only 10 per cent of the difference, training effort was not greatly different and, to their surprise, the levels of responsibility devolved to the work teams did not differ greatly. The major difference was the contribution of 'team leaders' to a number of key areas including inspection, rectification, routine maintenance and quality improvements, 'which was double that of team leaders in non-world-class plants. In most activities the team leaders played a pivotal role in world-class plants. . . These findings suggest that the role of the "empowered" operator in world-class manufacturing may have been overstated and that the crucial difference lies at team leader rather than operator level.'

There are, however, other fundamental differences between Western and Japanese relationships, primarily stemming from the fact that in Japan the customer usually has only one supplier for a particular component and that supplier will often be wholly or partially owned by its customer and may have only the one customer. In the West, the partnership will usually be between wholly independent companies, with the supplier not being wholly dependent on a single customer.

In Japan, the car assembly companies typically have not thousands but around 300 first-tier suppliers. The supplier is regarded as the expert in its components and has experienced design and engineering teams who will be deeply involved with the customer throughout the product development cycle. Often the customer will give only the broadest specification and the supplier will take on the responsibility of developing the system.

PARTNERSHIP SOURCING

Although in Japan the relationship is not always one of true partnership, often being epitomised by Yoshifumi Tsuji's comment at the head of this chapter, the concept of partnership sourcing seriously impacted on Europe with the arrival of Japanese automobile manufacturers in the 1980s and was given a Western twist. However, many of the 'drivers' were in place well before then, and the concept can now be seen almost as an *inevitable outcome* of the many new demands being placed on suppliers by customers, rather than as the introduction of a totally new concept.

The 'drivers' making partnership sourcing inevitable include:

Quality
- The recognition that a consistent high level of quality depends significantly on the performance of the entire supply chain

Cost
- Not just price but the consideration of all acquisition costs
- 'Conception to resurrection' costs and all 'cost in use' elements
- Target costing (defining the selling price and setting constituent elements accordingly)

Shortened product life cycles
- Need for faster response times
- Requirement to be 'right first time'

Concentration on core businesses
- Where most value can be added
- Where distinctive competencies exist
- Avoidance of unnecessary expenditure

Trend to black box assemblies/services
- Purchase of whole systems and services rather than components for sub-assembly
- Suppliers developing expertise applicable to a wide range of customers, hence spreading development costs

Competitive pressures making for lean supply
- Early involvement of predetermined suppliers for development of each individual component, system or service

- Pressure on inventory and all forms of waste, forcing closer matching of customer/supplier output levels and systems
- Need to optimise all linkages in the supply chain network (both internal and external)

Adoption of 'Best Practice' creating dependence
- Refined systems resulting from TQM, JIT, EDI etc. create customer dependence on suppliers
- Greater dependency requires closer integration of people, plans and systems, both internally and externally.

All of these trends are present in many businesses. They create the conditions in which partnership sourcing becomes inevitable but in themselves are *not* partnership sourcing. Partnership sourcing encompasses virtually all of these trends but it is bigger than the sum of its parts and adds to those parts.

Partnership sourcing was neatly described by the Confederation of British Industry in 1991:

> Partnership sourcing is where customer and supplier develop such a close and long-term relationship that the two work together as partners. It isn't philanthropy: the aim is to secure the best possible commercial advantage. The principle is that teamwork is better than combat. If the end customer is to be best served, then both parties to a deal must win. Partnership sourcing works because both parties have an interest in each other's success . . . It means rejecting the 'master–servant' syndrome where the supplier is merely told what to supply and the customer told the price. Instead the partners agree on common goals and build the commitment, trust and mutual support necessary to achieve them.

A key principle of partnership sourcing is that it is a *whole company* philosophy. It does not apply solely to the buyer–seller relationship but permeates the whole of both organisations from the chief executives downwards. It involves all functions and requires that both partners work together for mutual success, are open with each other and recognise that, as with the definition of quality, the ultimate beneficiary has to be the end user of the product or service.

Central to partnership sourcing is the establishment of a long-term relationship so that the environment is created in which the supplier has the confidence to invest in its design and development capability, its facilities and, in particular, in its people. Without good, well-trained and highly motivated people able to communicate directly with each other, no company is able to achieve anything. It is not necessary to have a long-term contract to achieve this relationship – once there is confidence between the partners, the only formal negotiations need be about price, although there will be continuous involvement in discussions on quality, new product development, delivery and management capabilities. The customer is not going to turn off the supplier nor will it seek annual tenders from competitors. The suppliers are stakeholders in the business of the customer and are treated as such. They become mutually interdependent; the relationship is one of trust, with both partners winning. If it is seen as a win–lose relationship, there is no partnership.

As a result, the supplier is able to participate fully in the development of new products and has far earlier sight of, and involvement in, the process. The supplier has to understand fully its customers' standards and targets and be able to respond to change requests; it needs to possess technical knowledge of the manufacturing processes and input into cost reduction and design change activities; it needs to be able to test its products to standards required by the customer and deliver trial parts from production tools; it needs to have state-of-the-art knowledge of its business and be able to generate improvements on existing products. All of this leads to a comprehensive interchange of information, often with the supplier being required to develop knowledge of related components even though they may not be its direct business. It leads to more 'black box' technology, with the supplier taking responsibility for whole systems rather than components. This in turn results in the elimination of sub-assembly operations in the customer's facility.

Sceptics have suggested that such concepts are merely an excuse for a powerful customer to put pressure on a supplier, to transfer the inventory carrying cost from the customer to the supplier, and that it works only in the good times. When the going gets tough the customer reverts to type and pressurises the supplier to cut prices. *If this is the case, the relationship is not a partnership.* The fundamental principle is that working together in an open and trusting relationship, with a recognition of the needs of the ultimate customer, can bring success and prosperity to all partners

With such a relationship the pricing equation fundamentally changes. The customer, with knowledge of the internationally competitive prices, aims to know the final selling price of the product and works backwards from there. Toyota buyers, for example, are networked throughout the world so that at any time they can check what other plants are paying for specific components or systems. Through value engineering the supplier develops the component to achieve the price the customer is prepared to pay. The price equation fundamentally changes to become:

$$PRICE - COST = PROFIT$$

The customer requires detailed knowledge of the supplier's costs – open book costing – so that they can work together to reduce these costs.

During the life of a product the customer will expect the supplier to offset inflationary increases by becoming more efficient, although customer-required product changes will be paid for. The customer will seek price reductions due to cost savings arising from improvements in productivity, scheduling, design and quality, resulting in the following movements in the financial equation:

$$PRICE - COST = PROFIT \uparrow \downarrow$$

In this equation the customer works with the supplier to help reduce its costs; as costs fall the supplier's profit will rise, and next time round the customer will expect to share in that increased profit through a price reduction. The equation shifts to:

$$PRICE - COST = PROFIT \uparrow \downarrow$$

But the supplier will continue to work to reduce costs so as to maintain an acceptable profit level. The cycle continues with the benefits shared. John Gillett, IBM's Procurement Manager, summarised the benefits of partnership sourcing as:

For the purchaser
- Joint development of the design, with early vendor involvement
- Reduced design lead times and fast introduction
- Product designed for value-added manufacture following early involvement of suppliers

- Product availability when the market place is ready
- Assured source of defect-free supplies on time
- Eliminates need for 'just in case' planning
- 100 per cent value added
- Working together gets cost out
- Lower paper processing costs

For the supplier
- Continuity of customer relationship
- An assured market
- Co-operation in the development of overheads and skills necessary to achieve customers' demands
- Better planning leading to more economic use of resources
- Lower selling costs leading to other customer opportunities
- Confidence to invest

It has to be accepted, however, that there is a potential downside. In some circumstances single sourcing may be a slightly more risky strategy and in the years of a high incidence of industrial disputes could not have been contemplated. Although there is a risk that such times will return, the concepts of the ascendant organisation – including the interdependence arising from partnership sourcing – make it less likely. There remains, of course, the disaster scenario and although in many businesses there will be alternatives, it is rarely easy rapidly to secure alternative sources of supply at the required specification, quality and cost.

The other side of the coin is complacency, and many find it difficult to understand how such long-term commitments cannot lead to the relationship becoming too cosy. Such attitudes fundamentally misunderstand the nature of the relationship which entails a search for continuous improvement and cost reductions. In any case, most companies single source – internally. The managing director of a small engineering company which has done it says people are needlessly nervous. 'I ask them, "How many paint shops do you have? How many computer systems?" They're single sourcing internally, but don't realise it.'

But how do you avoid complacency? The answer is to measure performance. Nissan's measurements system is based on five factors – quality, cost, delivery, design and development, and management. Each factor is broken down into numerous elements, targets are established and achievement measured on a quarterly basis. For example, delivery is broken down into production delivery, service delivery, load presentation and project management, and each of these into a further four or five measures. Overall delivery of production parts on time rose from 84 per cent in 1992 to 98 per cent in 1996. Every supplier knows his inventory performance on a monthly basis. Twenty-seven per cent of suppliers are responsible for 80 per cent of Nissan's expediting effort. They all know who they are. They all knew that in 1994 their delivery window would reduce from three to two hours and that greater emphasis would be placed on load presentation problems, for example, mislabelling and mixed stock concerns. Partnership sourcing does not result in complacency!

D2D (Design to Distribution Limited) is the manufacturing services arm of ICL and is responsible for technical services, fabrication and assembly, software, repair, refurbishment and recycling. As the 1994 winner of the European Quality Award it, not unsurprisingly, accredits its suppliers according to the quality standard they have reached. It has four grades of supplier:

Grade A: Quality activities fully endorsed by D2D
- ISO 9000 registration
- Self-assessment against a quality model, e.g. EFQM, Baldridge
- Long-term relationship with *its* suppliers

Grade A suppliers are only periodically assessed.

Grade B: Quality activities broadly satisfy D2D's requirements
- A plan is in place allowing the company to progress to D2D's requirements

Grade B suppliers' progress is monitored.

Grade C: Some shortfall in quality activities
- Quality activities not registered with accrediting bodies

Grade C suppliers are expected to commit to D2D's endorsed quality activities.

Grade D: Unacceptable level of quality activities
- Does not recognise the importance of quality activities

Grade D suppliers are required to take urgent action.

In total, quality comprises 40 per cent of D2D's overall measures of supplier performance with cost and service sharing the other 60 per cent equally. In assessing, for example, their freight agents they use criteria such as

Corrective action teams	Response to the unexpected
ISO 9000 registration	Price competitiveness
Delivered quality	Invoice quality
Response to tender	On-line information
Customer service	Off-line information
Operations meetings	On time delivery
Corrective action teams	Electronic links
Payment terms	Non-conformance

D2D regards regular performance reviews as the biggest single contribution to developing partnership relations and is very specific about the benefits. It sees them as follows:

For D2D
- Focused D2D attention and effort towards key vendors
- Vendor confidence and trust in D2D
- Vendor awareness of and measurement against D2D's key performance requirements
- Vendor actively involved in D2D's quality improvement process

For suppliers:
- Appointment of a vendor manager
- Greater visibility of D2D's/ICL's forward planning
- Joint quality teams established
- Provides the right D2D/ICL management audience for vendors
- Increased internal and external awareness
- More business, not just with D2D

While not all down to partnership sourcing, D2D is convinced that the practice contributed significantly to eleven years of continuously improving results, e.g.:

Delivery to required quality	20% to 99%
Delivery to required date	20% to 99%
Inventory turns	2–3 p.a. to 15 p.a.
Revenue	$150m to $450m
Staff	7,000 to 2,300

SUPPLIER DEVELOPMENT

One of the key elements of partnership sourcing is the willingness of the partners to work together for mutual improvement. Kodak has its quality improvement facilitators whose aim is to immerse both its own operations and suppliers in their quality culture. Glaxo brought together competing suppliers into one transparent team; Xerox has its supplier certification programme, Continuous Supplier Involvement, aimed at close operational linkages and has trained 30,000 of its suppliers' employees in its 'Leadership through quality' programme.

Nissan's Supplier Development (SD) concept began in late 1988 when the company commenced working with twelve suppliers, all of which had demonstrated a positive attitude to improvement and a willingness to seek Japanese performance levels. It is a never-ending process which is about changing people's attitudes, gradually altering their traditional ways of working and thinking and securing their ownership of and commitment to the new way. As such, it recognises that change cannot be forced through and requires investment in people, resources and time by both the customer and the supplier in anticipation of a considerable return. But it also recognises that, however committed the chief executive may be, real improvements take place only when managers, supervisors and operators share that commitment. The real work is at the sharp end.

Once suppliers are identified, bring them into the discussion process beginning at the top, but also involving people known to have real influence within their organisation. As a result, develop an initial work programme with a few suppliers with which you feel comfortable, both in terms of their attitude and the number you can manage. Nissan began with twelve, but for most companies this will be too many.

The SD approach recognises that the customer's team must not usurp the supplier's authority. Their role is one of education and training in quality and improvement techniques so that the suppliers themselves may identify areas for improvement. Then, for a period, they support the suppliers' initiatives, assisting in the development of improvement plans and monitoring progress. Specific areas include quality, production processes, stock control, maintenance, housekeeping and safety but they look in particular at the leadership given by managers. Do they have a philosophy compatible with the objectives and if so is it shared? What is the level of morale in the company?

The teams may work on non-Nissan activities – for the whole idea is to develop the total capability of the supplier, not just those elements which relate to one customer. Suppliers with multiple customers can often be confused by the different requirements of their various customers, and though this cannot be totally removed, it is recognised that the knowledge will be shared anyway.

Reorganisation, both structural and physical, often follows. Frequent outcomes include a move to cellular manufacturing systems, a desire to establish their own *kaizen* programmes and a major enhancement of the role of the supervisor. Also, there often comes a dissatisfaction with the performance of the suppliers' suppliers and the programmes have to be extended to the second-tier suppliers. In 1994 the DTI, in conjunction with Nissan, Toyota and Honda, organised a visit to Japan for a group of second-tier suppliers, extending the concept throughout the supply chain.

The tributes to this process have been many. VDO is a German company which assembles instrument clusters. Peter Callow, Managing Director, said that there were many MD-type reasons for being enthusiastic:

We use half the floor space, productivity increased by a conservative 50 per cent, work in progress reduced by thousands of per cent, end of line rejects decreased by 200–300 per cent and we measure throughput in minutes and hours rather than days, and all this has cost us next to nothing.

But there are other benefits:

All of our manufacturing staff have been involved in the process of improvement; they have been consulted, asked to identify problems, and most importantly have their ideas incorporated into the new ways of working. The use of multi-disciplinary teams has empowered people to make changes in systems, manufacturing methods and layouts. Very often it has been the first time that individuals in our teams have experienced that kind of freedom The ten-day improvement activities have acted as vehicles for education, training and development of many of our staff. Our experiences have made me realise how important is the manufacturing system as a whole, in particular we have begun to focus our attention on the issue of material handling and the role of our suppliers in improving our competitive position. The cynics, me included, have been silenced.

True to its word, VDO extended SD activities to its own suppliers. Nottingham-based Pressac supplies flexible and rigid circuits for VDO's instrument clusters. VDO introduced them to the quick changeover concept, which resulted in 80 per cent reduction in changeover times and, subsequently, to cell manufacturing and *kaizen* – resulting in 40 per cent labour saving, 40 per cent space saved, 85 per cent work-in-progress reduction and 80 per cent reduction in lead times. The techniques have been introduced in other Pressac factories and have been incorporated into a new £2 million facility.

The bottom-line impact is now very powerful. In January 1997, Renault announced that it aimed to sign 40 UK component suppliers in a fast-track recruitment programme, an action that would have been unthinkable a decade earlier.

HOW TO INTRODUCE PARTNERSHIP SOURCING

Because it is about relationships between different organisations, partnership sourcing is probably more difficult to establish than any other concept associated with becoming an ascendant organisation. More than anything else it demands trust and this does not come easily when antagonistic attitudes have developed over the years. The essential ingredients for a successful partnership include a genuine commitment at all levels of both organisations, with leadership from the top, coupled with open communications, information and genuine understanding of what is expected of each other. The true partnership means that the supplier also teaches the customer. This can only come about as a result of training, patience and the experience of working and learning together. Although the more advanced partner will normally take the lead; arrogance will cause failure.

The first task is to determine if this is the route you wish to take. It is not for everyone and the decision will not be easy. The greatest impact will be on the purchasing team and they will need to be convinced that there are advantages in this new approach, recognising that their skills may need to change and that other people – engineers, designers, quality assurance, trainers, and so on – will have an increasingly important part to play in the relationship. The people directly concerned must be fully involved in the decision-making process and then they have to be equipped to work in the new way.

I G Dewhirst, established in 1885, is Marks and Spencer's oldest and largest supplier. In 1992 Dewhirst restructured by establishing Strategic Business Units to provide greater focus on their relevant M&S departments, e.g. Shirts, Suits, Trousers, Blouses. 'But,' said Purchasing Director, Harry Douthwaite, 'we recognised that we could not achieve ultimate success without developing mutually beneficial strategies which embrace the needs of the customer, Dewhirst and the fabric and trim suppliers.' Therefore, in February 1993 they embarked on a supply-chain partnership programme, with the aim of improving the overall performance of the supply chain. Particularly, in a fashion market, they concentrated on the need to improve response times and flexibility, quality, planning and communication.

Dewhirst conducted a careful exercise to select their partners. They:

1. Conducted a Pareto analysis to determine the 20 per cent of suppliers which accounted for 80 per cent of spend.
2. Called together a selection of current and potential suppliers for a *common* briefing session explaining the concept and processes. All were given samples and details of the potential value of the business.
3. Held individual meetings with suppliers addressing their capabilities in areas such as product range, response times, innovation, obsolescence reduction, pricing and financial stability.
4. Prepared a short list.
5. Undertook informal visits to the short-listed companies for on-site discussions on all relevant matters, with specific attention to the management's attitudes.
6. Undertook formal visits to assess actual and potential performance in quality, cost, delivery, design and development and management attitude.
7. Made recommendations to senior management.
8. Conducted product trials (if necessary for new suppliers).
9. Gave final approval.

There are of course many more examples but the process and the areas of concern are unlikely to differ significantly. The CBI has pulled together a generic listing of factors a company might consider when choosing their first partners. I have simplified this and it is given in Table 10.2. The precise process and criteria will, of course, be specific to a company.

It is often said that customers seeking to implement partnership sourcing would fail many of the tests they set their suppliers. If this is the case, a key question is, *'Are you capable of managing such a relationship?'*

PARTNERSHIP AGREEMENTS

Most partnerships of this nature do not have formal agreements, and many argue that they should not need them, for the relationship is one of

Table 10.2   Choosing a Partner

What to do	Areas of interest
Identify candidates	Identify key suppliers which are close to the required standard
Review performance to date	Achievements Quality systems Development capability Attitude to change
Define minimum standards	Quality policy Quality certification Technology, e.g. JIT, EDI, etc. In-house design capability Supply capability – local/national/international Consistency of delivery of performance, service standard, product quality Attitude to total acquisition costs Willingness to change, flexibility of management and workforce
Assess management attitude	Identify key decision-makers and influencers Do they recognise opportunities for improvement? Is the management capable of taking partnership sourcing forward? Do they recognise they must play a key role?
Understand strategy	Do their long- and short-term priorities match ours? Are they willing and able to invest to achieve their aims? Is the supplier customer-driven?

trust and they are not partnerships in the legal sense. However, the partners may wish to record the nature of the relationship and in such instances the CBI has suggested a Partnership Agreement which includes the following terms:

- **Statement of principle**
  The partners agree in principle to work together in an open and trusting partnership deliberately to create a business relationship which is ethical and progressive, delivering tangible, measurable benefits to both partners over a long period.
- **Cost**
  Each partner will work year-on-year to ensure that total acquisition costs of items or services supplied will reduce.

- **Service**
  The supplier will work to ensure achievement of customer perform-ance and service levels of not less than *x per cent* timeliness of deliveries, *y per cent* quantity of deliveries and *z per cent quality of deliveries*.
- **Forecasts**
  The customer will provide accurate forecasts regularly. Such forecasts will provide *x* months of firm orders and *y* months' forecasted business volume.
- **Technology improvement**
  Each partner will work to improve the technology and process of manufacture of the materials and items supplied and will regularly review specifications to ensure maximum effectiveness of items supplied. As appropriate, technology improvement projects will be defined, agreed and implemented.
- **Continuous improvement**
  Both partners will implement a continuous improvement programme in their own business, apply it to the items supplied, and meet regularly to assess potential improvements.
- **Hardship**
  In the event that either partner gets into difficulty under the terms of this Partnership Agreement, they will have the right to approach the other partner requesting relief from hardship. At this point, both partners will meet to discuss openly the issues involved and the pro-active, positive solutions to them.
- **Cost structure**
  For each of the items or services supplied, an agreed open-book cost structure will be created (consisting of a formula containing materials, labour, manufacturing overheads, general overheads, profit, plus other categories, e.g. return on investment). These will be agreed at the initiation of the partnership and reviewed regularly in the light of the continuous improvement programme, cost reduction objectives and technology improvement objectives of the Partnership Agreement.
- **Materials**
  The customer will work with the supplier to minimise the cost of the supplier's material purchases, for example offering joint agreements for similar materials used in its business and offer to hold joint negotiations with material suppliers to minimise end-product costs.
- **Capital investment**
  Where expenditure on capital is required to be undertaken by the supplier to manufacture items on behalf of the customer, this will be

identified at the beginning of the partnership. The criteria for investment and pay-back and return from that investment will be clearly agreed and defined between the partners before any investment is made.

- **Management education and publicity**
  Each party will undertake to brief its management and staff regularly: initially on the nature of the agreement and subsequently on the status of development of the relationship between the two partners.

DEVELOPING THE RELATIONSHIP

In addition to establishing the Partnership Agreement it is critical that staff in both companies are kept well informed and are trained and developed in the new way. This can lead to joint review and improvement teams being established with, for example, the responsibility to determine where systems can be integrated through enhanced communication channels; sorting out problems and agreeing on performance measures.

It will also be necessary to define responsibilities and determine the resources required and by so doing develop an understanding of each other's business, but, above all, top management must set the example by behaving in the way they talk. In particular they must demonstrate that the partners are stakeholders in their business and must not walk away at the first difficulty.

These responsibilities are by no means exhaustive but they do give an indication of the areas that need to be continuously addressed if the initial enthusiasm is to be maintained. Ivor Vaughan, chairman of Rearsby Automotive, said of his company's relationship with Nissan, 'There's a lot to be said about partnership, but Nissan *lives* it. I am always referred to as *the* supplier. Nissan makes the commitment and its actions support it.'

Whatever the specific measures of benefit there is also the unquantifiable – the benefit that you are *the* supplier; that you will work together for continuous improvement; that both parties will have early sight of the other's plans; that in the tough times you will work together to pull yourselves out of difficulty; that you have the confidence to invest. Above all, there is the good feeling that comes from knowing that you are in it together for the long haul and that mutual interdependence means that neither can cast the other adrift simply because some predator comes up with a short-term, loss-leading price.

The relationship is not cosy – it is often very demanding – but the long-term benefits far outweigh the short-term difficulties that many experience when starting down the route. The very interdependence to which it leads becomes a strength, for while there is sometimes a concern about 'What will happen if the supplier goes under?' or 'I must not become too dependent on one customer' the very strength of the relationship helps prevent the worst from happening. Partnership sourcing does not necessarily mean *single* sourcing and you may decide that you wish to spread the risk. However, as confidence in the relationship builds, you may find that you are able to single source with much more confidence, and as capabilities grow so will the relationship.

Andy Dewhurst, Tesco's Trading Director responsible for frozen food, summed it up. 'To me, it's identifying the best suppliers to go forward with, concentrating suppliers into fewer hands and forming even close relationships than usual . . . The main advantages are lower cost, an improved investment climate, better product quality, improved logistics and better product development.'

If these objectives are achieved, Theodore Levitt's comment that 'Supplier partnerships require the same amount of attention as a good marriage' will, as with good marriages, reap benefits for both partners that are far greater than the attention given; and then, after a time, the attention becomes so natural that it is no effort at all!

11 Every Worker a Knowledge Worker

The basic economic resource – 'the means of production' to use the economist's term – is no longer capital, nor natural resources . . . nor labour. It is and will be knowledge.

(Peter Drucker, *Post-Capitalist Society*, 1993)

Said Ford to Mazda, 'How do you justify your investment in training?'
Said Mazda to Ford, 'We don't understand the question.'

(Stuart Hamer, Director of Education and Training, Ford of Europe, 1993)

GET THE BASICS RIGHT

The fundamental changes which have taken place in the world economy mean that advanced industrialised societies with their high wage and social costs can only succeed by having a highly trained, flexible and innovative workforce willing to accept devolved responsibility. In short, knowledge workers.

The term 'knowledge worker' is a vogue term; it generally refers to people working in the 'knowledge' sectors, or those who are expected to innovate or be creative. But if you use the term 'knowledge worker' to identify such people then, by definition, there must be those who are *not* knowledge workers. This is totally unacceptable.

In the ascendant organisation every worker is a knowledge worker.

In the United States, a 1991 report by the Secretary's Commission on Achieving Necessary Skills (The SCANS Report) said:

The message to us was universal: good jobs will increasingly depend on people who can put knowledge to work. What we found was disturbing: more than half our young people leave school without the knowledge or foundation required to find and hold a good job.

This condemnation has been echoed in many Western societies, particularly Britain where barely a month goes by without another report or politician denouncing the low standards of the education system and launching yet another corrective initiative.

The SCANS Report defines what it sees as the foundation of skills and personal qualities that lie at the heart of job performance. Although it regards these as 'Essential preparation for all students, both those going directly to work and those planning further education' they are so appropriate to the foundation skills needed in the ascendant organisation that I give them in full in Figure 11.1, 'A Three-Part Foundation'.

The SCANS report goes further, for in addition to the foundation skills it defines five competencies which it considers 'at least as important as technical expertise' and which 'are applicable from the shop floor to the executive suite' (except that in the ascendant organisation there is no executive suite!). Competencies span occupations and hierarchical levels although, of course, the balance will vary. While we might quibble with the detail, the listing is, again, so relevant to the ascendant organisation that it is given in full in Figure 11.2, 'Five Competencies'.

On the top of all this, there is the necessary technical knowledge for, however good the problem-solving skills or ability to keep records, unless the individual can actually do the job, whether it is engineering, nursing, accounting, deep-sea diving or operating a machine, no amount of foundation skills or competencies will achieve success.

The problem with The SCANS Report is that it is asking too much of the education system; it is applying the standards of the world of work to the world of education. When the education profession in most countries barely understands what is actually happening in the world of work; and after ten to twelve years of full-time education is still sending out half its pupils with inadequate literacy and numeracy, one cannot expect change to occur at a sufficiently rapid pace to match the changing demands of the world of work. We cannot wholly blame the educationalists.

Business has failed to communicate its changing needs, and the social mores in some countries are not conducive to supporting the teaching profession. However, if basic literacy and numeracy are the engines which drive all subsequent performance it is not unreasonable to comment that if the engines which determine aeroplane or automobile performance failed at the same rate as those determining people performance a certain amount of passion would be generated and not a few executives, managers and operators would lose their jobs! The business world has long learned that high quality and right first time is far superior to rectification. Nothing less should be required of the world of education.

Basic skills	Reads, writes, performs arithmetic and mathematical operations, listens and speaks
A Reading	Locates, understands and interprets written information in prose and in documents such as manuals, graphs and schedules
B Writing	Communicates thoughts, ideas, information and messages in writing. Creates documents such as letters, directions, manuals, reports, graphs and flow charts
C Arithmetic/ mathematics	Performs basic computations and approaches practical problems by choosing appropriately from a variety of mathematical techniques
D Listening	Receives, attends to, interprets and responds to verbal messages and other cues
E Speaking	Organises ideas and communicates orally
Thinking skills	**Thinks creatively, makes decisions, solves problems, visualises, knows how to learn, and reasons**
A Creative thinking	Generates new ideas
B Decision-making	Specifies goals and constraints, generates alternatives, considers risks
C Problem-solving	Recognises problems and devises and implements plan of action
D Visualising	Organises and processes symbols, pictures, graphs, objects and other information
E Knowing how to learn	Uses effective learning techniques to acquire and apply new knowledge and skills
F Reasoning	Discovers a rule or principle underlying the relationship between two or more objects and applies it when solving a problem
Personal qualities	**Displays responsibility, self-esteem, sociability, self-management, integrity and honesty**
A Responsibility	Exerts a high level of effort and perseveres towards goal attainment
B Self-esteem	Believes in own worth and maintains a positive view of self
C Sociability	Demonstrates understanding, friendliness, adaptability, empathy and politeness in a group setting
D Self-management	Assesses self accurately, sets personal goals, monitors progress and exhibits self-control
E Integrity/honesty	Chooses ethical course of action

Figure 11.1   The SCANS Report: A Three-Part Foundation

Resources		Identifies, organises plans and allocates resources
A	Time	Selects goal-relevant activities, ranks them, allocates time and prepares and follows schedules
B	Money	Uses or prepares budgets, makes forecasts, keeps records and makes adjustments to meet objectives
C	Materials and facilities	Acquires, stores, allocates and uses materials or space efficiently
D	Human resources	Assesses skills and distributes work accordingly, evaluates performance and provides feedback

Interpersonal		Works with others
A	Team member	Contributes to the team effort
B	Teaches	Teaches others new skills, coaches
C	Serves clients and customers	Works to satisfy customer's satisfaction
D	Leadership	Communicates ideas, persuades and convinces others, responsibly challenges existing procedures, practices and policies
E	Negotiates	Works towards agreement involving exchange of resources, resolves divergent interests
F	Works with diversity	Works well with men and women from diverse backgrounds

Information		Acquires and uses information
A		Acquires and evaluates information
B		Organises and maintains information
C		Interprets and communicates information
D		Uses computers to process information

Systems		Understands complex inter-relationships
A	Understands systems	Knows how social, organisational and technological systems work, and operates effectively with them
B	Monitors and corrects	Distinguishes trends, predicts impacts on system operations, diagnoses deviations in systems' performance and corrects malfunctions
C	Improves or designs systems	Suggests modifications to existing systems and develops new or alternative systems to improve performance

Technology		Works with a variety of technologies
A	Selects	Chooses procedures, tools or equipment, including computers and related technologies
B	Applies technology to task	Understands overall intent and proper procedures for set-up and operation of equipment
C	Maintains and troubleshoots equipment	Prevents, identifies or solves problems with equipment, including computers and other technologies

Figure 11.2 The SCANS Report: Five Competencies

A JOB WITH TRAINING – GERMANY

Vocational training systems vary greatly throughout the world but it is impossible not to mention the long-established German dual system which, even with its inflexibility, is often regarded as the model to which to aspire.

Briefly, in the (old) Federal Republic of Germany, 90 per cent of all school leavers receive vocational education and training, and in excess of 70 per cent enter training through the dual system under which, as apprentices, they spend about three days a week on in-company training and up to two days a week in a specialised training school. (Up to 40 per cent of the off-the-job training is in general education, including mathematics and politics.) Training is available for around 380 classified occupations ranging from motor vehicle maintenance to floristry. All firms which wish to employ an apprentice have to be approved by the local Chamber of Industry and Commerce as a training company. The local Chamber is responsible for the assessment of final examinations and is the awarding body for vocational qualifications. The cost of on-the-job training is borne by employers but the apprentices' pay is initially 30–40 per cent of that of the skilled worker.

However, the majority of firms choose not to be training firms. Of the 2.3 million companies, only about 500,000 provide training and only they are allowed to recruit young people. They often take on more than they can permanently employ, and at the end of their training about 60 per cent of all qualified apprentices leave for employment elsewhere. This is regarded by the training firms as part of their social responsibility and by many of the non-trainers as a free ride. I have difficulty in seeing it working well in many other countries!

The system is criticised for its inflexibility. Herman Schmidt, President of the German Federal Institute for Vocational Training, has pointed to the increasing difficulty in meeting new demands as agreed curricula rapidly became out of date. The system produces narrow specialists. He sees the future as moving towards a broader vocational education producing flexible generalists rather than one based on specialist skills. In the engineering occupations, recognising that within twenty years there will be virtually no unskilled workers and that skilled workers will take on more responsibilities, they have introduced the criterion to 'plan execute and control all work tasks within their occupation' as a less prescriptive and more project-based general competency (Schmidt, 1992).

However, the advantages of universal commitment outweigh the disadvantages of inflexibility. The amount of training is important, just as is the quality, although for those who enter higher education a system which can delay entry to the labour market to the late twenties or early thirties does suggest that more is not always better, and some Germans look with envy at the ability of the US and British systems to react rapidly to changing demands.

The key lesson from the German experience is not about structures or what is taught. It is that no young person should begin work without there being a commitment from the employer to provide training and from the individual to participate in that training. In the ascendant organisation such training will not be restricted to the narrow occupational requirements but encompass the broad range of foundation skills and competencies envisaged by The SCANS Report.

A JOB WITH TRAINING – JAPAN

The Japanese do very well without formal vocational qualifications. Alun Jones, Personnel Director of Sony UK, wisely commented on the great divide between the British and Japanese approach to training:

> The British are taught they have a responsibility to train people and tell them what is going on, otherwise they will not understand. The Japanese approach is from the opposite direction. They talk about an individual's responsibility to learn. It has a tremendous impact on what training means. While the British will lay on courses the Japanese see no need. They believe people will learn when they need to and if they are not motivated to find out then perhaps they should not be doing it anyway.

A 1979 study by the Tokyo Human Development Centre of the effectiveness of small group activities in Japan clearly illustrated employees' perceptions of the learning benefits of small group activities. The greatest benefits were in the personal development and satisfaction of the of the individual, with the more tangible measures showing lower positive impact:

	%		%
Improved skills	70	Improved efficiency	70
Job knowledge	84	Improved atmosphere	53
Motivation	68	Improved safety	48
Enjoyment of job	64	Improved quality	33

Although this survey dates from 1979, it is still quoted favourably by Japanese sources as being indicative of what they see as beneficial outcomes.

Therefore, for the Japanese, small group activities are not aimed at just achieving specific tasks; they are part of the overall education and learning experiences. The most accurate description is *near-the-job* training rather than on-the-job or off-the-job training. Near-the-job training involves studying what is going on, getting behind the obvious, using problem-solving techniques or the seven tools of quality control. The very nature of the activity is such that it enhances skills and confidence, aids personal development, increase the knowledge base and allows responsibility to be devolved. A virtuous upward spiral can be created, but it is a gradual process. If people are pushed too far, too fast and are expected to perform beyond their capabilities, they can easily become demoralised, switch off and turn the upward virtuous spiral into one which spirals downwards.

The Japanese, though, have the great advantage of slow-burn development. When it takes fifteen years from university graduation to become a manager, or eighteen years from high-school graduation to become a foreman, the need to develop people rapidly is simply not there. The university graduate is hired into a company, not an occupation, and during those fifteen years will be given a wide range of experiences in a variety of departments and divisions. They prefer not to allow specialisation to develop. They do not want narrow accountants, buyers or personnel officers. Their engineers will work in manufacturing engineering, production, quality assurance and purchasing. The aim is to develop people who have a broad understanding of the business acquired by experience and near-the-job training with instruction given by the immediate superior; by rotation of projects and assignments and often by considerable self-learning through self-study correspondence, television and radio courses. John Storey *et al.* found in their study of four blue-chip Japanese companies that 53 per cent of manual workers, 76 per cent of professional and technical workers and 73 per cent of managers undertook some form of voluntary self-development. (Storey, Edwards and Sissons, 1997, p.30).

The Japanese look for interaction and interchange between individuals, particular those in the same year or from the same university. Because of the seniority progression system under which it has been rare for the 'junior' to overtake the 'senior', the latter is not worried about teaching the former. In fact, it is regarded as a key responsibility of a manager to develop his staff, and his ability in this area is a significant factor in his overall performance assessment. Despite the beginning of the decline of the seniority progression system in favour of a merit-based approach, there has been virtually no change in their acceptance of this responsibility.

Some Japanese are, however, becoming dissatisfied with the traditional slow-burn development and as lifetime employment begins to break down and individuals increasingly choose to exercise their individuality, they are increasingly questioning a process which broadly provides for everyone to progress at the same slow pace irrespective of ability. In mid-1991 Daiken Trade and Industry (fibreboard manufacturers) announced its New Personnel System, which allows promising workers to rise through the ranks based on their expertise and merit as opposed to seniority. Said Personnel Chief Kazuhiro Izumi:

> We have to give people more training and more explanation about their training. People want to be told what their potential is and they want to know where their skills fit into the company's plans. Young people have lost loyalty because there are more jobs than people and so we want to give people more skill and make them feel useful.

One of the great criticisms of the Japanese development system is that individuals are only rarely told of their appraisals and that their careers, while planned, take virtually no account of the individual's desires. Izumi was reflecting the view that Japan's training practices were failing to keep pace with employees' expectations. In particular, Japanese companies have found that when they assign people to Western overseas locations with, usually, virtually no choice, no notice and no preparation, that their specific expertise does not match that of the professionals in the host country.

CONTINUOUS DEVELOPMENT

This leads to the point that the ascendant organisation will have a commitment to the continuous development of all staff.

This becomes particularly important at a time when most organisations have flattened their hierarchies. At one time those who envisaged that they had a career were able to look forward to rapid progress up the hierarchy. 'If I'm not promoted every three years I am failing!' But with flattened organisations, the elimination of jobs and more people competing, perceived promotion opportunities are no longer as obvious;

and a profound question must be, 'How do you motivate people when perceived promotion opportunities have disappeared?'. It then becomes imperative to motivate staff in a different way, particularly as people can be an appreciating asset; the longer their service, provided they are continuously developed, the more valuable they become.

What, then, is this concept of continuous development? I define it as:

A continuum in which in a structured way all people learn, are challenged and motivated so that they can grow and develop as individuals throughout their lives.

It is a continuum on two axes: the vertical, as the individual progresses upward through the hierarchy; and the horizontal, as the individual progresses over time, even if he or she remains at the same formal level. It is conscious and structured rather than accidental and haphazard, although some of the best learning opportunities arise in an unplanned way. It applies to all staff, not just a selected few. It refers to learning rather than training, although much learning can arise from training and development activities. It speaks of being challenged and motivated because personal growth comes not only from obvious learning experiences but also from assignments and projects. It refers to growth not just in the narrow sense of acquiring skills, but also in the development of the whole person. Finally, it is for life in two senses: it never ends and it is for the whole of life, not just for that part spent at work. A tall order!

The thought processes that went into my developing this concept took a long time to mature. One strand was my increasing dissatisfaction with the traditional concept of management development. The real break-through came when I realised that 'management' is not a separate career, that management education should not begin when someone is appointed a manager and that the real strength of an organisation comes from the continuous development of all people and not just a selected few. The focus has to move from management development, to helping people at all levels to learn, grow and develop throughout their lives.

This comes about not simply through training programmes but by involving people throughout the organisation in the continuous improvement of the business processes and in the development of their own skills, competencies and contributions. As we have seen, involving people in developing the culture of the organisation is critical to gaining ownership – but it goes further. It has to be a continuous process in which objectives are mutually defined, not as top-down targets to be imposed and measured on a pass/fail basis but as shared definitions of what is to be achieved; both in terms of tangible targets and in behavioural competences. We need to create a partnership between managers and staff in managing their overall performance.

To achieve virtually the same objective Sutcliffe Catering has introduced a different but no less valuable an approach. As a company with 2,700 separate business units it launched in 1995 a devolved and flexible programme, 'Steps to Success', which responds to the needs of individual members of staff. Under this programme the individual and his or her line manager review performance and then devise an improvement path using open learning materials, courses, assignments and so on, with the manager acting as mentor. A 24-hour helpline is available. Each individual builds up a portfolio of achievement which contains previous achievements as well as new skills. Once the portfolio is complete it is reviewed and guidance given as to the next steps, which might be more learning, a work-based project or other professional development. 'Steps to Success' is perhaps moving in the Japanese direction. It is entirely voluntary and, said Janine Whittaker, a learning and development facilitator: 'With this programme, we are turning [normal training] on its head by trying to get staff to take responsibility for their own learning' (Macqueen, 1996).

A word of warning – life is not perfect. While continuous development reaches throughout the organisation an organisation which ignores the specific development needs of its actual and potential managers does so at its peril. Identifying those who are likely to be able to progress through the managerial ranks and ensuring that they have the opportunities to develop and broaden their competencies and skills, is vital for all organisations.

This does not mean 'fast tracking'. Given the right opportunities and exposure, those with high ability emerge, and everyone, including their peers, recognise who they are. But avoid detailed succession planning. As an intellectual exercise it can use up many pleasant hours, but as a precise tool it is usually hopeless. People are rarely in the right place at the right time, and it is amazing how often, when forced to appoint unexpectedly, that the initially less-than-ideal person grows with the job. The critical task is to ensure that you have talent both in depth and breadth by appointing good people and giving them a range of experiences, assignments and training which prepare them for the future. And take risks. There is nothing more challenging, more daunting and potentially more satisfying for the individual and beneficial for the organisation than placing a manager in a role in which he or she lacks detailed knowledge. Provided you have confidence in the individual's overall capabilities, the task-specific knowledge, within reason, is the easiest element to acquire. Significantly, John Storey's *Managers in the Making* found that in four British and four Japanese companies the most significant factors impacting on 'Growing as a manager' were 'Challenging assignments' and 'Early responsibility'.

BEGINNING AT THE BOTTOM

Start at the bottom of the organisation, not at the top.

This thought is so blindingly obvious that in retrospect I wonder why it took me five years to realise it! This does not mean that the development of people at lower levels has been neglected, but that invariably it is regarded as something separate from the development of those at the top. In the ascendant organisation, however, many of the attributes once regarded as being the prerogative of people called managers, now become important at all levels in the organisation. Concepts such as teamworking, flexibility, *kaizen*, staff selection, process control, appraisal, JIT, training, total productive maintenance and so on become an essential part of the tool-kit at all levels. The ascendant organisation cannot wait until people reach a management position before being introduced to such concepts. An appreciation has to begin in the very first days of a career in the organisation, irrespective of the level at which the person is hired.

At the earliest stage the depth of knowledge is necessarily limited, but as people progress both in time and position, the initial appreciation progresses from awareness, knowledge, experience and understanding through to full capability. As per the definition, it is a continuum. Operational staff in the ascendant organisation will, then, have a wide range of capabilities, so far removed from the tasks of F. W. Taylor's operators as to be unrecognisable. They need to be flexible, to be able to contribute to improvement activities, to be quality conscious, to plan and deal with contingencies, to operate either alone or within teams, to work to and interpret instruction, to monitor and control progress and to practise care in all they do. They will use their brains as well as their hands. These capabilities will be the core. The technical tasks then become easy.

I now wish to put some flesh on the bones, for continuous development is not just a concept, it is a practical reality. But it is also a process which, like all other processes, has to be controlled; it is so important that it cannot be left to chance.

HOW TO INTRODUCE CONTINUOUS DEVELOPMENT

Step one

Ask the questions, 'What do people need to know to be able to do their jobs effectively?' and 'What competences and capabilities should they possess?' You will not get the full answers by asking top managers, for they have but limited knowledge of what their staff need to know and do to achieve the results. I did this when I first initiated the process. Asking directors what their people actually did was a salutary experience. Between us we came up with some 250 skills, capabilities and competences. When the training staff took over and started talking to the people actually doing the jobs, their initial listing exceeded 1,250! Therefore, begin by painstakingly questioning the people actually doing the jobs. Start at the bottom of the organisation and, gradually, patterns will emerge. There will be some common skills, competences, capabilities or knowledge that apply to most people at a given level irrespective of where they work in the company. There will be others which are specific to people within a function or business unit.

Step two

Begin the commonisation process. If the task is being conducted by a team, get them to share their knowledge. There will be much in common but some will have discovered areas that have been missed by others. At this stage, attempt the first rough tabulation – perhaps distinguishing as follows:

Core Skills	Attributes, knowledge, competencies, capabilities, which are common to all people in this role irrespective of where they work
Professional Skills	Attributes, knowledge, competencies, capabilities, which are specific to people in this position in this department/business unit/function etc.

Step three

Return to the departments and verify and/or amend the tabulation, seeking sign off – if appropriate – at manager level.

Step four

Add in the 'magic powder'. We all know people who have acquired all possible knowledge and skills but remain useless at their job. We also know people who have little experience but are superb. The difference is the 'magic powder' – it is specific to an individual and, by definition, cannot be defined in advance. You only find out what is missing, if you ever do, by observation, experience, analysis and discussion, and it can sometimes be a difficult process. I once spent hours with a manager trying to find out why he was not as effective as he might be. We concluded that it was his inability to see the wood for the trees. He was so involved with wanting to know the detail that he not only burdened himself with much unnecessary information, but also burdened his staff with putting it together. The result of our discussion was the development of a deliberate 'stand aside – give them headroom' plan, an art which often requires great self-confidence. The answer might have been different. No one knows until there is a totally open and honest joint assessment of needs.

On a formal basis, I translated 'magic powder' into 'personal effectiveness' and defined it as 'Development initiatives specifically tailored for the individual to enable each person to perform effectively at their existing level or above'. Such initiatives might include projects, assignments, transfers and external experiences. However, I still prefer 'magic powder'. It is much more evocative of what is really meant, and is readily understood by everyone.

Step five

Determine the delivery process. Some deliveries may be through formal training programmes, but learning is not simply about attending formal courses: it is active as well as passive. The responsibility for continuous development lies within the line department, shared between the boss and the individual. It is imperative that the individual examines and understands his/her own needs and objectives and agrees them with the boss. As with the Japanese approach, fundamental in the ascendant organisation is the delegation to line managers of the responsibility to assess training and development needs, and to ensure that these needs are met. Many of the professional skills can in fact only be delivered by the line department; they are too specialised to be delivered by anyone else. This involvement also creates ownership – the feeling that their contribution makes a difference, and it gives a sense of reality to the learning process. One of the most important core skills is therefore 'Training; coaching/mentoring' for, if those who have responsibility for developing others have not been taught how to do so properly and effectively, they cannot be blamed if they fail. Working together, systematically explaining, coaching and practising skills is easy to do badly and very difficult to do well.

It is clear that a well-trained, highly motivated workforce can be a sustainable, appreciating asset but many organisations are reluctant to train, because, 'We spend all this money training them and then they quit!' Continuous development can make a contribution to alleviating this problem. While little can be done to prevent the individual who is offered a massive salary increase from leaving, those companies which offer continuous development are more likely to retain staff than those who do not. One of my favourite aphorisms is, 'If you continuously develop and still lose significant numbers of people, you have got your development right and most other things wrong!' It is significant that companies which gain a reputation for high-quality training and development have no trouble in hiring good graduates. They may lose some of them but regard this as swings and roundabouts for they know that they are also able to recruit good people in their late twenties who have received their initial experience elsewhere. In fact, they do not want to be full of people in their thirties who have only worked for one company.

THE LEARNING ORGANISATION

Although another jargon term, the ascendant organisation is a learning organisation, which has been defined as 'An organisation which facilitates the learning of all its members and continuously transforms itself' (Pedlar *et al.*, 1989), or, as others might argue, 'A learning organisation continuously transforms itself and in the process continuously develops all of its members.'

However, an organisation by itself achieves nothing. It does not have a life of its own, it is not able to achieve anything without the intervention of people. It is the people who are able to create the climate in which the organisation is able to be transformed. A more appropriate definition of a learning organisation is therefore:

> One in which the people create the climate that facilitates the continuous development of all members who, as a result, are able continuously to develop their organisation.

I use the word 'develop' rather than transform. 'Develop' suggests a steady evolution, and in most organisations, if this is happening, the more radical transformation will not be needed.

Almost everything in this book is about learning and development and though in the learning organisation there is not necessarily a large amount of formal training, unless the people have the capability and opportunity to develop themselves and their jobs they will not be able to develop the organisation.

Peter Bonfield, when CEO of ICL, recognised this. He used the term, 'the resilient company':

> The resilient company is a learning company, it has processes for transferring intelligence throughout the organisation; it makes frequent adjustments to the company's course and thus takes advantage of any and all opportunities. The resilient company is not on autopilot.

In 1983, having recognised that it had to change from being a technology-driven to a market-driven company, ICL launched 'The ICL Way' with the message that it aimed not just at satisfying and delighting the customer but:

> The more we focused on the customer the more we realised that we had to become a fully open company. . . Because we are open, we are able to embrace new concepts swiftly and efficiently. By developing our people to think in an open way they are much more flexible and responsive to change. They embrace change willingly so that they can meet the challenges which come with openness. (Bonfield, 1993)

Bonfield argued that the key to ICL's resilience was the commitment and the professionalism of its people:

> Investing in people makes simple common sense in a business which changes as swiftly and radically as ours. To be resilient in adversity it is absolutely imperative that our people are able to respond and react in an innovative and entrepreneurial way. We have to recruit the best, nurture them and then let them create new opportunities for themselves

and for ICL . . . We have developed a culture of mutual support across the company . . . we have people from different divisions working together, all pulling in the same direction. And we do that with minimal central control or interface.

I do not give a step-by-step programme for achieving this Utopian condition, for it is not possible to teach an organisation to learn. It must learn to learn and it can only do this by experience ('it', of course, being the people in the organisation); by the mobilisation of all the knowledge and skills of all the people working together for the common good; by recognising that past success does not determine future success, indeed too much success can lead to complacency. Managers in such organisations are happy to devolve responsibility and to allow all people to contribute and to challenge the established way of doing things. They create an atmosphere which removes blockages to experimentation. However, people are also trained; it is critical to understand the correct techniques before you can go about breaking the rules. While the occasional genius may do everything wrong from the start, most of us are not geniuses. Even Picasso, who broke all the rules, understood and worked to them before he broke free and, in management jargon, created a paradigm shift.

Should we always be seeking the paradigm shift? The answer depends on where we are. Few would argue that moving an autocratic organisation to ascendancy is anything other than a paradigm shift, and moving to anything from apathy certainly is. Moving from functional chimneys to re-engineered business processes may well be. At the micro level, changing an airline's philosophy from one of flying planes to moving people is dramatic enough to deserve the term. Regarding people as possessing brains as well as hands requires a major paradigm shift for many managers.

But, and it is a big 'but', once you have become an ascendant organisation with all that entails, including the inherent capability to be able 'continuously to develop the people and the organisation', do you need any more paradigm shifts? As we have seen, continuous development of the small things creates the atmosphere in which major changes of the large can become the norm. I do not want to develop this into a circular argument, so therefore I conclude, rightly or wrongly, that the objective of an organisation which has reached this 'zenith' is to develop continuously so that it needs no more paradigm shifts! Except that once in a while . . .

12   Recognition and Reward

If top salaries are seen to reflect greed and the abuse of power an atmosphere can grow in which fiddling of expenses or other dishonest practices become commonplace.
    Philip Sadler, Vice-President, Ashridge Management College, 1993

THE PRINCIPLES OF PAY

> It is management's task 365 days of the year to motivate the workforce, not the bonus payment's on one day per year. The reward structure must be an outcome of good management, not a substitute for it.

There is no such thing as the perfect reward structure. Those which begin by being comparatively simple gradually become complex; those which initially motivate are quickly taken for granted; those which begin by being fair gradually take on the semblance of unfairness as adjustments are made in response to short-term pressures; payment by results systems become out of date as organisations move from a desire to maximise output to a need to achieve just the required output at a specified quality in a specified time.

New technology and working methods blur the distinction between white-collar and blue-collar work. Teamworking, continuous improvement, flexibility, devolved responsibility, the need for rapid response to customers' demands, the emphasis on quality, decentralisation and so on all pose dilemmas for traditional reward structures. Yet, with all the experimentation with new pay practices many fail to deliver. A Towers Perrin survey of over 700 organisations in the US, highlighted 'the problems with such pay practices, including over-complexity, and poor communication and implementation . . . Nearly half of the US organisations introducing competency-based pay approaches felt that they had not achieved their objectives in practice, and over 50 per cent still relied on traditional job evaluation approaches' (Towers Perrin, 1997).

How do we find a way through this maze if we are to develop a reward system appropriate to the ascendant organisation? Are there any principles which might help? While there is no magic formula, no single system which is right for all organisations, the answer is 'Yes'. The basic principles of a reward system within an ascendant organisation are as follows:

- It must be integrated with and support the organisation's values, strategy and goals.
- People at all levels are paid to achieve the goals and to improve performance. They should not be paid more for achieving what they are paid to achieve.
- It is management's job to motivate the workforce, not the reward structure's.
- While not absolutely identical at all levels, it must be transparent and help secure the commitment of everyone, not just a favoured few.
- Basic pay should be felt to be fair. Any additional elements should be applied equitably across the organisation and should be based on credible and fairly applied measures of performance, of both the individual and the organisation.
- It must be integrated with all other aspects of people management – leadership, teamworking, organisation, performance management, training and development and so on.

The ascendant organisation will have clearly defined its goals and behaviour and what it expects people to contribute. It is vital, therefore, that the reward structure contributes to achieving these ends. In so many organisations the reward structure has 'just grown'. 'It has been with us for ever' and while it may have been modified from time to time you can bet that that any synergy between the structure and the goals is by accident rather than by design. If this is the case, you can be sure that its impact will not be neutral – it is either for us or against us. Mostly, it will be against us.

The ascendant organisation works on the basis that the required quality and volume levels will achieved – they are not voluntary – and people should not be paid extra for achieving what they are paid to achieve. It does not want a payment structure such as piece-rates and production or quality bonuses which allow people to choose to achieve less than the required levels, nor to motivate them to hit or beat the target. If it achieves less, there will be waste in the system; if it achieves more, it will run out of stock. And because people are paid to think as well as do, it seeks continuous performance improvements throughout the organisation.

It is the managers' and supervisors' responsibility to motivate the staff, not the reward structure's, but many find it easy to hide behind the reward structure, believing that a bonus system will motivate people. It may do for a time, but for the majority of people the effects are not long-lasting. It requires effort and constant application to motivate people. How much easier it is for the lazy manager to rely on the reward structure! It follows that the basic wage should be 'right', that is, accepted as 'liveable' and equitable, both internally and externally.

The reward system must be transparent. This does not mean that everyone should know everyone else's pay, although if the system is equitable there is no great harm in this, but that the principles are known, are seen to be fair and just and that there are no hidden extras for a fortunate few. *The ascendant organisation wishes to secure the commitment of everyone, not just those at the top.* Again, this does not mean that, for example, a bonus formula should be exactly the same at every level; but it does mean that if some are able to share in the success of the enterprise, all should be able to share.

There needs to be room for pay progression, both as part of the performance management system (whereby corporate, business unit and individual objectives are developed, shared and assessed and individual development needs identified), and to encourage, recognise and reward both individual and group achievement. Some organisations may wish to recognise input as well as achievement, particularly at the operational levels. However, such recognition needs to take account of long-term overall performance, not just those elements which are tangibly measurable. The contribution to the team, a flexible attitude and innovation are not always tangibly measurable but may be far more important to the success of the enterprise than, say, an individual's attendance record.

THE PRACTICALITIES OF PAY

In considering the practicalities associated with these principles it will be helpful to divide rewards into broad categories: base pay and performance-related pay; and then consider the latter under two headings: rewards for inputs and rewards for outputs.

Base pay

It is fashionable for base pay to be criticised. Says Michael Hammer:

> In traditional pay systems, people are paid for seniority, for showing up, for following rules, for being pleasant to the boss, or, perhaps, even for performing and completing assigned tasks. But they aren't paid for producing results, which is ultimately the only thing that really matters. (1996, p. 57)

Hammer is wrong in two ways. First, in traditional pay systems there has always been some form of payment by results: piece-work remains endemic and has given rise to many problems – not least of which is short-termism, They need constant maintenance as the variables change, allow individuals to choose the performance levels they will achieve and prejudice the chances of participation in improvement activities. They fail to take account of the total contribution an individual can make either in teamworking or in small group activities. Standards are often slack, with 'beat the clock' being the name of the game, and those who play more craftily end up having the easier time, with a resulting feeling of unfairness and possible disruption. Management abdicates its responsibility to motivate the workforce and gives it to the payment system. Such systems have no place in the ascendant organisation.

Second, the ascendant organisation is different. People *are* paid to attend (and when they do not attend). They are also paid to achieve, for their commitment, their contribution to continuous improvement and innovation, and for their flexibility. Achievement is the norm and improvement is the practice. When you have a culture which *expects* the goals to be achieved and to be continuously improved, mechanistic payment by results systems are anathema.

But the basic pay must be right, meaning that it should be felt to be fair. 'Good' pay does not always motivate but 'poor' pay will always demotivate, so it is critical that the ascendant organisation pays constant attention to both its absolute and relative pay levels. No one in their right mind will turn down a pay increase and we all could do with more, but most people have an instinct about what feels right. They may not analyse it in depth but they talk with their colleagues, relations and friends and end up by feeling good or bad. Often, it is more to do with relativities than absolutes – unless everyone is paid so badly that they all feel a common grievance – and those relativities extend both inside and outside their company. Sometimes, people feel more aggrieved if they find their neighbour is earning £10.00 per week more for similar work than they do if they find that their chief executive is earning £100,000 more.

There remains much debate as to whether pay is a motivator or a hygiene factor. If you do not have a job then earning money is, usually, a motivator; and there will always be those who will fight to earn the extra buck. Few will turn down the offer of a pay rise, but for most people, provided the basic pay is felt to be fair, the possibility of extra money will not, in itself, bring about *sustained* extra effort. Most people settle into a norm of effort, satisfied with their earnings.

Performance-Related Pay

The PRP debate

Despite the weight of evidence favouring the view that 'pay for performance' does not have a long-lasting impact on company performance, it has in recent years become popular to advocate that a significant proportion of pay, particularly for senior executives, but increasingly reaching deeper into the company, should be related to company performance. A consultant-led industry has mushroomed to advise companies about exotic performance-related reward structures, and when they seek to sell to senior executives, who are those most likely to benefit, they find a ready market.

A great difficulty is that most people do not really know what they want from a performance-related pay system (PRP) or, indeed, what they can achieve – if anything! But we like the sound of them. Derek Torrington, of the University of Manchester Institute of Science and Technology, has said of PRP systems, 'They're like illicit love affairs . . . when you're not personally involved in one you feel you're missing out on something marvellous. When you are involved, you spend most of the time being miserable' (*Financial Times*, 15 January 1992).

Does PRP aim to assess the quality of input or the achievement of output? Is the reward to be related to an individual's or the team's performance. What is the team? Is the reward to be paid as merit and integrated into salary, or is it to be paid as a non-integrated lump sum? Or is it a combination of the two? If the organisation knows its long-term business goals, does the reward system support them? Is the system so complex that the individual can barely relate individual performance to reward? Is the same system appropriate for all people in the organisation? In a crisis situation, what will motivate people more – a large increase or a pay freeze? Derek Torrington was partially right. A *badly designed* performance-related pay system can create more misery then motivation.

Many argue that PRP just cannot work. Alfie Kohn wrote in the *Harvard Business Review,* 'Research suggests that, by and large, rewards succeed in securing one thing only: temporary compliance. When it comes to producing lasting change in attitude and behaviour, however, rewards, like punishment, are strikingly ineffective. Once the rewards run out, people revert to their old behaviour' (Kohn, 1993). Kohn supports the view that reward systems cannot be a substitute for good management. 'Treating workers well – providing useful feedback, social support, and the room for self-determination is the essence of good management. On the other hand, dangling a bonus in front of employees and waiting for the results requires much less effort.'

The Institute of Manpower Studies (IMS) has been researching the impact of PRP schemes for several years, and according to Research Fellow Marc Thompson, 'Across all organisations studied, the effect of PRP was at best neutral and mostly negative' (Thompson, 1994). The problem is that most organisations do not know if their PRP scheme is working, because they do not monitor it on that basis. Contrary to the argument that reward structures in the ascendant organisation must relate to the business strategy, such questioning by IMS 'usually drew blank expressions' Further probing often revealed that PRP had not been thought through from that standpoint. It was seen as the 'thing to do' – an act of faith.

This was very much the conclusion reached by compensation consultants, Bacon and Woodrow, who, in 1997, studied the impact on performance of financial participation schemes in 43 of the top 100 UK companies. Approved profit sharing schemes were used by 58 per cent of their sample and Save As You Earn by 93 per cent. They were almost universally thought to be 'a good thing', but few could give a reason for holding this view other than they were seen as a government-backed tax fiddle. Few companies had communicated the benefits of the schemes and 'fewer still attempt to integrate financial participation into a wider company philosophy or strategic process. As a result, the potential benefits for improvements in productivity have not been tested' (Sloan and Jackson, 1997).

We also need to remind ourselves that PRP came into vogue at a time when inflation and base salary increases were high. With general increases of around 15 per cent and, say, a 5 per cent performance budget it was possible to provide performance-related increases within a range of zero to 20 per cent, but with general increases at less than 5 per cent the room for manoeuvre on performance pay is greatly restricted. Performance pay can easily become higher than the general increase and while, to some, this may be a good thing it is much more difficult to control and can cause resentment. Barclays Bank experienced a series of 24-hour strikes in late 1997 due to attempts to change the balance between basic and performance pay when it was discovered that more experienced workers were to be held back in favour of younger 'high performing' workers.

In this debate on PRP I leave the last words to Andrew Lebby of the Performance Group of Washington DC, who in responding to Alfie Kohn wrote, 'Just as it is easier for some parents to show love with gifts rather than with hugs, it is often easier for organisations and managers to show gratitude with money than with words' (*Harvard Business Review*, November–December, 1993).

However, despite this 'non-provability' most managers and staff believe that 'it feels right'. In the IMS study over two-thirds of employees were in favour of the principle. The problem is in the practice.

Input-based performance pay

Input-based performance pay reflects an individual's contribution and is usually structured so that in individual can be awarded merit increases which take him or her along a salary range which usually has minimum and maximum salaries, or along a salary 'spine' which usually is a continuum containing the salaries of all people of all covered grades but which has 'bars' beyond which a person at a specific level cannot progress. Increasingly, employers are using broadbanding, that is, a small number of wide pay bands rather than a large number of grade-related pay scales. Typically, a normal pay scale has a median range width of 25–50 per cent for executive and professional staff and 15–20 per cent for non-managerial staff; whereas broad bands may stretch to 80 per cent or more. On close inspection, however, most broadband systems contain merit bars/or a number of defined jobs within the lengthened range, and individuals cannot progress beyond a specified pay level unless their performance warrants it on their job 'grows'. The reality turns out to be not very different system.

In such salary progression systems people receive merit increases which are usually consolidated into base pay. It is true that a high level of 'input' does not always result in a high level of 'output', for example, a salesperson can be very active but generate few orders. However, the ascendant organisation is interested in the *quality* of those inputs and when they are properly assessed 'activity' without 'result' will not score highly.

'Usually' is used four times in the above paragraphs (and it could have been more), for within this form there are many permutations, all with their advantages and disadvantages. Helen Murlis, Director of Compensation and Benefits of Hay Management Consultants, has summarised four of the most common systems:

1. Defined cash or percentage incremental steps.
2. Increments to a merit bar, then totally discretionary.
3. Discretion within a budget or 'merit pot'.
4. Variable cash or percentage increments within clearly stated guidelines.

Under the first option, the steps along the salary range are defined and, subject to satisfactory performance, individuals progress more or less automatically along the range. It is simple and easy to administer but is also rigid with no possibility of managers being able to fine-tune relative to degrees of performance. The vast majority of people progress to the maximum fairly quickly, for increases have to be 'significant' if they are to be meaningful. The results, in a low staff turnover situation, are high salary costs with large numbers of people at the top of the range. This has been a common experience in the public sector where salary progression, almost irrespective of performance, was long the norm.

Option two allows most people to progress to a certain level but then allows only high performers to progress beyond the 'bar' towards the maximum. This allows a greater control of costs but can also demotivate those who are stuck at the bar, which also sends messages about their promotion prospects. Such a system is wide open to abuse for it depends on an assessment of individual performance with considerable pressure being placed on the assessor to determine a rating which will allow the person to progress beyond the bar.

Option three, discretion within a budget or merit pot, is highly flexible, provides that the highest performers receive the greatest increases and ensures total cost control. However, it is potentially unfair, inconsistent and discriminatory, allowing 'blue-eyed boys' to emerge. Administration is highly complex and it requires a very high quality of management which may not exist.

The ascendant organisation will tend to favour the fourth option, variable cash or percentage increments within defined guidelines. Under such systems there are no specified steps along the range but, within guidelines, people can progress along the range at varying rates which are related to their overall assessed performance. The rate of progression can be flexed progressively or regressively as an individual's performance changes, although as a general principle an increase, once given, cannot be taken away. This system requires an effective method of assessing performance to avoid the 'blue-eyed boy' syndrome and, in order to control costs, may also need positive guidelines on the distribution of performance ratings. Without such guidelines, ratings will tend to drift upwards and, as merit increases are related to the assessment, the salary bill will also rise. This system can be difficult to understand and requires sophisticated management, which, by definition, the ascendant has!

The basis of an effective performance appraisal system has been described in Chapter 7, but having determined the method of evaluating performance, the actual methods of progression along the salary range are many and varied – they can be discretionary or fixed, constant percentages or constant amounts, progressive or regressive, large or small. What really counts is that people perceive they have been properly evaluated, their contribution has been recognised and valued and that they have been fairly treated in relation to others. Increases in the range of 2 to 5 per cent, depending on performance, seem about right, remembering that in this system such increases are additional to general increases. Further, the ascendant organisation recognises personal achievement in many ways – the 'Thank you for a great job', the night out or the refrigerator for the team – and, if this is done properly, salary progression is the cherry on the icing on the cake.

One of the great difficulties is determining how to bring teamworking into the equation. According to the American Compensation Association, 'When it comes to reinforcing team behaviour, the reward system is one of the most effective and influential tools' (*ACA Journal,* Spring 1996). Quoting Ed Lawler, they argue for a clear 'line of sight' between team performance and pay-out but one of the major problems is how to achieve this 'line of sight'.

Helen Murlis told me that much exploratory work on team rewards ends up by deciding on cash bonuses (which may work for one-off teams but when teamworking is the norm will be less appropriate), or by realising that an individual's general contribution to continuous teamworking can best be valued and recognised through a well-developed performance management process. The ACA's recommendation is to use skills-based and competency based pay to help organisations 'recognise individual development within a team environment' (a cop-out if ever there was one!) but also 'to use team-based performance management and rewards'. Their solution is to come up with systems such as gain sharing, goal sharing, group incentives, stock ownership or non-monetary recognition awards. These are moving towards 'output-based reward' territory and exhibit a total lack of understanding of real teamworking as I have described it. As we have seen in discussing performance appraisal, the contribution to the team is but one element. It is not difficult to assess and the ACA's contribution is yet another example of a vested interest attempting to make a simple concept, complex.

Some organisations consider their salary progression schemes to be totally performance-related with no general cost-of-living increases. Indeed in the Towers Perrin survey, 68 per cent of European respondents said they applied only merit/individual performance pay for their management and professional groups. IBM has long held this view, and Mercury Communications, a subsidiary of Cable and Wireless, rejected both job evaluation and grading. Instead, it established individual contracts, the main element of which is performance-related individual pay. Under this system, pay is based on the market worth of the individual and his or her performance assessed during the annual appraisal or performance review. There is no automatic cost-of-living increase. Mercury undertakes extensive pay research to determine that its salaries are correctly positioned in the market place and it is here that, like all such claims of 'no cost of living increases', the argument falls apart. Why is it that in the early 1980s such companies were giving merit increases of 15–20 per cent and in the late 1990s they are less than 5 per cent? The answer, of course, is to keep in line with the market, and market salaries increase broadly in line with general inflation. Let us not pretend that such systems are wholly merit-based and unrelated to the going rate of salary increase.

Output-based performance pay

Input-based performance pay usually results in merit increases which are consolidated into base pay. I use 'output-based performance pay' to describe discrete, non-consolidated payments based on defined elements of the organisation's performance.

One of the great difficulties for companies considering such schemes is determining whether they are primarily to be a reward for past achievement or an encouragement for future effort. Most schemes do not seek to distinguish between the two and end up hoping for the best of both worlds, often failing to achieve either. They may construct a formula-based profit-related scheme, some form of gain sharing plan or an *ex gratia* payment which allow staff to share in their company's success but can end up being a welcome but predictable annual bonus or, when the formula results in no pay-out, they can actually demotivate.

The often used argument about gaining employee commitment may have some validity, but when bonuses are related to corporate financial performance it is difficult for an individual to see how his or her performance can make much difference to the pay out. In any case few companies leave their scheme unchecked. If profits regularly rise adjustments to the formulae are made and few companies over the long-term average much more than 5 or 6 per cent. In January 1994, BT (British Telecom as was), Britain's largest private sector company, adjusted its ten-month-old PRP system for 26,000 of its managers and professional staff because its pay levels were regarded by top management as being over-competitive and the cost would exceed its planned overall increase for managerial staff. Concerned that its salaries were in the upper quartile of the market range, David Scott, BT's Industrial Relations Manager, was not worried about the demoralising effect: '[We] have to lose managers in the next financial year anyway' (*Financial Times*, 2 February 1994). This in a year in which BT made around £2.7 billion profit!

Systems aimed at encouraging future efforts can be constructed in so many different ways that avoiding pitfalls rather than enhancing performance becomes the prime consideration. Instead of analysing the thousands of permutations, I nail my colours to the mast and state that such a system is most likely to succeed when it is based on measured achievement against clearly stated, mid-term performance targets which are integrated with both the business values and needs, and when individuals are able to understand how their performance can make a contribution to that achievement. The same principles must be applied throughout the organisation. Beyond this, the permutations flow.

It must be based on 'measured achievement against clearly stated, mid-term performance targets' if it is to have any impact on real performance. If people do not know what is measured then it is impossible for them to know where their efforts should lie. If the targets are short term they lead to short-term actions which may not be in the long-term interests of the company; if they are long term they become so complex that it is impossible for people to see how they can have any real impact and then so many other variables come into the frame that clarity is the first casualty.

The system must be integrated with the organisation's values and business needs. It is simply no good emphasising long-term growth while rewarding short-term profit, or preaching that 'our employees are our greatest asset' but utilising a formula which rewards senior executives with bonuses of 30 per cent of base pay and operators with 5 per cent. In the ascendant organisation the formula must be transparent.

Perhaps the greatest practical difficulty is to devise a system in which the individual can appreciate how his or her contribution impacts on corporate performance and subsequent reward. Even in those areas where there is an apparent high correlation – for example, 'Selling more televisions increases profit' – life is not that simple. Discounts may be so high as to eliminate profit; it may be at the expense of quality or service and result in low repeat business or recommendations. Even when life *is* that simple, sales success is dependent on a wide range of product development, manufacturing, marketing and logistical support. An organisation may well make more money on support services than on direct sales. How, then, are the contributions to be assessed? Attempting to incorporate this degree of precision into a formula will result in so many permutations of such great complexity that the result will be total confusion – and bad feeling between departments and individuals. The individual must be able to make the link, but that is the responsibility of day-to-day management, not the bonus system.

How should an output-based system be constructed? There is no single right way and it may even vary within a company, although the ascendant organisation with its desire for equity and transparency will aim for flexibility within a consistent framework rather than inconsistency. Payments should be related to outputs which are determined in advance and are measurable – and this is a problem.

Target-setting is imperfect. It is extraordinarily difficult to determine the right measures and if they are correct at the beginning of the review period the chances are that needs will have changed by the end. If the measure is based on profit, what is profit? Particularly in multinational organisations, profits can be manipulated by transfer pricing arrangements which can be adjusted to changing tax regimes, or for strategic reasons to make the performance of a particular national company appear better than others. Even within a country, changes in transfer prices can have a dramatic effect on profitability. It may even be in the corporate interest that particular business units or national companies make a loss. Corporate financial performance may depend on exchange rate fluctuations as much as, if not more than, on real achievement. A company's share price may be affected more by overall market performance than by its own performance and the impact on measures such as earnings per share can be dramatic. Should the individual benefit or suffer?

The most popular methods of constructing performance rewards is to relate the reward to measures of real added performance such as growth in pre-tax profits, exceeding target pre-tax profits or earnings per share; and return on capital and cash flow measures are also frequently used. However, the ascendant organisation may wish to take account of non-financial indicators, recognising that long-term profitability will be optimised by attending to a wide range of performance measures such as sustained increases in customer satisfaction ratings or growth in market share. The targets may vary over time depending on the economic circumstances and the organisation's objectives.

IBM measures its 'Baby Blues' on seven parameters: revenue growth, profit, return on assets, cash flow, customer satisfaction, quality and employee morale. Rank Xerox had, up to the mid-1980s, a bonus system for senior managers only, in which 30 per cent of their remuneration was tied to the return on net assets employed and percentage revenue growth year on year. From the mid-1980s it increasingly introduced quality of service as measured by customers' perceptions of its performance against competitors. Headquarters staff were included in 1990 with the opportunity to earn a maximum of 2.5 per cent annually for meeting the customer satisfaction targets.

In 1995 Rank Xerox implemented an extraordinarily complex gain sharing scheme for 1,700 people employed at its Mitcheldean site in Gloucester. It is based on a formula which seeks to determine an added-value ratio by dividing net added-value by total employment cost (all elements of which were themselves carefully defined) and then compares actual performance against a target set at the beginning of the year. The surplus is shared 50:50 between the company and employees. In 1995, its first year of operation, the pay-out was £230 per employee, in 1996 it was £88 per employee and in the first quarter of 1997 zero. Said Robin Fyffe, HR Manager, 'The principles and formula of gainsharing are excellent for Rank Xerox: the task that remains is finding the means to persuade employees that they can deliver significant improvements in productivity and share the benefits that result' (IRS, 1997b). One of the great difficulties facing all such schemes is said to be that year on year performance improvements are difficult to achieve. They are if you rely on the reward structure to achieve them. Nissan, from 1993 to 1995 achieved 10 per cent per annum productivity improvement with no output-based reward structure. It was achieved through the capability of the management and the commitment of the workforce. Such results cannot continue – since then the target has been dropped to 5 per cent per annum!

From 1994, IBM has linked bonuses to business units and determined that 5 to 10 per cent of employees' pay will be linked to the performance of the business unit in which an individual works. Measures will vary according to the objectives of the unit. Those for the research centres will, for example, be very different from those for the PC business. This is entirely right.

Unfortunately, the more non-financial measures that are included the more complex the formula becomes and the more difficult it is for people to appreciate the impact of their efforts, which is why many still argue in favour of a few, clear measures of financial performance.

It is impossible to come up with a 'best-buy' package, but taking all of the foregoing into consideration and taking account of the objectives of output-based performance pay I conclude that it should contain no more than two elements – an easy to understand, universally applicable financial measure such as 'Growth in pre-tax profits' and one non-financial measure. If possible, this non-financial measure should be specific to the business unit or function. For example, in a product development function it might be based on a measure of 'New product lead time'; in manufacturing it might be based on 'Percentage straight through', i.e. the proportion of products which go through the entire manufacturing process without having to be rectified in any way; a sales operation might have a measure based on 'Repeat business'; customer service might have a measure based on 'Time taken to achieve a satisfactory outcome', and so on. It will be difficult but not impossible to devise an appropriate non-financial measure for every function within an organisation. But they must be simple. The Rank Xerox gainsharing formula is so complex that it is bound to fail.

How large should the pay-out be? The advice given by consultants Buck Patterson is typical: 'Bonuses should be of a size that is right for your company and this will depend on its position in the market, where it is in the growth-maturity cycle and a host of other factors.' Although they were speaking of bonuses at the top level, the words ring true throughout the organisation.

PAY AT THE TOP

Peter Drucker has long argued that a chief executive's pay should be limited to 20 times the average pay in the company. In American manufacturing companies, average pay in 1992 was $40,000 after tax and, said Drucker, 'You can live on $800,000!' Lester Thurow reported that in 1990 American CEOs were making 119 times more than the average worker, compared with a Japanese factor of 18 times (Thurow, 1993, p. 138). In Britain, the figure is around 35 times.

I have yet to meet a senior executive who is motivated solely by money; the most common motivator is the need to make things happen. Although few will turn down a pay increase, we do have to question whether the arguments in favour of the international market rate are anything more than mutual nest-feathering. When European executives begin to make favourable comparisons with their Japanese as opposed to their American counterparts, then they will deserve to have their comparability arguments taken seriously.

Despite the headline-grabbing multi-million dollar salaries paid to a few ('Disney chairman Eisner cashes in stock options for £91 million', or 'Toys R Us CEO gains $6.7 million bonus on top of $314 000 salary') a Towers Perrin study of more than 350 companies showed that in 1990/91 the average salary of an American chief executive was $1.4 million, inclusive of all cash and options. Clearly there are vast differences within these average figures, but when chief executives are paid $10,000,000 and more, even if the profit-related pay formula produces this result, we have to question whether the formula was properly set and whether the compensation committee was indulging in little more than mutual back-scratching.

Another very considerable benefit open to people at the top, but denied to most others, is the rolling contract, the value of which becomes evident when the individual leaves 'by mutual agreement'. In February 1994 John Cahill resigned as chairman of British Aerospace after only two years of a five-year contract. The formal announcement said little more than, 'This is an appropriate moment for him to relinquish the chairmanship.' But Cahill held options on 908,000 shares at an exercise price of 260 pence. At the time of the announcement the share price was 543 pence and Cahill stood to make £3.21 million although he waived salary payment for the remaining three years of his contract.

1997 research by Labour Research showed that, at least in Britain, the amount of the pay-out is falling, prompted by the Greenbury corporate governance recommendation that companies should move away from the typical three-year contract to one year. The average golden handshake fell from £406,000 in 1994 to £328,000 in 1997. But, says Labour Research, 'Huge amounts have been paid out in executive golden handshakes in recent years, even though they go to directors who have failed to keep their job and who have been sacked, resigned to pursue other business interests, walked away from companies because of clashing management styles or, occasionally, just because they have retired'!

The largest pay-off was made to Charles Mackay who resigned from car distributors Inchcape in mid-1996. He collected £760,000 for loss of office and a further £603,000 for his pension fund. George Greener, who resigned from BAT Industries 'by mutual consent', received £706,000 for loss of office and £585,000 towards his pension. Both were soon appointed to other top jobs, but Jon Richards, who quit as chief of Anite Software in March 1997 and received £323,000, had a clause under which he could pick up two further payments of £134,000 if he had not found another job by March 1998 or September 1998.

I do not blame the individuals concerned for accepting such generous treatment – there are few of us who would not take advantage of the opportunity. But the question has to be asked – is it right that senior executives should have long fixed-term rolling contracts when usually their only practical impact is to generate large pay-offs if the incumbent leaves early, for whatever reason? The answer is that it cannot be right. When everyone else in the organisation is on, say, three months' or one week's notice and rarely receives any other payment when they leave, there can be no justification for generous pay-offs applying solely to people at the top. This is thrust into relief when you realise that many of the largest pay-offs go to those 'whose presence is no longer required.' It appears that the only way to become rich is to foul-up in some way and be told to go! There is a moral and ethical dimension which appears to have been left to those of a left-inclined persuasion, such as Labour Research. It would be nice to hear more from the business community.

1993 research by Hay Management Consultants found that 74 per cent of directors had bonus schemes, 68 per cent of senior managers were similarly favoured, but only 20 per cent of other managers had schemes. In 1997, a survey by Remuneration Economics found that 75 per cent of directors received a bonus compared with 59 per cent of managers, with the average bonus for directors being £15,600 and for managers, £3,800.

The distribution of performance-based bonuses is shown by 1993 research from Monks Partnership. Eleven per cent of board directors received bonuses which exceeded 30 per cent of their salary, 22 per cent had bonuses of 20-30 per cent and 25 per cent received less than 15 per cent. Compared with these figures, senior managers were less generously rewarded – 5 per cent went over 30 per cent and 42 per cent received bonuses worth less than 15 per cent of salary (Monks, 1993).

Not only, then, are senior staff more likely to receive bonuses, but the more senior they are, the larger will be the bonus as a proportion of salary. Arguably, this might be correct if it could be demonstrated that company performance correlated with senior executives' pay.

In addition to cash bonuses, the ownership of shares in the company for which you work is often regarded as one of the most successful means of motivating people. Often such plans are put into place to make employees 'feel part of the company', but they will fail in this objective if their ability to share in success is limited to a 'Save as you earn' scheme at junior levels or is a result of concession bargaining, while senior executives have share options which enable them to make capital gains of many thousands of pounds. But there is little evidence to suggest that companies that operate such schemes perform any better over the long term.

In the United States, according to the National Center for Share Ownership, about 9,500 American companies, accounting for almost 10 per cent of the workforce, have employee share ownership plans, but in almost all cases workers own only a very small percentage of the total equity. According to Joseph Blasi of Rutgers University, most studies of such organisations agree that employee ownership confers very little competitive advantage (*The Economist*, 11 June 1994).

Such schemes in Britain allow executives to purchase shares between three and ten years in the future at the exercise price (that is, the price prevailing at the time the options were granted). Since 1984, when such schemes were first established, the stock market rise is resulting in very large pay-outs.

The size of executive share options can be seen from an analysis of exercised share options in the third quarter of 1993. Of 145 share options monitored by IDS *Management Pay Review* (February 1994) the average profit was £102,221 (139 per cent). Typically, the option was exercised after five years. The question has to be, why are such benefits denied to the majority of employed people?

Fortunately, there is now evidence to suggest that share option schemes are decling in favour of long-term incentive plans. A 1997 report from New Bridge Street consultants found that 19 of the FTSE 100 companies have announced that they are no longer granting stock options to their executives. Further, only 25 per cent of the compnies which established long-term incentive plans in 1996 intend to allow their executives to participate in share options (NBS, 1997).

If all of this made a difference to company performance there might be some excuse, for successful chief executives are a rare breed and the company depends – for good or ill – very much upon its CEO. But research into the pay of the directors of 77 of the Financial Times Top 100 companies concluded that there is no discernible relationship between their pay and their companies' performance (*IDS Top Pay Unit Review*, August 1991).

Alfie Kohn (1993) cited research by Rich and Larson, who examined compensation programmes and returns to shareholders in 90 US companies to determine if top executive incentive plans made a difference. They were unable to find any difference. In a rising stock market most executives stand to gain, irrespective of their own company's performance. A 1994 study by the National Institute of Economic and Social Research found that between 1985 and 1990 top executive pay increased in real terms by 77 per cent against 17 per cent real earnings growth. In March 1997 the *Financial Times* reported a study by JDH consultants of the accounts of 800 companies with combined sales of £677bn. It disclosed that remuneration is positively linked to performance in about 60 per cent of cases but that in 40 per cent there is an *inverse* relationship, with high-performing companies paying below average rewards! Commenting on this, Brian Friedman, a pay expert with Arthur Anderson, said that there was a complex and unclear set of relationships between pay and performance. He added:

This is in line with our own studies which showed an insignificant correlation between bonuses and shareholder return. Perhaps this suggests that in reality companies recognise the need to pay with regard to the employment market not just performance.

This view is supported by Towers Perrin, who commented in their 1997 study of European pay trends:

The general trend towards emphasising market rates in determining individual pay levels, at the expense of internal equity, is particularly evident in executive pay.

In other words, most companies can forget about sophisticated reward structures, as they are all con tricks designed to persuade the shareholders that senior executives' pay is 'scientifically' structured to encourage improved corporate performance. All you need do is pay the going rate and fire them without compensation if they do not deliver!

Philip Sadler, Vice-President of Ashridge Management College, has written:

Where the differential between the top person's pay and that of the rank and file is perceived as unjustifiably large, the consequences can be serious. Not only can it breed divisive class conflict and make wage restraint virtually impossible to achieve, it can also lead to a deterioration in the moral climate. If top salaries are seen to reflect greed and the abuse of power, an atmosphere can grow up in which fiddling of expenses or other dishonest practices become commonplace. (*Director*, September 1992)

How, then, in the ascendant organisation, should the top executives be rewarded? Again, there is no magic formula but there are some principles which are not a million miles away from the principles applied throughout the organisation. First, the salary package must allow the organisation to attract, motivate and retain the right people. We live in the real world and have, therefore, to compete with other organisations which might not see internal fairness as an objective and may wish to apply 'creative' reward structures to their top people. However, the ascendant organisation does see internal fairness as a factor and will not implement reward structures which might motivate those at the top but cause resentment everywhere else. Secondly, just as at other levels of the organisation, the basic salary must be recognised as the payment for doing the job the person is paid to do. If the key task is to improve market share by 10 per cent over the next three years and improve net profits by 5 per cent, that is the job the CEO is paid to do and, as with everyone else, you should not be paid more for achieving what you are paid to achieve. There can be no doubt that the CEO would, in any case, have had a hand in setting those targets!

And, it can be argued, they need no more than the right base salary to do what is required. As stated earlier, only a very few senior executives are motivated solely by money and if, as elsewhere, we accept that the base salary is the payment for doing the job and that we should not rely on the payment system to motivate, why should different criteria apply to the top executives? More than anyone else, they are motivated by the ability to make things happen. Provided the base salary is right, they do not need more to make them do their best for the company and its stakeholders, and if they are motivated by money (greed), their thinking is more likely to be short term (especially if the expected time in the job is short) rather than in the long-term interests of the organisation. Throughout my career, I and all other executives with whom I have worked, have done our best for our companies. A bonus for achieving or exceeding our targets is nice, and not refused, but it is not that which motivates us. Do not the teachings of McGregor *et al.* apply at the top as well as at the bottom?

Having said that, many will wish to establish performance-related pay for the senior team members, and much more difficult, therefore, is the reward for individual contribution, which is likely to form a higher percentage of their total pay than at other levels. The chief executive should be both leader and member of the team, and is probably more dependent on that team than anyone else in the organisation.

While most other members of the team (the organisation) have a reward structure which comprises a base salary and input and output-based performance pay, there is an argument that the CEO's and other top executives' variable pay should be related solely to outputs – no input-based element – and on outputs which are specifically determined in advance and are measurable. Here the same problems arise as at other levels: profits can be manipulated and performance affected by factors beyond the executives' control. Should non-financial measures of performance be included?

There is an argument that when someone is responsible for total performance the only credible measure is bottom-line profit, but there may be a case that one non-financial measure be included – for example a customer satisfaction index – if only to demonstrate to everyone else that other things are important. Such an indicator must be in place for, say, three years in order for there to be sufficient time to make an impact but not so long that it becomes routine. After that, choose something different to reflect the next non-financial priority.

The targets should not only be measurable, they should be adhered to. No allowance should be made for the unexpected. It is the top team's job to expect the unexpected! But what about the time scale? Quarterly, six monthly or annual measures lead to short-term thinking and are too short for the incumbent to have any real effect; and if it is longer than three years it leads to confusion as many different variables come into play. I would suggest that a two- to three-year average is about right with no pay-out being made until the end of the chosen period, meaning that when an individual is appointed from outside he or she should receive no output-based performance pay until the end of the defined period. After that the award will be based on the previous defined average.

I would also suggest that the period of notice for top executives should be no longer than that accorded to other people in the company. Remembering that in the ascendant organisation we have common terms and conditions of employment it is likely that the normal period of notice will be around three months. There is no logical argument that top executives should have a longer period, and if they foul-up they should go on exactly the same terms as any other member of staff! A fundamental objective is to build trust of the top and if top executives' reward structures are seen to benefit them however well or badly they and the company perform it does not exactly help.

None of this means that the top people should not receive substantially more than others. But what is the right money? Drucker's factor of 20, the Japanese 18, the British 35 or Thurow's American figure of 119? There is no absolute answer and in the end we are left with what feels right to all the stakeholders. There is no point in trying to create a formula. Pay is emotional and the best any organisation can do is to create a system at the top which it is not ashamed of, which it does not need to hide and which serves to motivate all the people and not just a few. If we have a top pay structure that we would rather keep secret then there is something wrong.

If the same rules apply to *every* organisation, the argument, 'We need to pay big money to get the right people' flies out the window. There is nothing wrong with stock options and everyone sharing in the success of the organisation. Indeed, it is to be encouraged. What is wrong is that a favoured few should benefit disproportionately, and when companies seek to disguise such benefits it does not actually suggest that they are proud of them!

Rosabeth Moss Kanter speaks of post-entrepreneurial pay systems, arguing that many organisations are gradually changing the basis for determining pay 'from position to performance, from status to contribution'. She is undoubtedly right that this is the way to go and she criticises merit pay for offering increases which are too small to be meaningful. Her solution is, 'Bucks for behaviour', and she advocates as many as five variables in determining pay:

- A guaranteed small amount based on level and position
- An individual merit component
- A group or division gain-sharing component
- An overall company profit-sharing component
- Short-term bonuses and awards for exemplary team and individual contributions. (Kanter, 1989)

This may seem ideal but it is so complex that it will be almost impossible to administer and difficult to understand. Therefore, it fails most of the tests of a genuinely motivating reward structure. More sensible, for people at the top, is to have a structure comprising just three elements:

- A liveable base salary
- An output-based performance element related to bottom-line profit plus one non-financial measure
- A long-term share option scheme.

That will achieve the right balance.

13 Trade Unions in the Ascendant Organisation

It used to be easy to hate managers, really easy, because they were so awful. It's a bit more difficult these days because they have become a bit cleverer. The company (Ford) seems to have realised that you can catch more flies with honey than vinegar.

Jimmy Airlie, National Officer,
Amalgamated Engineering and Electrical Union, 1987

In the past, activists had an ideological commitment to their union work. Now it is hard to find people willing to take on such responsibilities. But if employees do not see trade unions making a difference in their workplace, they won't become members.

Keith Sissons, Director, Industrial Relations Research Unit,
University of Warwick Business School, 1997

THE DECLINE OF TRADE UNIONS

For the greater part of the twentieth century large-scale enterprises were highly centralised, with rigid hierarchies and power based on a 'control' philosophy. Scientific management rigidly defined jobs, breaking them down into simple tasks, reducing the skill and discretion levels. Labour was hired and fired according to demand; and large indirect departments removed authority from the front line-managers and supervisors. While trade unions abhorred many of these practices, it was these very conditions that led to their growth and success, often built on the view that there was an inherent conflict of interests between labour and capital. Paradoxically, during their period of greatest power, trade unions reinforced many of the central tenets of scientific management. By insisting on narrow job definitions, thereby protecting skills and restricting flexibility; by insisting that 'an operator is an operator is an operator'; and by rejecting management attempts to use the brain as well as the hands, they gave a further turn of the screw of scientific management, resulting in the contribution of all operators being far less than their inherent capability.

Trade unions developed in many different ways. Their structures may be based on the industry (as in Germany, although the metalworking agreement covers thirteen different industries); the company (Japan); political or religious tendency (France); industry sector (USA); or have just grown (UK). They may be centralised as in Germany and Sweden or fragmented as in Japan where there are thousands of individual company unions. The basic drives may differ. To stereotype these drives, American unions are economically motivated and Japanese unions are essentially collaborative. German unions have a strong social agenda, French unions have a political agenda but exercise this in the large state enterprises and have little influence elsewhere. British unions combine economic objectives with class-based politics, but were partially marginalised by their inability to attract members in the new industries, and by government hostility during Conservative government years of the 1980s and 1990s.

Negotiations may be centralised but take place at different times of the year, as in Germany; or decentralised but take place at the same time, as in Japan (the *shunto* – the spring offensive – which is an offensive in name only); they may vacillate between centralisation and decentralisation, as in Sweden; there may be pattern bargaining, as in the USA; or a mixture of everything, as in Britain. Legal frameworks differ, the range of services varies widely and the level of professionalism differs greatly.

Trade union power and influence reached its peak in the 1950s to 1970s when, in Britain, membership peaked at some 12.5 million. Since that time there has been in almost all countries a steady and dramatic decline in membership and most have seen their influence wane – first in France in the 1950s, followed by the USA in the 1960s, and the UK in the 1980s. In Britain, 1996 membership stood at 7.2 million, representing 31.3 per cent of employees. According to the International Labour Office's World Labour Report, union density in Spain is down from 18 per cent in 1980 to 11 per cent; Italy has seen a fall from 44 per cent in 1980 to 34 per cent; Japanese density rate has dropped from 30 per cent in 1982 to 24 per cent. In the USA, where in 1954, 35 per cent of the workforce was unionised, the 1995 figure was 14.9 per cent. In Germany the figure is 34 per cent, although some 90 per cent of workers are covered by union agreements. It is simply no good pointing at the political persuasion of the government or the structures of trade unionism, suggesting that one country has got it right and that if only the others would emulate it they, also, would be rejuvenated.

The structural reasons for the decline in trade union membership are well known: the changing structure of industry, declining plant and company size (it's easier to recruit in large companies than in small), decentralisation, increased unemployment and the ending of full employment as a strategic goal, the expansion of the service sector, the increased employment of women, expansion of part-time employment, government hostility, the decline of traditional institutions, and so on. All of these factors impact on both the absolute numbers and the percentage of workers in trade unions.

In almost all countries, trade union membership levels are now higher in the public sector than in the private, often by 20 to 30 percentage points. The 'typical' trade unionist is today more likely to be working in a government office or teaching than to be working at a lathe in a privately owned engineering company.

There are always plans to increase membership and on many occasions trade unions in almost all countries have sought to recruit in under-represented areas, particularly among women and in the small and medium enterprises (only 16 per cent of companies with fewer than 25 employees were unionised in Britain in 1996), with some short-term success at a huge cost per new member but with little long-term impact. Spurred on by some successes in the United States where young, dedicated organisers were hired to act as recruitment squads to go into an area and almost inspire people into membership, the British TUC in 1997 hired some twenty young people for an 'organising academy' where they receive twelve months of training to help unions organise among the 16 million non-union members. They will have a tough job. A 1997 poll among young workers carried out by the public sector union Unison found that while they were concerned with low pay, lack of training opportunities and limited chances of promotion, most saw the trade union as an irrelevance in improving their position. To repeat Keith Sissons, at the head of this chapter, 'If employees do not see trade unions making a difference in their workplace, they won't become members.'

However, despite these grandiose attempts to hire 'young, dedicated people' the British Labour Research Department found that the most powerful recruitment method is face-to-face contact, with trade union representatives approaching non-union employees and persuading them of the benefits, particularly when there is a trigger such as a pay claim, the need to defend jobs, health and safety issues and so on. They highlighted the need for representatives to have access to new recruits, keeping in touch, prioritising needs, encouraging attendance at TU courses and so on. In simple terms, it is about getting the basics right (Labour Research Department, 1997).

However much trade unions may seek to increase their membership and increase their influence, they will fail unless they are able to demonstrate their relevance on two levels. First, on a national scale, they must show that they can have a meaningful and constructive role in assisting national competitiveness and, second, at company level the critical issue is to determine their role in organisations which have responded to the long-term, fundamental changes in industrialised societies by totally changing the way they manage the employment relationships. In short, what is the role of trade unions in the ascendant organisation?

THE NEW AGENDA

An early attempt to address the national agenda was contained in *A New Agenda – Bargaining for Prosperity in the 1990s* prepared by two British trade unions, the GMB (a general union covering a wide range of occupations in many industries) and the Union of Communication Workers (UCW). Much criticised by other unions and, perhaps, a document before its time, they said, 'Trade unions should wish to work together with employers and government to create a successful industry, a strong economy and a caring society in the 1990s.' In discussing what they refer to as the revolution of rising expectations, they said:

> Performance levels must reach record heights if Britain is to enjoy economic success . . . Achieving them requires more than cost cutting. The pressure to improve the competence and the commitment of employees is increasing. Customers are demanding ever better goods and service. This means scrapping penny-pinching attitudes to investment in training. *Britain's workers want greater opportunities to develop their talent . . .* They wish to escape the drudgery of dead-end jobs and take pride in work that is both worth doing and done well.

In 1997, when approaching the general election, the British Trades Union Congress published *Partners for Progress,* a title which very accurately reflected the theme of New Unionism. Said the TUC:

> The theme of this statement is partnership, a recognition that trade unions must not be seen as part of Britain's problems but as part of the

solution . . . At the workplace social partnership means employers and trade unions working together to achieve common goals such as fairness and competitiveness . . . At the national level partnership means Government discussing issues with employers and trade unions on a fair and open basis where a common approach can reap dividends, for example attracting inward investment and promoting training and equal opportunities.

The TUC recognised that good quality and secure jobs cannot be created by government but that government's role is to create the framework and to direct resources to priority groups. It wants unions and employers to work together on policies which will support jobs, such as 'investment, training and fair labour laws and practices which will minimise industrial disputes and which will promote equal opportunities at work'.

A great difficulty is how the rhetoric of the top can be translated into practice in the workplace, and a key issue for trade unions must then be, 'In this new environment can we define and provide a service which members, actual and potential, want?' and, in this, members play a vital role. They *are* the union but also see themselves as its customer. Customer requirements change, often rapidly and erratically. The customer pays a price, the subscription, for a service. Many regard it as an insurance premium to provide protection in time of need. If the price is too high in relation to the service, the customer, if he or she has a choice (and, increasingly, the trade union's customers do have a choice), will no longer wish to pay. The individual member is primarily interested in 'What will the union do for me and my colleagues in my company?' And when the basic pay and other benefits are right and when the employee feels valued as an individual, the answer is often, 'Not much.'

The GMB–UCW *A New Agenda* said:

Technical innovation is causing rigid production methods to give way to flexible manufacturing systems offering reliability and variety at low unit cost . . . In future even greater weight needs to be attached to team work, motivation and commitment. Success and security, profitability and prosperity require that management and labour work together to make the best use of the talent available in each enterprise.

In discussing the fresh approach, they added:

The New Agenda would make the quality of output rather than the price of inputs the centrepiece of talks between trades unions and employer . . . work organisation, training and quality should form the focus . . . Discussions should concentrate upon productivity and ways of bringing the ingenuity of employees to bear on question of quality.

The Rover Group's 'New Deal' is a classic example of a company and a trade union seeking to take a major step in the new direction. In seeking to offer enhanced security it ended distinctions between white and blue-collar workers, ended demarcations, introduced a new disputes proce-dure, guaranteed job security and introduced teamworking. When launching it in 1992, George Simpson, Chief Executive, wrote to all employees, saying: 'Necessary reductions in manpower will be achieved in future with the co-operation of all employees through retraining and redeployment, natural wastage, voluntary severance and early retirement programmes.' There were to be no more compulsory redundancies. But, it has to be said, Rover was only able to offer this *after* it had implemented tens of thousands of compulsory redundancies. The demand for its products and the number of people employed was about in balance. Several years earlier it would have been impossible to give such a guarantee.

Blue Circle Cement, a company which has a history of both innovative deals and troubled labour relations, was faced with fierce competition and an uneven recovery in the building materials market. After a two-year journey of discussion, consultation, negotiation, hostility, mistrust, confrontation and exhilaration the company signed a ground-breaking deal with three unions, the AEEU, GMB and TGWU in May 1997. The company gave a commitment on employment security, guaranteeing that under normal circumstances any staffing reductions will be handled by voluntary means and the unions undertook to recognise and support business goals and objectives and encourage best practice throughout the company. In addition, the deal provided for succession planning, multi-skilling and training; no automatic replacement of leavers; redeployment within departments and sites; harmonisation of manual and white-collar terms and conditions, a rolling three-year pay deal and a written understanding that 'should industrial action be taken by the recognised trade unions then the spirit of this agreement will have been broken and as such the benefits of this agreement would no longer apply to those individuals involved'. Symbolically, the deal was signed by the President or General Secretary of the unions.

The Blue Circle deal is an extreme example of a trend which is gathering pace. As part of the move towards an emphasis on individualism and teamworking, companies are seeking an increasing amount of creative input from their workforce and often the key relationship is becoming the direct relationship between the individual and his or her immediate boss. Good internal relationships in such organisations do not primarily depend on the relationship between the company and the unions but on the face-to-face relationship between individuals. It is based on a belief that if staff are not treated properly, with respect and trust, they cannot be expected to behave similarly towards their customers, either internal or external. It involves a belief in the goals of the organisation and is totally removed from the imposed compliance on which traditional trade unionism thrived.

There remain some in the trade union movement who have failed to perceive that long-term fundamental changes are taking place. We have seen in Chapter 3 the reaction of the Canadian Autoworkers Union. Many local trade union officials see teamworking, with the new-style supervisor working directly with employees, as a mechanism for by-passing them whereas in the 'good old days' the trade union official used to by-pass the supervisor by going direct to the manager. Even the sophisticated European Metal Workers' Federation, in referring to decentralised structures, states, 'Management sees these forms of work organisation as a means of weakening the trade unions. . . it is extremely dangerous for both workers and their trade unions if management is allowed to proceed without control.' They are mistaken. Managers' objectives have been to ensure that their company responds positively to the changing environment and this response has created the basis for new relationships. The danger to trade unions lies not in managers going on the offensive against them but in their failure to recognise and respond to these changes.

Some are responding. Sigi Roth of IG Metall is thinking about the role of teamworking in Germany. He aims for a high degree of decentralisation and self-organisation, with tasks shared to a much greater extent than at present. This means workers not just moving around within the manufacturing operations, but rotating through areas such as material supply, quality control and maintenance. He seeks an environment with high-quality working conditions and human-oriented values in which goals are agreed and manning levels co-determined, particularly with reference to the integration of older and disabled workers and the training of unskilled and semi-skilled workers. He looks for group discussions to be held during working hours involving a self-confident, critical and highly qualified workforce, and for spokespersons to be democratically elected and then have involvement at all levels of decision-making within the company.

The European Metal Workers' Federation is thinking constructively about the future role of trade unions, and in 1992 produced a document, *Mechanical Engineering in Europe in the Year 2000*, which outlined its views. It recognised that the move to employee involvement impacts on the relationship between management and the workforce, dissolves the old blue-collar–white-collar demarcation and rejoins the Taylorist separation of planning from execution. But it also recognised that reorganisations can lead to employment instability, especially when markets are saturated and there is no economic growth. In such circumstances, 'Since this aspect of productivity is completely neglected by management, the task of maintaining a balance between the two dimensions lies with the unions.' For them, this must lead to more free time for workers for training/reskilling and for improving working conditions, with at least 5 per cent of annual hours being allocated to these tasks.

The European Metal Workers' Federation is also concerned to achieve 'a more integrated firm, characterised by a more horizontal hierarchy and above all by the dynamic involvement of all the workforce in decisions concerning the present and future operation of the company'. To achieve this, workers and unions must play an active role in work and company organisation concepts, personnel development, technical and production process concepts and even in the actual production conception. In particular, they aim for the humanisation of work, 'To eliminate pressure and stress to provide the necessary staff and rest periods, to carry out a reasonable volume of work and allow for necessary breaks.'

However enlightened a company might be, the traditional role of trade unions does not go away. In organisations which are devolving responsibility to local management, there is great potential for managers to abuse their powers and it becomes increasingly important that local trade union representatives have sufficient skills and understanding to allow them to respond in an informed way to local initiatives.

Trade unions must, therefore, continue with their traditional roles representing effectively those employees who have a grievance or who are subject to the company's disciplinary procedure. Even in the most enlightened company, there will still be individuals who do daft things, and in such circumstances the individual's and employer's interests will diverge and high-quality, third-party representation is needed. The British Trades Union Congress, in its evidence to the House of Commons Employment Select Committee, quoted a survey which showed that 93 per cent of respondents chose, 'To protect me if problems came up' as a 'very' or 'fairly' important reason for joining a trade union. But this protection is not only needed in times of relationship difficulties; it manifests itself in very practical ways. In 1996 trade unions pursued over 150,000 personal injury claims and won more than £330 million in compensation for their members!

Many trade unions throughout the world are rapidly extending their range of financial services, providing benefits for members only. This is particularly prevalent in the USA. These benefits extend to savings plans, insurance, assistance with loans for house purchase, credit cards, road rescue services, discount travel, welfare assistance, convalescence and support services and private medical insurance. In 1985, the American AFL–CIO recommended a Union Privilege Benefits Program designed for former members whose branch was dissolved because of plant closures. Designed to provide ongoing benefits for laid-off workers the programme attracted four million associate members.

In 1994, however, the AFL–CIO produced, rather belatedly, a significant review of the future role of trade unions which sought to define a new model incorporating five principles:

- A rejection of the traditional dichotomy between thinking and doing, conception and execution.
- The redesign of jobs to include greater variety of skills and tasks and greater responsibility for the ultimate output of the organisation.
- A flatter management structure.
- An insistence that workers, through their unions, are entitled to a decision-making role at all levels of the enterprise.
- The rewards realised from transforming the work organisation to be distributed on equitable terms agreed upon through negotiations between labour and management.

The first three of these principles are common with those of the ascendant organisation. The fourth, however, seeks to extend significantly the influence of workers 'through their unions' on the strategic decisions of the organisation. For example, on the acquisition of new technologies, changes in products or services, how much work will be done, where and by whom? Their argument is that, 'Because workers have long-term ties to their jobs, they bring a long-term perspective and can be counted on to promote policies designed to ensure that businesses have long-term futures and can provide long-term employment at decent wages.'

Unfortunately, the history of the trade union movement, particularly in the United States, has been one of resistance to change, protection of the status quo, insistence on the seniority principle, the stifling of innovation, the protection of jobs through costly lay-off agreements and, in the good times, the maximisation of wages almost irrespective of the impact on the employer. In seeking to establish a model in which strategic decisions are made jointly between management and workers, the AFL–CIO presupposes a responsibility which, in the majority of cases, has not been demonstrated. This is reinforced when their comments on the fifth principle state that, 'This means, in the first instance, a negotiated agreement to protect income and employment security to the maximum extent possible.' They fail to realise that such negotiated agreements can give but short-lived security.

Real security comes from working in an organisation which is able to anticipate and respond rapidly to customer demands. As we shall see shortly, trade unions can have a partnership based on mutual recognition and respect and *can* make valuable contributions to the strategic direction of the enterprise. Even when such partnerships exist, there will be different objectives and trade unions have the right to express their views. In the end, however, the management of an organisation is paid to make decisions affecting its long-term future and that responsibility cannot be shared. The established American unions, in coming to the opposite conclusion, are leading their members down a blind alley.

TRADE UNIONS IN THE ASCENDANT ORGANISATION

To use the GMB–UCW terminology, there can be a 'new agenda' for trade unions in the ascendant organisation. What should this be? First, the organisation and the union can establish a partnership in which they jointly commit themselves to the success of the enterprise; the company recognises the right of its employees to join the union and for the union to represent its members; and the union recognises that management must exercise its right to take action in the interests of the organisation. The precise regulation of such relationships will depend very much on the history and legal framework within which they operate but the principles are sound and universal.

Even such seemingly innocuous proposals are controversial. Nissan in the USA made the conscious decision to set up in Tennessee, a Southern 'right to work' State, and successfully fought off a long campaign by the UAW to secure negotiating rights. In the UK, however, we established a single union deal with the AEU from the very start. Provided the union is committed to the success of the enterprise no one need fear it and in preventing some of the potential excesses of free market management the union can play a role that in the long term is beneficial not only to its members but also to the management.

Unlike most who write on trade unions, I have faced them at their most hostile. In five years at the Ford Dagenham Metal Stamping and Body Plant, I personally handled hundreds of strikes, have been involved in numerous physical confrontations, have had my office smashed up around me, have been in the middle of several demonstrations and once, for several hours, personally confronted several hundred rioting production workers, eventually going among them to face-off to the leaders. I was at the front line of the revolution where, to some of the extremists, those who supported the Communist Party were regarded as right-wing, class collaborators. I can therefore say with some authority and not a little understatement that if the unions are not prepared to work with management for the success of the enterprise and look only to defend their members, restrict flexibility, cause disruption, create tension and secure the greatest gain for the least effort, they are to be resisted.

I have constantly emphasised that if employees are to contribute continuously to improving productivity which might eliminate their particular job, they must have security of employment. And I do distinguish between employment security and job security. As we have seen, Nissan's consultation with employees on how best to handle the anticipated 1994 car market decline, led above all to a call for job security, with a clear recognition that this would mean some voluntary job losses and retraining. Trade unions are coming to recognise the distinction between employment security and job security, between employment and employability. In these rapidly changing times the successful organisations will be those who offer the former but gain acceptance that job flexibility can make a significant contribution to that end.

However, to suggest that all organisations offer this commitment would be crazy. We were able to do so, as was Rover, because our staffing levels were 'about right'. We had already achieved a high degree of leanness, our core processes were clearly defined and much of the peripheral work had been contracted out. If necessary, some could be called back in. But many organisations are not yet in this position. Many still have excess staff numbering in the thousands. No organisation with that type of surplus can offer security of employment. When, however, it has gone through the reduction process, it should then offer security for those who remain. When they are at this 'about right' level, all organisations should seek to accommodate marginal fluctuations. The costs are small and the potential benefits great.

Within the increased emphasis on individualism and teamworking, companies are seeking an increasing amount of creative input from their workforce. With the condition that the trade unions must also be working for the long-term success of the enterprise and its employees, it is clearly possible to envisage a scenario in which they welcome this trend as an important step on the road to genuine employee involvement. They must not interpret it as an attempt by management to divorce employees from their union but as an opportunity to achieve what they have claimed to be seeking for years. Management inspired teamworking provides the unions with the chance to gain real influence in areas that are fundamental to success – organisation structures, work methods and patterns, facility layouts, the environment, training, product changes, new technology and so on, not with a view to resist such change but to facilitate it in a manner beneficial to both employees and the company.

Some trade unions are able to make constructive contributions in this area and genuinely inform their members of the potential problems if lean production and control of the processes are pushed too far. Much of manufacturing work remains tough and, as shown in Chapter 3, one of the neglected areas of management is ergonomics, the physical interface between people and process. This is one of the areas in which trade unions can make a significant impact – but not simply by being awkward. 'Easy working' improves the working environment, product quality and productivity. Most managements and trade unions have barely begun to address these issues in a constructive way. The unions of the future must, and if they do they will find that they can have a real impact where it matters to most employees – in their place of work.

Another factor is that, with declining membership, unions, though recognised as the bargaining agent, no longer represent much of the workforce. The Germans have long lived with this situation and get over it because the theoretically non-union Works Councils represent employees, not union members. Many unions have, however, refused to represent non-members, even though they have accepted that the pay deals they negotiate will cover union and non-union members alike. In Britain, the 1997 Labour Government, at the time of writing, has still to determine whether, if a union represents more than 50 per cent of workers, the company must afford it recognition.

Nissan's Company Council was very much influenced by the German model. While recognising the Engineering Union as having sole representational rights for all employees below managerial level (including engineers, shop-floor workers, indirect workers, supervisors, and so on) we thought it was more likely that manual workers would join the union than white-collar workers. The Company Council was therefore structured so that all employees, union or non-union, would have representation. Our belief was that about 70 per cent of our total population would join the union, with a higher proportion among shop-floor staff. Over the years membership has fluctuated between 25 and 45 per cent (still above the UK private sector figure). We also thought that, as in Germany, active trade union members would be elected to the Company Council. This did not happen.

This creates a problem for trade unions in such companies, for this experience is not unique. The message for trade unions must be that in such organisations they have to make extraordinary efforts to demonstrate their relevance. The national officers of the Engineering Union originally believed that simply signing a single union deal with Nissan would result in employees flocking to join. It did not. They have to earn membership. Nissan must be the only company which has (in 1988) invited the President and General Secretary of a Union to address all employees in an effort to increase membership and in which the Personnel Director wrote to all employees extolling the virtues of trade union membership, emphasising that success had to be three ways – the company, the employees and the union!

Bill Jordan, when President of the AEEU, wrote:

One thing took me completely by surprise. We had difficulty recruiting members into the union at Nissan. We asked for the opportunity to talk to the workforce and I was surprised to be given that opportunity on the day that the managing director was to address the whole workforce. Having talked about what had happened in the previous year, he then to my utter astonishment, personally introduced me as a leader of a union with whom the company had nothing but the very best of relationships, and suggested that it was in the interests of everyone in the company to be part of the Union. How many MDs would take time out to promote that sort of harmony? (Jordan, 1991)

The problem for most unions in such organisations is that it is not management opposition but a co-operative management style that contributes to low membership. Old-style union officials were brought up on the assumption that there was an inherent conflict of interest between capital and labour and that a worker's first loyalty was to the union. Adapting is difficult.

It is about time that trade unions realised and acted on the fact that what unites people because they are all employees of the same company is often stronger than what divides them because some are skilled and others semi-skilled, some are supervisors and others supervised, some are blue-collar and others are white-collar. When you have teamworking, flexibility of working practices and common terms and conditions of employment, there is no case for having separate bargaining units within the enterprise. There is no reason why a supervisor cannot sit on the same side of the bargaining table as the people who work for him or her, nor why, on that same side, there cannot be engineers, finance staff and other white-collar employees. Those who argue that this cannot work have not seen it in operation.

However, surprisingly, it does place a considerable new responsibility on the management negotiators, for although everyone may be sitting around the same table this does not mean that different interests disappear. There remain areas in which supervisors have a different interest from engineers, maintenance staff from operators, and so on. But if management negotiators seek to bargain separately with these different groups it will not take long for the whole thing to collapse. The way through this conundrum is to allow technical side discussions to take place, always with the chairperson of the employees' side present, and to insist that nothing can be agreed until it is brought back to the common table and accepted by all representatives. Placing on management negotiators the responsibility of balancing conflicting interests presents a new and very demanding task.

The trend towards performance appraisal and merit pay provides opportunities for trade unions to play a new and constructive role. For so long, their attitude has solely been one of saying that irrespective of ability all should be paid the same and then protecting the inefficient. This must be modified to include encouraging and rewarding the efficient but in such a way as to ensure that it is done fairly, that equal opportunities apply to all, that the appraisal and merit system is equitably applied and is relevant to all elements of performance (not just the tangibly measurable), and that all are given the opportunity to progress. Further, there is now no logical case why the terms and conditions of employment should differ between white-collar and blue-collar workers. Instead of seeking to perpetuate differences of treatment, all unions should seek to establish timetables within their negotiating groups for complete harmonisation, with the only difference being pay and closely related elements.

Along with this goes flexibility. Unions should be seeking to eliminate all management and trade union restrictive practices which inhibit what people do. The GMB–UCW New Agenda says, 'Unions must escape from a self-defeating fixation with tightly specified job descriptions and embrace the adaptability that comes from broader job definition.' Managers are also backward, in retaining their love of job evaluation and job descriptions which are their equivalent of trade union restrictive practices. The unions and managements that succeed in the future will be those which seek jointly to break out of this straitjacket.

Change is now the only constant. Trade unions must encourage and support change. We are past the time when every change of technology, working practice or staffing level can be the subject of negotiation. Instead, when decisions affecting these issues are being pushed way down into the organisation, the unions have a real opportunity to facilitate change in a manner beneficial to both employees and the company. To do this they must first demonstrate that their approach is constructive and directed towards success and growth; and secondly they must make a real effort to train their representatives in understanding these issues.

Unions have barely penetrated the growing band of non-core workers, and when such people are often less well treated than their permanent full-time colleagues, they have a glorious opportunity to make a difference. But it requires effort, and such attempts as there have been were short-lived and resulted in high cost per new member. John Monks has great concerns in this area, particularly with regard to the training of the peripheral workers. He said to me, after visiting Nissan, that, to say the least, he found a certain incompatibility between the desire of many organisations to reach world-class standards and the increasing use of peripheral workers with low levels of training. John was clearly highlighting a potential problem and he uses this in his campaigning rhetoric, but at the grass roots, the British trade unions have only rarely reached the starting gate.

Companies, broadly, get the unions they deserve, and if managers abuse their authority they deserve to be checked. Remembering that the relationship that really counts is that between *individuals* in the place of work, constructive unions *can* be genuine agents of change. To do battle with trade unions simply because they are trade unions is short-sighted. I have, literally, battled with the extremes of trade unionism and know that many executives who claim not to be 'anti-union' but 'pro-worker' speak with forked tongues. There is nothing wrong with wanting an easy life, wanting to treat people well and finding it more comfortable not having to negotiate with trade unions, but it is what employees want that counts. If employees feel the need to have a trade union represent them, who are managers to deny recognition?

In the past, trade unions have opposed change, but they can have a constructive role provided they are prepared to change their approach. If they wish to oppose, management must recognise that such opposition, if supported by the workforce, will make it more difficult to progress towards becoming an ascendant organisation. Management must then determine its strategy accordingly and resist.

Some may have the luxury of being able to indulge in confrontation, as did those of us in the British car industry in the 1970s. Others may seek to de-recognise the union, as a few British companies have done in the 1980s and 90s or as has long been the case in the United States. However, it is difficult to be confrontational and constructive at the same time, and, if the objective is to move towards a constructive relationship with a trade union rather than obliterate it, management will almost always have to take the first step. The culture change process is long and difficult. To this, I now turn.

14 Becoming Ascendant

There is nothing permanent except change.

Heraclitus, 501 BC

We trained hard and it seemed every time we were beginning to form into teams we would be reorganised. I was to learn later in my life that we tend to meet every new situation by reorganisation. And a wonderful method it can be for creating the illusion of progress while producing confusion, inefficiency and demoralisation.

Gaius Petronius, 1st century AD

There is nothing more difficult to handle, more doubtful of success and more dangerous to carry through than initiating change in a state's constitution. The innovator makes enemies of all those who prospered under the old order, and only lukewarm support is forthcoming from those who would prosper under the new.

Niccolò Machiavelli, *The Prince*, 1514

We all resist change – unless it is our own idea. Then we want everyone to accept it! Virtually the whole of Part II has been about 'becoming ascendant', but having the ingredients and making the cake are very different things. With the same ingredients one cook can create a disaster and another a masterpiece. This penultimate chapter is concerned with the total change process. The great cooks vary the ingredients and introduce their own special something, so, as always, it is indicative rather then prescriptive.

HOW *NOT* TO CHANGE

Mick Crews, who moved from the business world to the voluntary sector, tells the delightful story of the Change Agent, who, after a long period seeking to implement change in a variety of businesses, had just been appointed to the position of Group Stability Agent in a large organisation. His task was to ensure that the Chief Executive's policy

246

of 'No change whatsoever' was implemented to the letter. On meeting a former colleague, he was asked:

> 'That must be difficult for you after all those years as a Change Agent. Don't you need to develop a vast amount of new material and programmes?'
> 'Not at all. I just use the same programmes I developed when I was a Change Agent. Nothing really changed then, so I don't see why anything will change now!'

The late Christopher Lorenz of the *Financial Times* reported a KPMG Management Consulting survey of change management. 'Most of its 250 corporate respondents are running four or more different types of cross-functional change programmes. With ample justification, KPMG doubts whether many of them are being properly integrated.' It warns of the need for co-ordination and prioritisation, 'so that the change machine does not get out of control'. Lorenz also cited Boston Consulting Group's report that in many large US companies up to 15 process improvements are under way, 'But these seldom added up to a coherent programme' (*Financial Times*, 27 July 1993). When Heraclitus and Gaius Petronius made their comments on the ancient world, they were also making accurate predictions about twentieth-century business!

Michael Beer, Russell Eisenstat and Bert Spector told of the major US bank which announced a company-wide change effort in the mid-1980s. The new CEO carefully reviewed the bank's purpose and culture with his top executives. They produced a mission statement and hired a new Vice-President, Human Resources, who established company-wide programmes to push change deep into the organisation; he developed a revised organisation structure, introduced new performance appraisal and reward systems, conducted attitude surveys, and so on. Two years later, nothing had changed. What went wrong? Just about everything. Say our trio of authors, 'Every one of the assumptions the CEO made about who should lead the change effort, what needed changing and how to go about doing it was wrong' (Beer *et al.*, 1990). Maybe Mick Crews's story was not a joke!

A paradox of the change process, for those who believe it has to start at the top, is that chief executives have usually reached their position as the result of success in an environment which values strength measured by decisiveness, direction, the ability to take the tough decisions and by short-term results. Such people may see the need for change but have great difficulty in implementing anything other than a centrally directed, top-down process. And their problem is that most people like the established way, whether it is always sitting at the same table in a restaurant or conducting their business in their accustomed fashion. They resist change that is thrust upon them.

The most difficult organisation to change is the one which is large and comfortable, well established, making good profits, often in a mono-polistic position; 'Why should we change?' Such organisations, whether in the private or public sector, became fat and complacent. Managers have their perks and staff their ever-rising salaries; share holders have their dividends and suppliers their profits. There is little need to worry about competition. This (apathetic) organisation may even think that it is responsive to customer needs. It has what it believes to be a good product-development programme and it determines the pace of innovation, for each product must achieve full profitability before the successor comes on to the market. It has established ways of doing things which, although at one time may have been innovative, have become so embedded in the organisation, so accepted, that no one even considers challenging them. This applies not only to the products or services actually offered to the customer but also to the way of providing them. In fact, all the ingredients making for future disaster! Two examples of comfortable organisations were BP and IBM.

BP

An example of a change programme that did not work as well as planned is the experience of BP, the petro-chemical company, employing in 1990 some 120,000 people world-wide. Robert Horton, with a highly successful track record with BP in the USA, took over the top job in 1990. He inherited a large, comfortable, matrix organisation, multi-layered and bureaucratic, with a headquarters staff of 2,200 and nearly 90 committees. A questionnaire sent to 150 top managers and 4,000 other staff, had revealed widespread ignorance of BP's strategy and voiced strong criticism of its multi-layered committee structure and review process, which virtually institutionalised second-guessing. Horton was determined to change the culture and initiated a programme which formally was called Project 1990 but within BP came to be known irreverently as 'Horticulture'.

Building on his American experience, Horton sent out a three-page 'Vision and Values' statement to all employees. It aimed for a new, slimmer headquarters, no longer working in large, hierarchical depart-ments but in small, flexible, cross-functional teams; and instead of a formal organisation, the emphasis was to be on informal networking with open and informal communication. 'Managers are there to support and empower their staff, not to monitor or control their activities.' Horton sought 'Openness, care, teamwork, empowerment and trust' and said that the current appraisal system was wholly deficient in coping with teamworking and should focus more on interpersonal skills and the ability to motivate staff.

Along with this, the matrix organisation was changed to give business streams primacy over the old geographical regions. Headquarters staff was cut to 400 (except that 800 of the operational headquarters jobs were retained but relocated) and about 70 of the committees were abolished. Throughout the organisation BP shed some 8,000 jobs.

BP had both hard and soft objectives. A £750 million per annum cost-cutting programme was to be accompanied by a programme aimed at making the company more open and caring. But in December 1991 a top management review said, 'As we remove complexity in our organisation and reap the benefits of *Project 1990* job security becomes an increasing concern.' One aspect of the project, personal development plans, was redefined by staff as 'personal departure plans'. If people do not feel secure, their commitment is difficult to achieve.

The great problem was not in seeking to combine hard and soft objectives, but that Bob Horton was said not to walk like he talked. At the pre-launch conference, a senior executive was reported as saying, 'Do we really believe that Bob is going to stop second-guessing his top colleagues? That's the only way all this change will work: if the top managers behave differently, managers will take their cues.' Another said, 'I don't believe he'll really change his spots. If he trusts you, you get delegated authority heaped upon you. But he will want to be involved in every significant decision. . . he instinctively wants to be seen as hands on. But he also wants to be seen as an innovative leader' (*Financial Times*, 30 March 1990).

Project 1990 declined as a programme not because its objectives were wrong, but because of the failure of the people at the top to walk like they talked. A personnel officer said, 'Open, empowered – great. But when we saw that the company was not living by that credo, scepticism grew and now has turned to cynicism', and a consultant added, 'Throughout the two years staff have consistently said there was talk but little action. This must reflect on the wisdom of such grand schemes' (Miller, 1992).

Despite all his efforts to cut costs, BP remained under considerable financial pressure – but Horton, an advocate of the primacy of the shareholders, insisted on maintaining the dividend. Four months later, he resigned. The other directors made it clear that the resignation was not entirely voluntary and that it was about personality rather than policy. His replacement, David (now Lord) Simon, said, 'This is about the style of running the company at the top. It is not about changes in strategy.' Under Horton, BP had refused to cut its dividend in spite of falling profits and rising debt levels. In August 1992 BP cut its dividend for the first time since the First World War and said it was reducing staff by 11,500 worldwide. In December of that year it announced a further 9,000 job losses. 'Horticulture' was over.

IBM

IBM was long held by many to be the epitome of success. In 1984, profits after tax exceeded $7 billion, and in 1990, $6 billion. By the late 1970s, 70 per cent of the world's computer applications were centred on IBM mainframes and mini computers and by 1980 it had 38 per cent of industry revenues and 60 per cent of its profits. As IBM moved into the 1990s, Sir Edwin Nixon, Chairman of IBM UK, was able to say 'IBM United Kingdom Holdings Group experienced its 37th year of growth.' In 1986 IBM ranked first in the *Fortune* magazine ranking of the best-managed companies.

IBM was committed to change. Founder Tom J. Watson Jnr. said in 1962, 'I believe that if an organisation is to meet the challenges of a changing world it must be prepared to change everything about itself except its basic beliefs.' These basic beliefs are, 'Respect for the individual, the best possible service to our customers and the pursuit of excellence.' According to Len Peach, then IBM's UK Personnel Director, 'Respect for the individual' meant 'Full employment, promotion from within, equal opportunity, pay for performance and single status.' Common factors included, 'Drawing out the best of individuals' energies, talents, skills. creativity and adaptability.'

In 1989, when visiting IBM's production plant in Havant, Hampshire, I was told that 90 per cent of staff were involved in improvement activities, that simultaneous engineering had been introduced to reduce product lead time; and that they were moving from 140 suppliers to 40 and from 2,000 parts numbers to 120, with suppliers becoming responsible for designing their own parts. They had an extensive programme for recognising individual and team achievements and in 1989 implemented 779 improvement projects, with £14 million saving. Many other initiatives were in place and everyone was genuinely proud of their success.

In that very year, however, IBM's Fortune ranking had slipped to 45th and in 1992 the company lost $4.97 billion. In 1993 some 85,000 people left the company. The group took an $8.9 billion pre-tax charge to cover the payouts to people leaving the company and the closure of factories and offices around the world. What went wrong?

Basically, the computing world changed more rapidly than IBM. Its success in the 1960s, 1970s and 1980s was due to its large mainframes, based on solid-state memory chips, each costing millions of dollars with profits to match. It was the low-cost silicon microchip leading to low barriers to entry, few real product differences, vigorous price wars and slim profit margins, that ended IBM's dominance. Open systems, allowing customers to integrate equipment produced by a variety of manufacturers, had taken over from the proprietary system, and the new companies were able to develop technology more quickly and respond to customer needs more effectively.

When John Akers took the helm at IBM in 1985, he recognised that their products were lagging behind the competitors' and were grouped in families which could not connect to each other. He saw that the company was technology-driven rather than customer-driven and decreed that this must be reversed. Five years later Jack Knehler, IBM President, said:

> The new IBM is market driven . . . IBM aims to offer information technology solutions . . . IBM will bundle computer hardware, software and support service to provide turnkey systems designed to meet the specific needs of individual customers and industry sectors . . . IBM has not made major investments in applications software in recent years . . . it has had to turn to third party software developers in recent years . . . IBM recognises that its field sales force is ill-equipped for solution selling. (*Financial Times*, 27 April 1990)

But the reforms were too little, too late. In 1984, IBM's revenues were $46 billion and it was building a company capable of handling a predicted $180 billion revenue which did not materialise. In May 1991 IBM was forced to cut the price of its high-performance workstations by 60 per cent to compete with Hewlett Packard, Sun and the myriad other competitors appearing in the market place.

In April 1991 one of the most infamous meetings in IBM history took place. Akers attended what was thought to be a routine meeting of middle managers at its New York headquarters, and told it to them like it is. He repeated what he had said to his top corporate management team two days earlier. He said that he believed that the messages from the top get 'filtered' on their way through the organisation and that, 'I'm sick and tired of visiting plant after plant to hear nothing but great things about quality and cycle times and then to visit customers who tell me of problems. If the people in labs and plants miss deadlines tell them their job is on the line . . . the tension level is not high enough in the business, everyone is too damn comfortable at a time when the business is in crisis.' Revenues in the first quarter of 1991 were down by 5 per cent over the previous quarter and profits were down by 50 per cent.

Akers directed his diatribe across all of IBM's divisions. Of the USA he said, '20,000 people four years ago delivered $26 billion dollars . . . now [we] have 25,000 people who in 1990 delivered $27 billion . . . unsatisfactory . . . Where's my return for the extra 5,000 people? Where's the beef? What the hell are you doing for me?' On people management he said, '[Its] not good enough. Our people have to be competitive and if they can't change fast enough, as fast as our industry . . . goodbye . . . half of one per cent MIA'd [sacked through management-initiated attrition] from laboratories and we have the nerve to think this is performance based? [We] need a forced march on the MIA problem.'

IBM was managerially inflexible. In the thirty years to 1986 it had the same top-down functional organisation in every country, with fourteen layers of management. In 1989, 55 per cent of non-manufacturing employees in the UK were in the support sections with only 45 per cent in the front line.

Despite IBM's efforts to change during the second half of the 1980s, it had clearly not done enough, it had not led the change process and for too long behaved as though the years of success would continue. I remember being frustrated towards the end of each year as the special offers came out. 'Buy now and we can knock 25 per cent off the price', or 'Our prices are going up on 1st January – if you get your order in now we can let you have it at this year's price even though it won't be delivered until next year', or 'We're updating the model shortly, we can't tell you exactly what the improvements will be, but if you order now you'll be near the head of the queue.' All indicative of the monopolist who does not really have to try.

But change continued – substantial job cuts (voluntary, but usually on the basis of generous offers which were difficult to refuse), restructuring into thirteen highly autonomous business sectors each measured by their individual revenues and profits, the elimination of much of the corporate bureaucracy, reducing management layers (in the UK from seven to four) and spinning off activities such as property services and professional training into new companies. In 1992, IBM split off its personal computer division, eliminating the boundaries between development, manufacturing and distribution to speed product development time, and reducing the bureaucracy needed to achieve a price change – allowing decisions to be made at division level in days rather than at corporate level in weeks or months.

On 26 January 1993 John Akers announced he would step down and the company slashed its dividend from $1.21 to 54 cents, the first time it had cut the payout to shareholders.

The lesson of the IBM story is not one of failure to change but of failure to change in the good times before the need to change was thrust upon it. The time to implement major change programmes is when the organisation is able to be pro-active rather than reactive, when people do not feel threatened. As the gardener once said, 'If you weed before you need to weed you never *need* to weed.'

Jaguar

Another lesson is to have regard for the whole organisation, not just part of it. Ford found this out when it acquired Jaguar in 1990. The previous chairman, Sir John Egan, had done a marvellous job on the sales and marketing side, projecting an image of a high-quality, high-prestige product, and had dramatically improved distribution, particularly in the USA; but he did not fundamentally change Jaguar's manufacturing, which Bill Hayden, previously Ford of Europe's Vice-President, Manufacturing, subsequently compared to a Russian car plant in Gorky! In early 1990 Jaguar was experiencing 2,500 defects per 100 finished cars. Ford introduced a transition team, whose job it was to conduct an in-depth examination of Jaguar.

The transition team found that: 'People in Jaguar want to do well, building on the company's reputation for producing distinctively styled, luxury saloons and sports cars', but it identified many problem areas not conducive to producing good quality and high levels of customer satisfaction: 'Poor housekeeping, lack of measurement and data, incapable processes, sloppy discipline and poor material handling.' It found that throughout Jaguar there was a lack of adequate management. Specific criticisms included:

- Compromised quality is being accepted by management throughout Jaguar – an inadequate and inconsistent approach in respect of the removal of the poor disciplines which compromise quality.

- Records and paperwork are in many cases dirty, unreadable, lost, poorly stored and filed.
- There are many examples of processes which are not capable of providing consistent, good quality.
- Insufficient data is being collected. Analysis is poor and dissemination is inadequate.

In short, poor leaders and managers were neither able to motivate the workforce nor control the processes. The change process had barely impacted on manufacturing and this prejudiced the chances of success in those areas that Egan had genuinely improved.

SUCCESSFUL CHANGE – THE ROVER GROUP

Sir Michael Edwardes, Chairman of British Leyland in the 1970s, had the task of implementing the blood-letting process, and though both demanding and exhausting such a process is not that difficult; the narrow focus concentrates the mind. But in the late 1980s and early 1990s The Rover Group (to give it its new name), having learned much and made steady progress with its then Japanese partner and shareholder, Honda, decided that a change of gear was needed. They developed a strategic vision aimed at repositioning the company for success in the late 1990s. This vision included moving the product up-market, growing in Europe, reducing its break-even sales level, increasing employee involvement and commitment, improving its image with greatly enhanced customer satisfaction and moving to a business unit focus.

To achieve such objectives Rover recognised that it needed to act on many fronts at the same time, but also that each was dependent on the other. With regard to the people issues, it would be seeking considerable improvements in the flexibility, mobility and teamworking activities which had already begun in 1987, when the Board and executive committee were trained in total quality and had launched a Total Quality Improvement programme. Team and cell working had been introduced, but this was not enough. Rover sought to move away from what many still called their 'megaphone management' style, towards an open and honest style which treated people with respect and dignity.

Rover recognised that if it were to succeed, the trade union role was critical and union leaders were brought into the thinking process at a very early stage, before anything was formally published. They even brought together 400 shop stewards to discuss the issues, a practice previously considered impossible. They recognised that job security was of critical importance. All the preliminary work culminated in September 1991, when Rover management formally presented to the unions a document *Rover Tomorrow – The New Deal* with the headline 'We need a workforce distinguished only by individuals'/teams' contribution to the company'. Not exactly the stuff of tabloid newspapers, but meaningful to those who needed to know.

Of central importance to the subsequent discussions was the fact that Rover and the unions did not seek to tie them into the bi-annual pay and conditions negotiations. Management laid out its long-term vision, recognising that it could not get there in one step, and invited middle management, the trade unions and employees to share that vision. The subsequent agreement in March 1992 was very little different from the original document, which was based on the type of package initiated by Nissan (Rover had visited Nissan as part of its researches). It introduced single status aimed at eliminating the 'them and us' syndrome, payment by credit transfer and a commitment to no lay-offs: 'In the event of a problem which disrupts production, all employees will be engaged in worthwhile activities and be required to co-operate with efforts to maintain productive output.' Continuous improvement was built in as 'a requirement for everyone'. 'There will be maximum devolution of authority and accountability to the employees actually doing the job.' Productivity bonuses were to be progressively phased out and, most critically: 'Employees who want to work for Rover will be able to stay with Rover. Necessary reductions in manpower will be achieved in future with the co-operation of all employees, through re-training and re-deployment, natural wastage, voluntary severance and early retirement programmes.'

Things did not go smoothly. The deal, advocated by the trade unions, was accepted by a slim majority of 168 votes out of 23,754. When I visited Rover in 1997, it was clear that at shop-floor level much remains to be done; some shop stewards, and no doubt some managers, still speak of the 'good old days'. The level of knowledge of the control processes remains limited and its application at shop-floor level irregular. The capability of first-line supervisors needs to be enhanced. But it is a long-term programme, the product is excellent, quality dramatically improved and motivation greatly enhanced. Rover, now taken over by BMW, is one of the success stories of the European automotive industry.

Rover, and many others, have shown that you do not need a greenfield site to make major changes. Indeed, those who point to the advantages of a greenfield site or a Japanese parent as the reasons for success are often

simply seeking excuses for their own inactivity. They point to the favourable circumstances of one company and because they do not enjoy such advantages argue that they are a condition of success. They are not.
The key to success is not a greenfield site but a greenfield mind!

HOW TO BECOME AN ASCENDANT ORGANISATION

You will now have a good idea of what an ascendant organisation is, and know how not to implement a change programme. You will also know that if a revolutionary change is needed there will not have been enough evolutionary change in the past. You know that you *must not*:

- Begin before achieving some understanding of what you wish to achieve
- Believe you have a monopoly of wisdom and know the full results and impact in advance – you will not even know all the questions, let alone the answers
- Impose a 'big bang' new concept from the top
- Concentrate on short-term results, either financial or non-financial
- Bring in an outsider to take responsibility, or remove responsibility from accountable managers in favour of 'facilitators'
- Talk in vague terms of 'culture change'
- Use off-the-peg panaceas
- Produce a written statement and think you have done all that is necessary
- Simply concentrate on the vision and strategy and then lose interest in the 'doing'
- Talk one way and act differently, or give out inconsistent messages
- Ignore the key implementers until late in the process
- Believe that by changing the structures and processes you will achieve the objectives
- Negotiate a little at a time without a perception of the long-term plan.

You know that leadership can exist at all levels and, indeed, one of the tasks in moving to an ascendant organisation is to provide the environment in which such leadership can flourish. However, in moving to the 'how', I speak for simplicity of the whole organisation. 'The top team' means the chief executive, immediate reports and other key individuals respected for their capabilities and influence. But the process can start at any level, division, location or geographical area, although

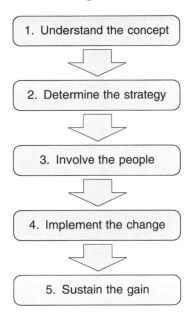

Figure 14.1   Becoming Ascendant

without corporate commitment, freedom may be limited and the ability to spread the word restricted. The process is much the same wherever you start. However, to omit steps in the process, without good reason, will result in a weakening of commitment and make it more difficult to sustain any advances made.

At all times it is important to remember that the old has to continue alongside the new – it must continue to operate effectively while change is going on around it. Concentration on the harvest due in five years may result in this year's crop being neglected and if this happens too frequently there may not be a fifth year!

The five stages of becoming ascendant are shown graphically above (Figure 14.1).

Understand the concept

One of the great problems facing any change programme is that someone in top management becomes inspired by a new idea and seeks to implement it without a real understanding of what it is about. Often it is a result of reading a book, attending a conference or visiting another company but rarely does the initiator get below the surface of the idea and achieve a true understanding of the underlying thinking and the implications for the company. Reading one book is insufficient. Read many others. Visit companies from which you feel you can learn and talk to people who have been through a similar process. Begin by analysing where you are now before you seek to determine where you want to be. Usually, an outside agent can best help you through this process as long as the agent is the servant, not the master.

In reading this book you may already personally have completed and analysed The Ascendant Organisation Questionnaire given in Appendix Two and you may wish to share your new understanding with your colleagues. You will find that they have different perceptions of 'where we are now'; they may even not share an understanding of 'why we are in business', and certainly they will have different views on 'where we want to be'.

There will also be many different levels of understanding and only rarely have I found a shared perception of the present, although future perceptions are often much closer. This process will allow the top team to gain an understanding of the type of organisation they currently are, even 'why we are in business', before they begin to consider the future.

Seek to gain 'knowledge' as well as 'know-how'. Assess what your competitors are up to and what might be the impact on your products or service, or on your suppliers. Begin to define specific business needs that should be addressed, but keep it broad at this stage. Remember Ivor Vaughan's 'stand' (see Chapter 8). If you have to prove every detail in advance then it is not a 'stand', not something in which you passionately believe.

Hopefully, this process of gaining understanding will lead to the conclusion that it is not possible to be precise about the future, that it may be unclear and subject to many complex, conflicting and changing pressures, both internal and external; that future progress will depend on gaining ownership throughout the organisation, so that people are motivated by diagnosing problems for themselves and initiating action rather than by vague talk of 'culture change'. Behaviour is shaped by the way people are managed, and the great thing about moving towards an ascendant organisation is that the process through which people go is a living example of the concept in action.

Some argue that trade unions and/or middle management should be brought in at this very first stage, and in some circumstances, particularly at plant level, this may have validity. However, there is also strength in the argument that top management needs a period of internal contemplation and most organisations will choose this option before deciding to extend the process.

There is a paradox, however. If the top team is convinced, the great danger is to fall into the trap of wanting to direct the change, whereas what is really needed is for the people in the organisation to find out for themselves what the top team wants them to find out. 'But,' the CEO may argue, 'isn't that like re-inventing the wheel?' Yes it is, but there is no harm, in fact there are positive benefits, in people finding out for themselves. And their conclusions may be different, for views change depending on your position - but I guarantee that, provided the process is followed, there will be a high level of agreement as to the broad direction.

Leadership and example will still be required – do not assume that things happen by themselves. Leadership must be continuous and consistent. The great danger is for the top team to produce the concept or written document and think it has done its bit. Until the ascendant organisation is a reality, the top team must be there to support, reinforce, cajole, assess and to be a sounding-board – but not overtly to direct.

Before moving to the second step, the top team may decide that it wants to do something that sends out a signal. Ralph Stayer, of Johnsonville Sausages, said, 'Just start, don't wait until you have all the answers. Start by changing something visible. I stopped tasting sausages!' (Stayer,1990). But beware of empty gestures – if the rest of the organisation is not ready then such actions may be premature and treated with cynicism. Above all, do not prematurely change things which affect other people, but remember that when the rest of the organisation is changing, nothing is better than specific examples from the top.

Determine the strategy

The essential task for top management is to establish the broad direction and strategy. You must determine where you are today and where you wish to be in, say, five years time and write it down, but not in tablets of stone. But this alone is not enough – the determination to see it through is also needed. Top management must therefore also recognise that the journey of change is full of rocks which need to be identified. These rocks can include militant trade unions, inflexible senior management, demoralised supervisors, a poorly educated workforce, investors looking for short-term results, customers seeking attention now, suppliers who cannot keep up, and so on. If these rocks are not identified you may as well not start on the journey, for you will then be surprised when they appear and you will either founder, stop or turn back. You must determine what you will do about the rocks – go round them, smooth them or even blast them away. But, also realise that the destination will change as you go along. Nothing stands still and if, in five years time, you arrive where five years before you said you wanted to be, you will be out of date. The target may move further out, sideways, or may even come towards you!

Some 2,500 years ago, Sun Tzu, a Chinese military strategist wrote, 'All men can see the tactics whereby I conquer but what no one can see is the strategy out of which great victory is evolved', a statement as relevant to the top management team today as it was to the Chinese military of 500 BC. The top team is concerned with the strategy – the dynamics of the process, not the detail – but it has to understand how the elements of that process fit together and react upon each other. This is true whether you are seeking revolutionary or evolutionary change.

Involve the people

The next steps depend partly on the size of the organisation. Dowty Seals, a small manufacturer with a 320-strong workforce, diagnosed at top level that it was getting smaller, losing out on business and that there was a lack of direction and enthusiasm. Change was needed and the top management group decided that the best way for them was to talk directly with the whole workforce reasoning that change would not be accepted if the staff felt their future was secure. By taking staff into their confidence, a programme was initiated which resulted in a change from a centralised structure to focused business units, manufacturing cells and a reduction from eight to four levels between the MD and the shop floor. As a result, order to delivery time was reduced from sixteen weeks to two, work in progress was cut by 40 per cent, profits rose and motivation was much higher. This was not a move to an ascendant organisation and the implied threat challenges my argument emphasising the need for security, but unfortunately life is not simple. All any organisation can do is what is right for it in its circumstances and there will always be examples of organisations which break all the rules and succeed.

The essential point, however, is that this step begins (and in small organisations perhaps ends) with the involvement process. In large organisations it simply is not possible for everyone to be involved in the strategic debate but equally you will not achieve long-term ownership if communication is restricted to a one-way information session – the very antithesis of the concept of communication in the ascendant organisation.

You will fall at the first hurdle. People in the middle of an organisation and those at the periphery want to be able to contribute to forming the new way. How can you expect them to develop infectious enthusiasm if they have not been part of the process? 'Sharing' can only be achieved if it is a fully participated process. Again, an excellent way of beginning is to use The Ascendant Organisation Questionnaire and plan your change programme on the basis of its results.

It is vital to remember that this may well be the first time that many in the organisation have had anyone seek to 'share' anything with them. The top team often fails to realise that people at lower levels do not have their perspective. Because senior executives spend a considerable proportion of their time meeting people from other organisations and are frequently away from the four walls of their own business, they fail to appreciate that many people are restricted in both their contacts and their experience. Ask senior executives if they gain from their external perspectives and the answer will always be 'Yes'. Ask them if they would lose by being restricted to their four walls and the answer will again emphatically be 'Yes'. They cannot therefore expect everyone else immediately to share a perspective which they will have developed over many years of both internal and external experience. People respond by seeing things for themselves rather than by being told what others think they should think!

The ways in which people can share in the process will vary with the type of change you are seeking. When discussing quality, I emphasised the approach of bringing together the diagonal teams and such an approach can also work when tackling broader issues. After your initial analysis you may choose to cascade the discussions vertically through the organisation, or involve middle managers or supervisors as discrete groups. You may repeat the Questionnaire exercise at all levels throughout the organisation. Some may permute any combination. Others, with strong trade unions, will seek to involve them at this stage. One example was in the General Motors Cadillac Engine Plant in Livonia, USA. When starting their change programme, Irving Bluestone, then the UAW director of the Union's GM department, said:

> Truly successful endeavours in employee participation in decision making are not developed by management and simply handed down to the union and workforce. A successful improvement programme derives from mutually agreed upon understanding in which the union and management are co-equal in planning, designing and implementing the employee involvement process. (Nora, Rogers and Stramy, 1986)

Although not all managers would entirely agree with Bluestone, his personal track record was such that he was listened to carefully by GM management.

Whatever the actual structure of the groups handling this stage, similar golden rules apply as when seeking to integrate quality into the organisation, and for the same reasons:

- Members must have high personal credibility and be trusted.
- Members must be innovators, achievers and effective communicators.
- Members must represent all parts of the organisation and retain full normal responsibilities.
- The facilitator must be trusted and must contribute significantly to the process while not owning it.

Ownership is paramount and, particularly in large organisations, the groups must be able to contribute actively to the thought processes and refine the broad strategy and draft documentation of the top management team. Remember, the top team does not have a monopoly of wisdom but wisely heeds what others have to say. The group will know far more about the nuts and bolts of the organisation and top management will learn much from this. This is the beginning of the process of sharing the vision and each organisation will have to decide how many people are involved. Too many and it will become a glorified talking shop; too few and the result will be nothing more than handing down the tablets of stone. You may wish to involve a few doubters at an early stage. There are advantages – the doubters may become early converts and/or their questioning will challenge the values of the majority; and disadvantages – they may weaken the group. On balance, a small number should be involved. If the concept is so weak or the majority so uncommitted as to be unable to withstand criticism, it is better to find out sooner rather than later.

If, in a multi-location organisation, it is decided to establish a series of groups based on divisions or location, the results will differ from location to location. This does not matter. Provided the analysis is properly done, it is inevitable that the history, market circumstances and personalities will lead to different answers. Indeed, if everyone came up with the same answers, that would be the time to worry; the top team would have been too prescriptive. Some may even decide it is not for them. Again, this does not really matter. After a few months, they will either be shown to have been right, or they will decide to learn from the others, or their conclusion will be proved wrong, in which case they will, one hopes, change.

This process seeks to achieve a shared understanding of the strategy, the involvement of key implementors, the placement of the initiative in the hands of people in places where the practical issues manifest themselves, and a diagnosis of the detailed change requirements. It can help prepare the organisation for the change process by questioning and weakening commitment to the existing way of doing things. It can also help to build the essential critical mass within the organisation. How large this needs to be is a question for debate but it is often suggested that it is the square root of the number employed. Although it is impossible to be precise, there can be little doubt that a comparatively small group of people who know what they want can greatly influence a large group who, initially, do not mind what they get.

The groups should not at this stage seek to make changes to the formal structures, systems, rewards or procedures of the organisation. They are the tip of the iceberg, and only in very exceptional cases will such changes have any impact at this stage – except to confuse. Good people can work well irrespective of the organisation structure and to seek to force them into the straitjacket of premature organisation change will result in mistakes that later will need confusing revision. Better to let any changes result from an emerging need, rather than to predict.

Implement the change

Involving the people and implementing the change are not discrete steps. They overlap and combine; often they will be simultaneous, and are separated here only for descriptive convenience. Remembering that the ascendant organisation achieves the right balance between commitment and control, implementation eventually involves everyone in the organisation in doing practical things differently.

It can take many forms. George Stalk and Thomas Hout, in *Competing Against Time*, speak of pilots and breakthrough teams. 'Pilots are a good way to energise those parts of the organisation where good people are ready to go and where local trial and error experimentation is the right way to get solutions.' They advocate sheltering the pilots both physically and politically, particularly keeping 'senior people with turf issues out of the pilot itself'. Pilot activities work best when an organisation wants a demonstration of what can be achieved and knows that it will achieve early success. Breakthrough teams are multi-functional managerial teams, brought together for a period to achieve radical goals, like 'collapsing time in half', or substantially challenging the organisation's assumptions, for example, 'How to establish an around the clock global short-term money management function in the company'. Say Stalk and Hout:

> In this way, the change process is neither top-down nor bottom-up, but really driven from the middle and co-ordinated at the top by those who settled on the vision. The able middle managers are in the best position to do the cutting-edge learning that will reshape the company's practices. (Stalk and Hout, 1990, pp. 217–22)

Involving the key middle managers in 'doing' is clearly correct, but the great danger is isolation: Stalk and Hout's 'breakthrough teams' can easily become 'special' and work for short periods *because* they are different. If the lessons are applied widely, that is fine, but the ascendant organisation uses the talents of all the people, gives to all the freedom to do their own thing, to re-invent the wheel, to make their own mistakes and learn from them. The ascendant organisation involves everyone as the normal day-to-day way of doing business. It achieves its shared values by using the talents of everyone, not by imposition or by peering over the fence at what someone else is doing.

Having said that, it is vital that goals are set and performance measured at corporate level; but within these targets, sectional goals must be determined by the sections themselves, perhaps on a cascade basis. At an operating division an introduction goal may be nothing more than, 'Within one year involve 50 per cent of the people in small group activities', thus concentrating solely on the process, leaving that 50 per cent to define their own specific improvement objectives. Alternatively, the divisional objectives may be performance related within a framework of achieving them by involving the people. Some may seek to combine the two, making the decision either as the result of a top-down directive or following a consultative process.

In summary, unless you achieve genuine employee commitment to change in an organic way, no amount of management theorising or pontification will achieve anything that will last beyond the flavour of the month panacea. We must remember that directors and managers actually deliver very little. It is the people in the front line, the sales people, operators, teachers and their immediate supervisors, who deliver. Some leaders may inspire, but unless they achieve the hearts and minds conversion of the front-liners and have the capability to make that inspiration last, the benefits will be but short-lived. Eventually, even the forces of inertia will arouse themselves to resist change!

Then:

> # GET ON AND DO SOMETHING

though not everything at once. In 99.9 per cent of cases that will be both impossible and undesirable, but keep an eye on the vision, seeking to ensure that all elements are integrated. I am a great believer in involving the people in setting goals and targets to act as motivators, and in going for early success. There is nothing like a sense of achievement to enhance self-esteem and spur further efforts. What is achieved, within reason, does not really matter as long as it is something that is meaningful to that group. As with integrating quality; training and development needs will quickly become identified as will necessary support from other functions. The organisation must be aware of this and be ready to respond speedily to the demand, otherwise frustration will quickly set in. Supervisors will need to be trained in facilitating and coaching and in problem-solving techniques, but such training must be against a background of an understood need. There is nothing worse than a comprehensive training programme set up in advance with nothing to do thereafter except wait for the rest of the organisation to get ready.

It is here that the top team must be seen to be making its very visible contribution – perhaps abolish the executive dining room or remove reserved car parking spaces – or stop tasting sausages!

Create indicators of progress: not, 'How far we have progressed to becoming an ascendant organisation' – that will be impossible to measure – but measures of achievement against specific targets. Gradually it may be possible to make these measures common across the groups, sections or divisions or even the organisation, but be patient: this could take years. Or the top management may decide that a small number of important measures of corporate performance should be made known quickly so that people will understand how the total effort is progressing. Top management must never be successfully accused of failing to tell it to people like it is.

It is important to take away feelings of insecurity, because if people feel threatened by change, they resist it. In Chapter 2 we saw that the behavioural scientists put security as a base need which has to be satisfied before an individual can move on to a 'higher' need. But we have also seen that flexible organisations are moving to flexible employment practices and the traditional type of security is no longer the norm. However, within the revised definitions and practices, we also know that it is possible to achieve a different type of security, and that includes equipping people to be able to cope with change.

There is however a first time, the beginning of a new set of experiences, and if an organisation has yet to make the step-change transition brought about by the restructuring needs it would be irresponsible to guarantee existing employment levels. It may be necessary to go through the restructuring process before seeking to move to an ascendant organisation type of culture, for to attempt both at the same time will, to say the least, send out confusing signals. Confrontation and construction normally lie uneasily together.

However, when the first traumatic step is under way, it is important not simply to take away the feeling of insecurity but to give a feeling of security, remembering, of course, that we are all subject to the vagaries of the market place. But in seeking to change to becoming an ascendant organisation, I advocate that no one, except top managers, should compulsorily lose their employment because they cannot make the transition from the old to the new way. It is not their fault. They have been hired and trained to behave in a different way and why should they be punished if management wishes to change the style? Some may have to change their job within the organisation, and if others wish to go voluntarily, this option can be made financially attractive if the organisation can bear the cost – but seek to avoid dismissals. That takes away the threat, the insecurity, and makes acceptance easier.

It is easy to argue that if people cannot adapt, 'We'll fire them anyway.' That is not the way of the ascendant organisation, which seeks to treat people properly and with respect, including those who leave. Those who remain observe how those who leave were treated, and to believe that their attitude is not affected is to suffer a delusion.

Sustain the gain

Launching any programme is easy, sustaining it is extremely difficult. Once achieved, even in the ascendant organisation which should be self-sustaining, it is not easy to maintain. The easy thing is to revert to type, especially when the going gets tough. It is for this reason that top management must stick in there all the time, not just at the strategic stages. It must be aware of all the stakeholders – the employees, investors, customers, suppliers and the community. John Neill, Chief Executive of Unipart, who turned a sickly British Leyland subsidiary into an independent world-class automotive component supplier, referred to all having the same destiny:

> If you run a traditional Western model which is a power-based, short-term relationship between a company and its stakeholders, those businesses will fail. If you put the interests of one group continuously above the interests of another you will hit the wall when you come up against companies that build high quality and enduring relationships with all their stakeholders. (*Works Management*, September 1992)

This does not mean that everything remains unchanged. As previously stated, if in five years time we are where we aimed for five years before, we will be out of date, ossified in a time warp.

However, in order to sustain the never-ending change process of an ascendant organisation, a number of guidelines for top management are evident. Top management must:

- Maintain its long-term commitment to all aspects of the change process and ensure by its behaviour and requirements that everyone recognises this.
- Ensure that the direction and environment are maintained, support provided, lessons spread and people developed, so that at all levels and throughout the organisation good people are given the responsibility, the authority and the resources to make good decisions and are held accountable for those decisions.
- Regularly review progress against the strategy, adjusting as appropriate, recognising when desirable, cajoling when needed and acting when required.
- As the needs become evident, facilitate changes to the structure, reward systems, working arrangements, development programmes, processes and procedures, and so on, to ensure the organisation responds positively and consistently and encourages further initiatives.
- Ensure that career progression is based on success in the new way.
- Continuously communicate the principles and objectives to all stakeholders: the shareholders, suppliers, customers, unions and staff and ensure that their interests are properly balanced.
- Benchmark the competition, not forgetting the need continuously to improve the product and service and to remain profitable.

- Never cease to learn, do not be impatient, take the tough decisions at the right time to remove the rocks, and pray that sufficient progress is made in the good times so that it will see you through the next recession!

Living through a total change process is perhaps one of the most demanding, most exciting and most rewarding of all business activities. Machiavelli called it difficult, doubtful of success, and dangerous. The three D's of Japanese manufacturing are dirty, dangerous and difficult, and that is a reason *for* change, not an excuse for inaction!

15 The End of the Beginning

This is not the end. It is not even the beginning of the end. But it is, perhaps, the end of the beginning.

(Winston S. Churchill, 10 November 1942)

If this book is to have any impact, this final summary chapter must be the end of the beginning. Part I concluded with a chapter titled 'Conclusions – and Beginnings', and defined the ascendant organisation:

> The ascendant organisation combines high levels of commitment of the people with control of the processes to achieve a synthesis between high effectiveness and a high quality of life leading to long-term, sustainable business success.

It is not my intention to repeat here what I called the emerging conclusions from Part I, for Part II has been concerned with the practicalities and has attempted to show 'how to' progress to becoming an ascendant organisation. This final chapter will pull out some of the key requirements.

THE CULTURE

- All organisations, even those which have never heard the word, have a culture, either implicit or explicit. It does not have to be written down, but doing so can assist the definition of the shared values. True commitment has, though, to be earned and it is earned when the culture is 'lived'.
- Strong cultures can contribute to decline, because that very strength makes it difficult to change when needed. Only cultures which encourage flexibility and adaptive behaviour can achieve long-term success.
- The ascendant organisation recognises that it is people who make things happen and the culture is as much, if not more, about how people relate with each other as it is about the objectives.

269

- The people employed by the ascendant organisation are just as much part of it as are other stakeholders. They are not 'our people'. The greatest asset of all the people in an organisation is customers.
- It is concerned with treating all people with respect, trusting them, valuing their individual contributions and providing opportunities for them to grow throughout their lives. It permeates all relationships, processes and objectives and encourages flexibility and adaptive behaviour. Only such cultures can achieve long-term success.
- A culture must integrate with all expressed values and support, and be supported by, the business strategy.
- If the organisation has an expressed mission that, too, must integrate with the culture. It must not be a 'motherhood and apple pie' statement. It must inspire and require effort to achieve.
- Although it forms the bedrock of the organisation, it is valuable at lengthy intervals (maybe five years) to involve people throughout the organisation in reviewing it. 'Are we behaving as we ought?' 'Do we need to modify anything in the light of changing circumstances?'

LEADERSHIP

- Leadership in the ascendant organisation is about creating the conditions in which all people can perform to the maximum of their potential. It sets the tone, part of which is responding to the needs of all stakeholders and is about working through and with people.
- Leadership is not just about transformation. It exists at all levels and it is a key task of the top leadership to create the environment in which leaders can grow and flourish throughout the organisation.
- At the top, the leaders provide the direction and determine the goals. They seek to align the organisation, that is to make sure that everyone and every unit are working together within the same broad principles and business strategy to achieve shared objectives.
- Leaders seek to ensure that the organisation structure is such that it focuses on the essential flows of the business processes but they are not hidebound by them. They hire good people, and genuinely devolve responsibility and accountability and allow headroom, recognising that good people can work effectively within most structures; but if these structures need modifying to accommodate them, then they make sure it happens.
- Key attributes of leaders in the ascendant organisation include an intuitive empathy with the needs and desires of people at all levels,

respect for all and the ability to inspire and motivate. They are members of the team as well as leaders of it. Such leaders set high standards and lead by example. They are concerned with the 'how' as well as the 'what'. They constantly challenge, seeking both continuous improvement and, periodically, fundamental change. They are both intuitive and logical. They have a vision of where they want the organisation to go and the ability and passion to take it there.

- Some people are 'born leaders'; most leaders are made by experience.
- Leaders, and managers, exist in a time continuum. They must build on or redirect the work of their predecessor, undertake their own initiatives and prepare the ground for their successor. In the ascendant organisation they do not seek short-term success at the expense of the long term.
- Management is about the organisation and development of resources. Managers are more concerned with doing things right than doing the right thing, with a shorter time-scale than the leader. But a manager who cannot also lead is, in the ascendant organisation, a waste of space.

LEADERSHIP IN THE FRONT LINE

- Supervisors, if carefully selected, well-trained, highly motivated and given the status and pay appropriate to being the professional at managing the processes and the people, can make more difference to the long-term success of an organisation than any group other than top management. And even here, it is the supervisors who deliver top management's policies in the workplace.
- Appointment to the position of supervisor is seen as the beginning of a career, not the end of it.
- In the ascendant organisation, the supervisor exercises technical leadership (can understand the current technology and appreciate and deploy the new); applies modern techniques and processes; creates a positive environment for the people and identifies development needs and ensures they are met.
- The supervisor takes on many of the responsibilities which in other organisations have been assumed by functional specialists, including cost control, team selection, communication, training and process control, achieving schedule and quality, inputting into new products, and so on, and must therefore be regarded and paid as the

professional at managing the production process. The supervisor is at the same level as all other professionals.

- The supervisor is a member of the team as well as leader of it. The high-calibre supervisor – like all leaders – devolves responsibility, thus achieving commitment, and creates the environment in which the prescribed tasks and processes are properly performed.
- By increasing the influence of the staff, the role of the supervisor changes and grows. The 'influence pie' expands.

SINGLE STATUS

- You do not get a first-class response from people who are treated as second-class citizens.
- Common terms and conditions of employment are a necessary but not sufficient condition for achieving that first-class response. Nevertheless, the ascendant organisation begins to eliminate, as a precondition for behaviour change, illogical differences in the way people are treated; and aims for total elimination of such differences.
- The ascendant organisation does not give benefits to senior executives that are denied to others.

TEAMWORKING

- A team is a group of individuals who work together to achieve a shared objective.
- Such teams have positive leadership. In this they are different from work teams or groups which are based on organisational and/or physical structures.
- In the ascendant organisation the leader of the team is fully accepted as a member of the team.
- The team in the ascendant organisation works together for the success of the enterprise.
- The ascendant organisation comprises numerous interlocking teams – the day-to-day work groups, the project teams, task forces and *ad hoc* groups. Teamworking is the norm on a day-to-day basis and special 'teambuilding' activities are rarely needed.
- Teamworking operates just as successfully in an office environment. The physical layout, with genuine open areas, can greatly help.
- The ascendant organisation works very hard at creating teamworking among the top executives, recognising that this is the most difficult group in which to achieve success.

- Successful task or project teams comprise good people who learn together, explore their tasks, develop their own way, establish their goals and measure their progress. Often their families are involved in social events.

COMMUNICATION

- We all communicate all the time. Verbal communication is but one aspect. The ascendant organisation sends out messages when it eliminates illogical benefits, when the senior people are approachable, when distinctions of dress are removed and when, for example, the toilets on the shop floor are to the same standard as those in the offices. It has a 'no door', not an 'open door' policy.
- The ascendant organisation distinguishes communication from information. Communication is about a genuine multi-lateral exchange of views. It occurs when a senior person can speak directly to anyone without them feeling threatened.
- If something is worth communicating, it is worth communicating quickly and the only way to do this is every day, face to face. If it can wait for the monthly magazine or the corporate video, it is information, not communication.
- 'The communicator is king' and it is a top management responsibility to equip all managers and supervisors to be able to communicate effectively, not simply through meetings and discussion, but also by their demeanour in the morning and participation in social activities in the evening.
- The ascendant organisation communicates at all times – in the bad as well as the good. Most communication is about matters affecting the group, and the ascendant organisation is not concerned that everyone should get exactly the same message at exactly the same time: the important point is that the group shares what is important to it in its way. When the process is in place for the small issues, it then becomes easy to communicate about the big issues.
- The ascendant organisation communicates more rather than less, because it trusts people and believes they have a right to know,
- The top executives ensure that they get out to where the action is. They are available at regular intervals to communicate face-to-face with all the workforce, to give the big picture in the way only they can, and to allow anyone to question them directly. This is not by-passing the immediate management, but adding a different dimension.

INVOLVING PEOPLE

- The ascendant organisation does not speak of 'empowerment' but of genuinely ensuring that responsibility, authority and accountability are held in the most appropriate part of the organisation. Rather than the centre 'giving power' to the business units, the business units 'take power' from the centre.
- The ascendant organisation understands the difference between involving people and Employee Involvement. Employee Involvement involves the representatives in a formal process. Involving people ensures that all people throughout the organisation are fully involved in those aspects of the business they can influence and are fully informed about those aspects they cannot.
- Involving people at their place of work includes genuine multi-lateral communication, ownership of the standard operation by the people doing the job, full participation in the change processes, definition of the objectives, problem-solving and improvement activities. It takes people beyond the prescribed tasks into the discretionary, and values individual contributions.
- The ascendant organisation creates the environment in which such involvement is part of everyday life. It recognises, therefore, that if it is to have a philosophy which involves people, it has to involve people in determining that it will involve people. Once it becomes the norm, it ceases to be 'voluntary'.
- By involving people in 'local' issues, the ascendant organisation develops them so that they are able to contribute effectively on the major issues. It includes both core and non-core employees in the processes.
- If the organisation has trade unions, it encourages their representatives and officials to contribute in a constructive way, recognising that, representing the collective view, they bring a different perspective and that if this challenges management's conventional wisdom, that is their role.
- The ascendant organisation is not greatly concerned about big presentations, but recognises that in some circumstances they are valuable. The important point is to ensure that people know that their contributions are valued. Such recognition is developed in a myriad ways appropriate to the personalities and the people.
- The ascendant organisation does not theorise, discuss, debate or negotiate about involving people. It just does it – at all levels all the time.

- The ascendant organisation believes passionately in *kaizen*, continuous improvement, recognising that the people doing a job know more about that job than anyone else. The managerial responsibility is to create the environment in which that knowledge is brought out and is used for the benefit of the organisation. It aims to achieve an environment in which all staff are motivated to contribute those hundreds of 0.01 per cent improvements – and then modify the standard operation. It recognises that contributing small improvements greatly improves the chances of large improvements being generated and accepted.
- As *kaizen* develops, it can become increasingly sophisticated, but in so doing, it can generate more enthusiasm, not less.

FLEXIBILITY

- The ascendant organisation aims for flexibility within a consistent framework.
- It has a framework which does not restrict what people do. Therefore it eschews rigid organisational structures, fixed employment patterns unchangeable processes, immutable rules, detailed job descriptions, analytical job evaluation and precisely defined job titles and 'grades'. It recognises that people grow and develop their skills and competencies and that the organisation must adapt to them, rather than they to the organisation.
- The organisational structure is an outcome of good management, not a substitute for it.
- Flexibility in the ascendant organisation is about being able both to have an impact on the business environment and to respond to changes in that environment. It is about pro-active, evolutionary change and continuous improvement which avoid the need for violent, reactive change.
- People have the freedom to make decisions and, particularly in service organisations, it is recognised that it is at the face-to-face level that this freedom can make a significant difference.

PERFORMANCE EVALUATION

- Performance evaluation is part of an overall performance management process which supports the culture of the organisation, values all the elements the organisation values and assists in driving it in the direction it wishes to go.

- It satisfies the fundamental principles of being objective, consistent, open and motivating, and is fair and seen to be fair.
- It incorporates achievement against previously agreed goals and the individual's contribution to the team. It is a genuine two-way process, not a top-down evaluation.
- It is forward-looking, seeking to develop and grow all people throughout the organisation.

COMMITMENT IN AN INSECURE ENVIRONMENT

- The ascendant organisation, through effective management, seeks to offer security: not simply through long-term employment but by valuing everyone, by ensuring they know where they stand and by developing transferable skills so that employability as well as employment become important.

CONTROL OF THE PROCESSES

- The starting point for control of the manufacturing processes is the standard operation, the currently known best way of performing a task so as to achieve the required quality and productivity levels in a safe manner.
- The ascendant organisation seeks to ensure that the standard operation is always followed – until it is improved, usually by the people doing the job.
- In the ascendant organisation the standard operation is the property of the people doing the job. It is not imposed on them from the outside. The operational team, instead of being controlled by the standard operation, has control *of* the standard operation.
- The actual manufacturing process, whether it is cellular manufacturing, batch production, or line-paced volume production has to be right for the organisation but the ascendant organisation recognises the needs of the people and ensures that they are able to influence and control. There is proper integration of machinery and people and not domination by the former of the latter.
- Manufacturing cells are a particularly effective method of improving production, allowing simplification, increased productivity, an improved environment, more responsibility and greater involvement.

- The ascendant organisation simplifies before automating and then only automates at the appropriate level. It does not believe in automation for automation's sake, recognising that too complex a system is unreliable and expensive to maintain and that it is only people who can make further improvements to the processes and products. Machines, by themselves, improve nothing.
- The ascendant organisation devolves responsibility to the work groups, whatever the structure of the manufacturing processes. This can extend way beyond quality and productivity into team selection, purchasing decisions, work scheduling and the very structure of the group. There are many levels of the autonomous work group and each organisation has to make its own decisions as to how far to go.
- Total productive maintenance recognises that the people using equipment have a better feel for it than anyone else and involves them fully in the maintenance of their facilities. Maintenance then becomes a partnership between the operators and the professional maintenance teams. The objective is not simply to ensure the facility operates to its specification but also to improve it.
- The ascendant organisation seeks to eliminate waste in all aspects of its work. It removes buffer stocks, eliminates non-value-adding work, minimises changeover times, reduces inventory and controls its logistics. It concentrates on doing 'just' what is necessary 'in time', but recognises that such systems can easily become fragile. Therefore it aims to achieve the right balance between security, flexibility and waste elimination.
- In particular, the ascendant organisation aims for the right balance between its JIT minimum inventory philosophy and the appropriate logistics control systems. It recognises that, as with physical automation, it must simplify before introducing complex systems and must involve the people who will use the system.
- The ascendant organisation regards housekeeping as a fundamental aspect of workshop management. It is systematic about it, places responsibility where it belongs – with the people doing the job – and establishes control processes to ensure the high standards are maintained.
- Visible management is vital. This means managers being visible and relating to the people throughout the organisation, not just by 'walking around' but with purpose. It also means ensuring that the performance of each group is known to everyone by the visible display of information prepared by the group in a relevant way.

- The ascendant organisation recognises that the elimination of waste potentially increases the intensity of work and therefore concentrates enormous efforts on the ergonomic aspects of job design, seeking to eliminate problems at source through product and facility design. It then assesses the tasks and ensures that those people directly affected are fully involved in subsequent modifications.

INTEGRATING QUALITY

- In the ascendant organisation achieving high quality is not voluntary.
- The ascendant organisation regards high quality as the norm and does not need initial capitals like TQM. Quality does not give a competitive advantage. It is the price of staying in business and therefore is fully integrated into the business. It is no longer special.
- Quality focuses on customers, who are often irrational, illogical and whose views are constantly changing. Therefore, the quality of a product or service is the customers' perception of it, taking into account their total experience of those features they consider important. These are many and varied.
- Therefore, the ascendant organisation gets close to its customers, seeks to understand their needs and forms partnerships with them.
- It recognises that its front-liners are key links in this partnership.
- Internally, the ascendant organisation trains the staff and controls its processes to ensure delivery of consistent high quality, and determines internal performance measures which correlate strongly with customer requirements.
- The ascendant organisation designs for quality and, through the simultaneous engineering process, integrates customer needs, suppliers, production and marketing. In the process it reduces the time from conception to delivery and also concerns itself with disposal and resurrection. It recognises that top management does not have a monopoly of wisdom as to what is a good product or service, and devolves responsibility to those directly involved.
- The ascendant organisation does not rely on a few mavericks, but spreads innovation and commitment to quality throughout the organisation. It recognises that without everyone's commitment, the formal systems do not work for long.
- Within the ascendant organisation there are no change agents, but everyone is an agent for change. The standard operation is the starting point for quality improvements.

- The internal customer is vital. You never knowingly pass errors to the next person. Staff are encouraged to flag up their mistakes and are never criticised for so doing.
- Recognising human fallibility, the ascendant organisation seeks to 'foolproof' the physical process as much as possible.
- Quality circles are the cherry on the icing on the cake. They work when there is already a commitment to quality, and it is the total commitment to involvement and improvement that is important. The process is as important as the results and the organisation benefits from the experience the participants take back to their normal job.
- The ascendant organisation speaks not of the cost of quality but the price of poor quality – that price can be to go out of business.
- Bureaucratic systems, such as ISO 9000, do not in themselves set quality standards. They determine detailed procedures and rules which may help those who already have a commitment to quality but will make those with bureaucratic inclinations even more so inclined. The ascendant organisation uses such standards positively and learns from them.
- Benchmarking is a valuable tool – but in addition to making comparisons with competitors, the ascendant organisation seeks to understand the 'best in class', whatever the business in which it occurs, and uses that information to help determine where it wants to be. It also seeks to understand what is the 'best possible condition', even if no one has yet attained it.
- The ascendant organisation determines its key measures of externally assessed quality success and establishes key internal measures which correlate with the external. It fully involves the staff in this process.
- Change to processes, structures, and so on, result from a perceived need, not precede it, and may require fundamental challenges to the established way of doing things.
- Techniques for improving quality are tools, not a religion.
- Top management attention has to be maintained for ever.

PARTNERSHIP SOURCING

- The ascendant organisation is interested in the quality of its relationships with its suppliers and therefore develops long-term, mutually supportive partnerships.
- Partnership sourcing is a whole company philosophy which depends on relationships throughout both organisations and in which both are

stakeholders in the other. The supplier knows that in all normal circumstances the business is secure.

- Because of the depth of the relationship, partnerships can only exist with a comparatively small number of suppliers, the vast majority of whom will be the single source for a component or service.
- The customer will assign people specifically to work with its suppliers to develop their capabilities in design, manufacturing, quality assurance, delivery, management and any other areas relevant to the relationship – but will not usurp their authority and responsibility. Ascendant suppliers will assign people to work with their customers.
- The financial relationship changes from 'Cost + Profit = Price' to 'Price – Cost = Profit'. Rather than expecting continuous inflationary increases, the target is real price reductions due to increasing effectiveness and volumes.
- The ascendant organisation measures the performance of its suppliers and sets demanding improvement targets. In so doing it avoids complacency. The ascendant supplier will measure its customers!

KNOWLEDGE WORKERS

- In the ascendant organisation every worker is a knowledge worker.
- The ascendant organisation continuously develops all staff. Continuous development is a continuum in which, in a structured way, all people learn, are challenged and motivated so that they can grow and develop as individuals throughout their lives.
- The ascendant organisation builds on performance management – a partnership between managers and staff in which the business strategy, objectives, organisation requirements and individual evaluation and needs are integrated.
- All young people receive thorough training – on, off and near the job. They work for formal qualifications in specific skills but also develop broad competencies in teamworking, innovation, flexibility, problem-solving, and so on.
- In the ascendant organisation many of the attributes once regarded as the prerogative of managers become the natural currency throughout. All people use their brains as well as their hands. Therefore the development of these attributes begins as soon as people join the organisation, at whatever level – and all subsequent development builds from the bottom-up.

- The development of managerial skills and competencies is not reserved for people at or approaching management positions, but identifying those who are likely to progress through the managerial ranks is vital. Such people will be given the opportunity to develop and broaden their competencies and skills. High-potential people are placed in challenging positions.
- The ascendant organisation does not spoon-feed people. They take on considerable responsibility for their own development, and line managers regard it as part of their responsibilities to facilitate this process. Often it is only line managers who are able to provide the necessary knowledge and coaching and, therefore, a key part of everyone's training is being trained how to train. All staff participate in developing other staff.
- The ascendant organisation seeks joint agreement on roles, account-abilities, objectives and competency requirements as a means of measuring performance and on development and performance plans.
- The ascendant organisation encourages learning of all types and provides the necessary resources.
- Skills training is systematic and assessed. It seeks to answer the question, 'How do you *know* the staff are properly trained?'
- The ascendant organisation seeks to define in all people the 'magic powder' element, that elusive 'something' peculiar to an individual which will enable the person to perform better than he or she had thought possible.
- Non-core, as well as core, staff are properly trained and developed.
- The ascendant organisation both learns and forgets. People create the climate that facilitates the continuous development of all members who, as a result, are able continuously to develop the organisation.
- As a result, the ascendant organisation seeks to avoid the need for the traumatic paradigm shift but from time to time recognises that such a shift is necessary, but without the trauma!

RECOGNITION AND REWARD

- The reward structure reflects the view that it is management's job 365 days of the year to motivate the workforce, not a bonus payment's job one day of the year. Therefore, it is an outcome of good management, not a substitute for it.
- The ascendant organisation has a long-term horizon. Although it values good short-term results, it does not risk the long term for the

sake of the short term. It invests in people, product and facilities for long-term success.

- It takes into account the interests of all stakeholders, not just the financial investors,
- It values non-financial as well as financial performance, particularly when seeking to determine future performance. Judgements are made on the basis of long-term performance.
- In the ascendant organisation the reward structure is integrated with and supports the culture, business strategy and objectives.
- The ascendant organisation aims for transparency and seeks the commitment of everyone, not just a favoured few.
- For the vast majority of people short-term payment by results systems have no place and skill-based pay is questionable.
- In the ascendant organisation people are paid to attend (and when they do not attend). They are also paid to achieve, for their commitment, their contribution to continuous improvement and innovation and for their flexibility.
- Basic pay is 'right', meaning that it is felt to be fair.
- Performance-related pay (PRP), if introduced in the ascendant organisation, is designed to reinforce the culture, is clear as to the targets and standards, enables performance to be tracked, and ensures that people are able to impact on that performance. It is clear about the benefits to be gained.
- Performance-related pay is divided into two elements – input-based and output-based.
- Input-based performance pay reflects an individual's contribution and provides merit increase which are usually consolidated into base pay. It is based on a performance assessment which is as objective as possible.
- Output-based performance pay is based on measured achievement against clearly stated, mid-term performance, both financial and non-financial, which are integrated with the long-term goals of the business.
- It should contain no more than two elements, one based on a clear measure of financial performance and the other on a non-financial indicator.
- The ascendant organisation relates its performance bonuses as closely as possible to the business unit in which people work. It extends the bonus to all employees, not just to those at the top, and ensures that it is equitable.

- The ascendant organisation makes no secret of pay levels, being confident that they will be seen to be internally and externally fair. The top executives do not receive 'excessive' pay in relation to others and if there are share options they are available to all.
- The structure of top executives' reward packages is not significantly different from those of all other staff. And is structured around three elements – a liveable base salary; an output-based performance element related to previously agreed financial objectives plus one non-financial measure; and a long-term share option scheme.
- The contract of employment for top executives is not significantly different from that of other staff. In particular, the period of notice is the same and, in the case of poor performance, the senior executive 'goes' in exactly the same way as any other poor performer.

TRADE UNIONS

- The relationship that really counts in the ascendant organisation is that between individuals, not that between the representatives of trade unions and the representatives of management.
- Trade unions can have a constructive role in the ascendant organisation provided that they are committed to the success of the enterprise and they consider carefully their changed role. They ask, 'Can we provide a service which our members want?' and seek to become involved in the 'new way' where it matters to their members – on the shop floor – ensuring that there is no abuse and that the benefits are equitably distributed.
- They seek to represent both core and non-core employees.
- The new agenda for trade unions in the ascendant organisation is about the quality of outputs as much as the price of inputs.
- Trade unions retain their traditional roles but in a modern way, while at the same time accepting that teamworking, employee involvement, flexibility, and so on, have resulted in employees recognising that their only real security comes from working for a successful enterprise.
- The ascendant organisation does not resist constructive trade unionism but opposes those who attempt to be destructive. It recognises that it is what employees, not management, want that counts.
- In the ascendant organisation what unites people because they are all employees of the same organisation is stronger than what divides them because of their different levels and roles.

THE CHANGE PROCESS

There are many different change processes depending on the area of the organisation to be changed – the whole culture, quality, teamworking, reward system, and so on. However, running through the 'How to' sections there have been common threads:

- At the top level, analyse where you are now and seek to establish a common understanding of where you want to be. Benchmark the opposition, 'best in class' and seek to understand what 'the very best possible' might be – even if no company has yet attained it. But do not be precise: you will not get it right because you will not really know what goes on throughout the organisation. It is top management's job to create the framework which liberates people throughout the organisation to determine the detail. Writing down the first thoughts is a great discipline, but make sure it *is* first thoughts and not 'tablets of stone'.
- Appoint the best people to develop the concepts but ensure that they do not think they have a monopoly of wisdom. Make sure they consult widely and involve all the stakeholders, including non-core workers and trade unions if appropriate, and particularly the middle managers who will often feel the most threatened but who will be the key deliverers of change.
- Allow gun-jumping – provided the people concerned have thought it through. 'Ownership' is critical. Do not worry about the wheel being re-invented. Let people do their own thing and make their own mistakes, but ensure they learn from their mistakes and from each other.
- Perhaps send out signals from the top. Change something which is visible and symbolic but choose the timing carefully, otherwise it may be seen as a cynical exercise.
- Take away insecurity – but in some organisations you may have to go through the traumatic 'downsizing' before you can even begin to think this way. Although no one is protected from the vagaries of the market place, remember that it is not individuals' faults if they are unable to make the change. They have been hired and expected to behave in a particular way and it is management's responsibility if a change takes place. Individuals may have to change their job or may choose to go with generous financial payments, but do not dismiss them. If people think that they will lose their employment if the changes go through, they will make sure that nothing happens.

- Trust people. You will get surprises. It will not happen the way you thought, but it will be all the better for that.
- Encourage experiments, provide training.
- List critical success factors and, where possible, measure, but often the change will be a 'stand'. If you have to prove it, you do not believe in it; and do not forget that that which is measured is often not important and that which is important is often not measured. Do not start by changing the structures or processes. Leave them alone. If the need arises it will become obvious to everyone. Maybe you will be able to abolish many of the previous bureaucratic systems which inhibited flexibility – but this can only come at the end. Too early, and you will make some horrible mistakes.
- Top management's interest must be sustained throughout. It is no good setting the train in motion and walking away. It will be a long haul.
- Outsiders can help; they can ask the difficult questions but they must never take over. Ownership must rest within the organisation.
- Remember that the old must continue for a considerable time to operate beside the new. Not everything can change at once.

THE FINAL MESSAGE

Remember, we all have a part of our organisation we can influence. We do not have to wait for the change process to start from above us. Do not miss out the planning and understanding, but avoid paralysis by analysis.

There comes a time when you have to make a stand and just do it!

Today is a great time to begin!

Appendix One: The Japanese 'Target'

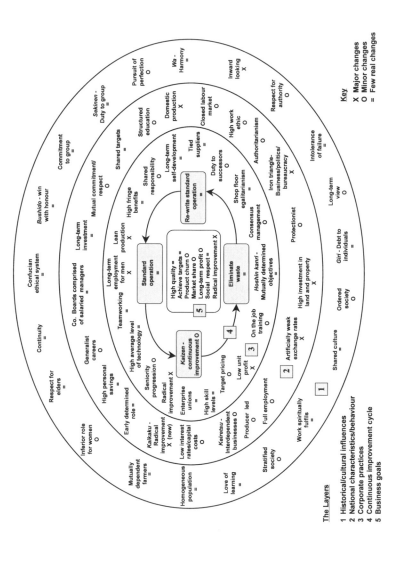

The Layers

1 Historical/cultural influences
2 National characteristics/behaviour
3 Corporate practices
4 Continuous improvement cycle
5 Business goals

Key

X Major changes
O Minor changes
= Few real changes

Appendix Two: The Ascendant Organisation Questionnaire

Note: This questionnaire and the associated assessment techniques are copyright to Peter D. Wickens and Organisation Development International (UK) Limited. It is given in this book for the sole use of individual readers who personally wish to assess their own organisation. Any reader or organisation wishing to use it beyond this personal assessment must gain permission from the author and Organisation Development International (UK) Limited. Its use by organisations can only be undertaken through Organisation Development International (UK) Limited and payment of the required fees. The questionnaire and the assessment process may not be amended in any way by anyone other than the author or Organisation Development International (UK) Limited. (Approval for use should be sought from the address given on page xiv).

This questionnaire comprises twenty sections each containing two statements. Please follow the instructions given below to enable you to develop the 'footprint' of your organisation. The word 'staff' is used throughout the questionnaire to cover all people, other than 'managers'.

1. Read each pair of statements in the questionnaire very carefully and allocate a score to each statement in the pair indicating your personal perception of your organisation's (or your part of it if you prefer) 'performance' against that statement. Remember, you are recording *your* perception, not how you feel your organisation would wish to be seen. You have 5 points to allocate to each pair. A score of 0 (zero) indicates total disagreement with the statement and a score of 5 indicates total agreement. *The total score of a pair must not exceed 5, and in many cases the total is likely to be considerably less than 5.* You may, for example, totally disagree with both statements, in which case your score would be 0 – 0.

Acceptable scores are therefore:

0 – 0	0 – 1	0 – 2	0 – 3	0 – 4	0 – 5
1 – 0	1 – 1	1 – 2	1 – 3	1 – 4	—
2 – 0	2 – 1	2 – 2	2 – 3	—	—
3 – 0	3 – 1	3 – 2	—	—	—
4 – 0	4 – 1	—	—	—	—
5 – 0	—	—	—	—	—

The blanks in the above table indicate spaces where the scores would be unacceptable. For example, 1 – 5 and 2 – 4 are not acceptable because their totals exceed 5.

Do *not* just put down and stick with your first thoughts. As you proceed through the questionnaire you may well wish to revise your original scores.

2. After completing the questionnaire, transfer the score for each statement to the appropriate box in the Score Sheet (while not consecutively positioned, each one of a pair is in the same column); then add-up each horizontal line to give a total for each organisation type. Please note that there is no section for 'Apathetic'. 'Apathetic' is shown in the Nine Alpha Organisation Footprint as a small circle in the centre.

3. Transfer the total score for each organisation type onto a blank Nine Alpha Organisation Footprint (two are given) by marking the appropriate axis at the relevant point, e.g. a score of 17 would be marked two-fifths of the way between 15 to 20.

4. Join the marks. This gives the 'footprint' for your organisation. The lower your total scores, the closer you will be to 'Apathetic' in the centre.

QUESTIONNAIRE

Score

1.A	This organisation achieves high levels of performance by combining commitment of people with positive controls of processes and procedures.	
B	*This organisation is characterised by management behaviour which is perceived as legitimate and acceptable.*	
2.A	Flexibility and co-operation are the norm, with staff deciding on accepted methods and practices.	
B	*There is little flexibility. Externally imposed standards are clearly defined and adhered to.*	
3.A	This organisation is characterised by high levels of coercive management behaviour and rigid controls.	
B	*This organisation is characterised by a high level of individual commitment to organisational goals and low levels of control.*	
4.A	All staff are dedicated to promoting teamwork and harmony.	
B	*Adherence to clearly defined standards is evident.*	
5.A	A high level of teamwork, co-operation and harmony exists across all levels and functions.	
B	*Individuals are allowed little discretion and judgement.*	
6.A	'Superiors' impose their authority on employees to achieve results.	
B	*All staff enjoy a high level of individual discretion and judgement.*	
7.A	All staff are responsible for developing and improving processes or procedures which then serve as controls to ensure success.	
B	*Managers act as if only they have knowledge and experience to control and improve processes.*	

Score

8.A	Top-down imposition of rules and procedures and coercive behaviour by managers create a negative response from staff.	
B	*All staff are highly motivated and eager to meet goals and targets.*	
9.A	Staff feel protected and comfortable. They are content with their position and the organisation's future.	
B	*High standards are achieved through clear explicit procedures.*	
10.A	There are high levels of pressure to conform to demands of 'superiors'.	
B	*This organisation has little control and little co-operation. Staff pursue their own agendas and goals.*	
11.A	Decision making is delegated throughout the organisation within clearly defined authorities and controls.	
B	*Decision making is centred at the top where managers are perceived to have most experience and knowledge.*	
12.A	Systems and procedures are adapted by staff to meet their own needs.	
B	*Clear procedures, standards and rules exist and staff comply with them.*	
13.A	Management behaviour and restrictive rules create an 'us versus them' climate.	
B	*A high level of individual commitment and flexibility exists with little influence and control from management.*	
14.A	Behaviour is governed by people in positions of power.	
B	*People do what is important to them.*	
15.A	Employees are managed and controlled by rigid managers and formal procedures.	
B	*Staff are free, creative and innovative. They achieve agreed goals and targets by using their initiative.*	

Score

16.A	Staff know their business, share a common goal and continuously improve the processes.	
B	*Managers know their business. Their decisions, experience and wisdom determine which changes and improvements are implemented.*	
17.A	A top-down management style prevails.	
B	*All staff are self-motivated to achieve their goals and targets.*	
18.A	A low degree of co-operation and commitment exists, motivation is generally absent.	
B	*A high degree of co-operation and commitment exists; controls are generally absent.*	
19.A	All staff are skilled in many tasks; their behaviour is goal directed and guided by standard operating procedures.	
B	*Staff are single skilled; their behaviour is determined by their 'superiors'.*	
20.A	Staff do what they are told to do.	
B	*Staff do what they personally want to do.*	

SCORE SHEET

						Totals
Ascendant	1a	7a	11a	16a	19a	
Anarchic	6b	10b	14b	17b	20b	
Ardent	3b	8b	13b	15b	18b	
Amiable	2a	4a	5a	9a	12a	
Authoritarian	1b	7b	11b	16b	19b	
Autocratic	6a	10a	14a	17a	20a	
Alienated	3a	8a	13a	15a	18a	
Absolute	2b	4b	5b	9b	12b	

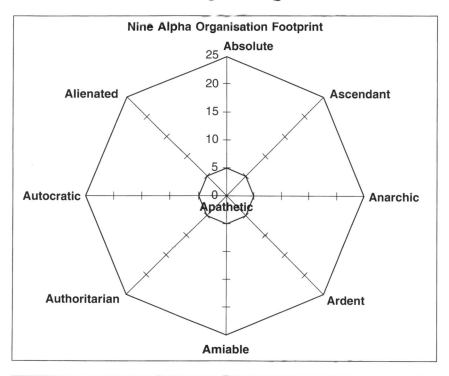

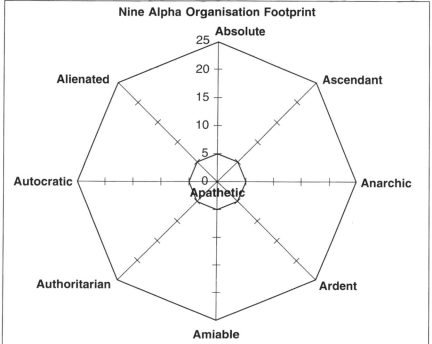

References

Note: This listing contains some references which are not specifically quoted but which have been used in the preparation of this book.

A. T. Kearney (1992)	*Total Quality Management: A Business Process Perspective*	A. T. Kearney Inc.
Abegglen, J. (1958)	*The Japanese Factory*	The Free Press, New York
Adler, P. S. (1993)	'Time and Motion Regained'	*Harvard Business Review* (Jan.–Feb.)
American Compensation Association (1996)	'Teams, Pay and Business Strategy'	*ACA Journal* (Fall)
Anderson Consulting (1993)	*The Lean Enterprise Benchmarking Project*	Anderson Consulting
Armstrong, M. and H. Murlis (1994)	*Reward Management* (3rd edn)	Kogan Page, London
Barnett, C. (1986)	*The Audit of War*	Macmillan, London
Beer, M., R. Eisenstatt and B. Spector (1990)	'Why Change Programmes Don't Produce Change'	*Harvard Business Review* (Nov.–Dec.)
Belbin, W. M. (1981)	*Management Teams – Why they Succeed or Fail*	Heinemann, London
Bennis, W. (1992)	*On Becoming a Leader*	Century Business, London
Berggren, C. (1993a)	*The Volvo Experience*	Macmillan, London
Berggren, C. (1993b)	'Volvo, Uddevalla – a Dead Horse or a Car Dealer's Dream?'	Royal Institute of Technology, Stockholm
Berggren, C., T. Bjorkman and E. Hollander (1991)	*Are They Unbeatable?*	Royal Institute of Technology, Stockholm
Berggren, C. and M. Nomura (1997)	*The Resilience of Corporate Japan*	Paul Chapman, London

Binney, G. (1992)	*Making Quality Work*	The Economist Intelligence Unit, London
Binney, G. and C. Williams (1995)	*Leaning into the Future*	Nicholas Brealey, London
Bonfield, P. (1993)	*Building a Resilient Company*	Management Centre Europe Conference (May)
Burns, P. and R. Savers (1988)	*Participative Management and Employee Involvement*	Ford Motor Company
Carlzon, J. (1989)	*Moments of Truth*	Harper & Row, New York
Chadwick, P. (1993)	'Supervisory Roles, Responsibility and Training in British Industry'	Peter Chadwick Ltd.
Clark, J. (1995)	*Managing Innovation and Change*	Sage, London
Confederation of British Industry (1988)	*Statement of Principles on Employee Involvement*	CBI, London
Confederation of British Industry (1991)	*Partnership Sourcing*	CBI, London
Conference Board of New York (1993)	*Does Quality Work?*	Conference Board of New York
Deming, W. E. (1982)	*Out of the Crisis*	Cambridge University Press
Development Council of Sweden (1984)	*Volvo, Kalmar Re-visited – Ten Years of Experience*	
Drucker, P. (1993)	*Post-Capitalist Society*	Butterworth-Heinemann, London
Epps, T. (1987)	Untitled	European Metal Workers' Federation Conference (April)
European Foundation (1997)	'Employee Direct Participation in Organisational Change', in P. Edwards, *The Changing Employment Relationship*	European Foundation

European Metal Workers' Federation (1992)	*Mechanical Engineering in Europe in the Year 2000*	
Feigenbaum, A. (1983)	*Total Quality Control* (3rd edn)	McGraw-Hill, Maidenhead
Ferdows, K. (1992)	'New Mandates for Global Manufacturers'	European Manufacturing Management Conference, Geneva (June)
Foster, M. and S. Whittle (1989)	'The Quality Management Maze'	*TQM Magazine* (vol. 3, May)
Fucini, J. J. and S. Fucini (1990)	*Working for the Japanese*	The Free Press, New York
GMB/Union of Communications Workers (1992)	*A New Agenda*	GMB and UCW, London
Guest, D. (1984)	'What's New in Motivation?'	*Personnel Management* (May)
Hackman, J. R. and G. R. Oldham (1985)	'Motivation Through the Design of Work'	*Organisational Behaviour and Human Performance* (vol. 16, no. 2) in T. Robertson and M. Smith, *Motivation and Job Design,* Institute of Personnel Management
Hamel, G. and C. K. Prahaled (1994)	*Competing for the Future*	Harvard Business School Press, Boston
Hammer, M. (1996)	*Beyond Re-engineering*	HarperCollins Business, London
Hammer, M. and J. Champy (1993)	*Re-engineering the Corporation*	Nicholas Brealey, London
Hammer, M. and S. A. Stanton (1995)	*The Re-engineering Revolution*	HarperCollins, London

Handy, C. (1987)	*The Making of Managers*	National Economic Development Office, London
Handy, C. (1993)	'What it Takes to Make a Manager'	*Director* (Dec.)
Handy, C. (1994)	*The Empty Raincoat*	Hutchinson, London
Harbour, M. and J. Brown (1993)	*Customer Driven Quality*	National Franchise Dealers Association, Rugby
Hatakeyama, Y. (1985)	*Manager Revolution*	Productivity Press, Portland
Hay Management Consultants (1996)	*Broadbanding*	Hay, London
Herzberg, F. (1959)	*The Motivation to Work*	Wiley, New York
Hitchens, D. A. and K. Wagner (1985)	*Productivity, Machinery and Skills in a Sample of British and German Manufacturing Plants*	NIESR, London
Holloway, J.	'The Red Rose of Nissan'	*Capital and Class*, No. 2
Hopson, B. and M. Scally (1989)	*Twelve Steps to Success through Service*	Lifeskills Publishing Group, Leeds
Howard, G. (1993)	'Design for Assembly'	Automotive Vision
IG Metall, RKW and VDW (1992)	*Nine Principles: Towards an Innovating and Social Industrial Culture in the Machine Tool Industry*	IG Metall
Imai, M. (1989)	*Kaizen: The Key to Japan's Competitive Success*	Random House, New York
Industrial Relations Services (1997a)	'Competency Profiles and Merit Pay at Reigate and Banstead'	*Pay and Benefits Bulletin* (July)
Industrial Relations Services (1997b)	'Sharing the Gains at Rank Xerox'	*Pay and Benefits Bulletin* (Sept)
Industrial Society (1996)	*Managing Best Pactices No. 28 Job Evaluation*	Industrial Society, London
Ingersoll Engineers (1991)	*Change: The Good, The Bad and The Visionary*	Ingersoll Engineers Ltd.
Ingersoll Engineers (1993)	*The Quiet Revolution Continues*	Ingersoll Engineers Ltd.

298   *References*

Ingersoll Engineers   *The Way We Work*   Ingersoll Engineers
  (1996)   Ltd

International Labour   *World Labour Report*   ILO, Geneva
  Office (1994)

Jackson, J. (1997)   *Dynamic Organisations*   Macmillan, London

Jacques, E. (1961)   *The Measurement of*   Tavistock. London
                            Responsibility

Japanese Auto   *Japanese Automobile Industry in*   JAWU, Tokyo
  Workers Union   *the Future*
  (1992)

Jordan, W. (1991)   'Working with Japanese   Anglo-Japanese
                            Investors: The Trade Union   Economic
                            Response', in *Japan and the*   Institute, London
                            Regeneration of British
                            Industry

Kamata, S. (1983)   *Japan in the Passing Lane*   Allen & Unwin,
                                                            London

Kanter, R. M. (1989)   *When Giants Learn to Dance*   Unwin Hyman,
                                                            London

Katzenbach, J. R.   *The Wisdom of Teams*   Harvard Business
  and D. K. Smith   School Press,
  (1993)   Boston

Koestler, A (1960)   *The Lotus and the Robot*   Hutchinson and Co.,
                                                            London

Kohn, A. (1993)   'Why Incentive Plans Cannot   *Harvard Business*
                            Work'   *Review*
                                                            (Sep.–Oct.)

Kotter, J. P. and   *Corporate Culture and*   The Free Press, New
  J. Heskett (1992)   *Performance*   York

Krafcik, J. (1986)   *A Methodology for Assembly*   IMVP, MIT
                            Plant Performance
                            Determination

Labour Research   *Organising for Union*   Labour Research
  Department (1997)   *Recruitment*   Department,
                                                            London

Lamming, R. (1993)   *Delivery-on-Time Initiative*   I.Mech.E, London

Lane, C. (1989)   *Management and Labour in*   Edward Elgar
                            Europe   Publishing,
                                                            London

Lawler, E., S. Mohrmon, and G. Lapford (1995)	*Creating High Performance Teams*	Jossey Bass, San Francisco
Lazonick, W. (1990)	*Competitive Advantage on the Shop Floor*	Harvard University Press, Boston
Lehndorff, S and G. Bosch (1992)	*Working Time and Operating Hours in the European and Japanese Car Industries*	Institut Arbeit und Technik, Gelsenkirchen
Lewchuk, W. and D. Robertson (1996)	'Working Conditions under Lean Production'	*Asia–Pacific Business Review* (vol. 2 no. 4)
Macqueen, J. (1996)	'Personal Development for the Whole Workforce'	*Employee Development Bulletin,* Industrial Relations Services (Oct.)
Maslow, A. (1970)	*Motivation and Personality*	Harper & Row, New York
Mayo, E	'The Social Problems of an Industrial Civilisation' in D. S. Pugh, *Organisation Theory* (3rd edn)	Penguin Books, London
Monks Partnership (1993)	*Incentives for Management*	Monks Partnership, Saffron Walden, Essex
McGregor, D. (1960)	*The Human Side of Enterprise*	McGraw-Hill, New York
Miller, P. (1992)	Untitled	*Communications Review*, no. 2 (April)
Miller, K. Lowry, (1993)	'The Factory Guru Tinkering with Toyota'	*Business Week* (17 May)
Mintel (1993)	*Quality Assurance and the Customer*	Mintel, London
Mintzberg, H. (1975)	'The Manager's Job – Folklore and Fact'	*Harvard Business Review* (Jul.–Aug.)
Mito, S. (1990)	*The Honda Book of Management*	The Athlone Press, London
Monks Partnership (1993)	*Incentives for Management*	Monks Partnetship, Saffron Walden, Essex

300 *References*

Morton, C. (1994)   *Becoming World Class*   Macmillan, London

Moto, I. (1982)   'Class Struggle in Post-War Japan'   *AMPO Japan-Asia Quarterly Review* (vol. 14, no. 3)

National Economic Development Office (1990)   *The Roles, Competences and Training of Supervisors*   NEDO, London

NEDC (1991)   *What Makes a Supervisor World Class?*   NEDO, London

NEDC (1991)   *The Experience of Nissan Suppliers*   NEDO, London

New Bridge Street (1997)   *Paying for Performance*   New Bridge Street, London

Nikkei Research Institute (1990)   *Sixth Annual Survey on Japanese Youth*   NRI, Tokyo

Nikkei (1995)   *Contemporary Enterprises*   Nikkei, Tokyo

Nomura, M. (1992)   *The End of Toyotaism*   IG Metall Conference, Frankfurt

Nora, J.J., C.R. Rogers and J. Stramy (1986)   *Transforming the Workplace*   Princetown Research Press, New Jersey

Oakland, J.S. (1990)   'TQM: One Way to Delight your Customers'   *Works Management* (May)

Ohno, T. (1988a)   *Workplace Management*   Productivity Press, Portland

Ohno, T. (1988b)   *Toyota Production System*   Productivity Press, Portland

Oram, M. and R.S. Williams (1995)   *Re-engineering's Missing Ingredient*   Institute of Personnel and Development, London

Ouchi, W. (1981)   *Theory Z*   Addison Wesley, Reading, Mass.

Parker, M. and J. Slaughter (1988a)   *Choosing Sides: Unions and the Team Concept*   South End Press

Parker, M and J. Slaughter (1988b)   'Managing by Stress: The Dark Side of Teamwork'   *Industrial and Labour Relations Report* (Fall)

Pascale, R.T. (1990)   *Managing on the Edge*   Viking, London

Pedlar, M.,
  T. Boydell and
  J. Burgoyne (1989) — 'Towards the Learning Company' — *Management Development and Education* (20.1)

Peters, T. (1988) — 'Leadership Excellence in the 1990s' — *Journal of Management* (vol. 7, no. 5)

Peters, T. (1992) — 'Perfection is not Enough' — *Works Management* (Dec.)

Pinchot, G. and
  E. Pinchot (1993) — *The End of Bureaucracy and the Rise of the Intelligent Organisation* — Berret-Koehler, San Francisco

Pugh, D. S. (ed.)
  (1993) — *Organisation Theory* — Penguin Books, London

Quinn, J. B. (1990) — 'Ford's Team Taurus 1988', in *International Motor Business* — The Economist Intelligence Unit (April)

Rhys, G. (1992) — *The Motor Industry: A Wider Vision* — SMMT Conference (Sept)

Rich, J. T. and
  A. Larson (1987) — 'Why Some Long Term Incentives Fail', in H. R. Nalbantian (ed.), *Incentives, Co-operation and Risk Sharing* — Rowman & Littlefield

Robertson, D. (1992) — *New Management Techniques and the Development of a Trade Union Counter Strategy* — TIE/Vauxhall Motors Shop Stewards Conference (Jan.–Feb.)

Roth, S. (1991) — *Analytik '91* — Hamburg (Nov.)

Roth, S. (1992) — *Japanisation or Going Our Own Way* — IG Metall

Roth, S. (1993) — 'Lean Production in German Motor Manufacturing' — P+ *European Participation Monitor* (no. 5)

Royal Society of Arts
  (1995) — *Tomorrow's Company* — RSA, London

Schmidt, H. (1992) — *Skills for Europe: 1993 and Beyond* — Conference, London (Sept.)

Scholtes, P. R. (1987) — *An Elaboration on Deming's Teaching on Performance Appraisal* — Joiner Associates Inc.

Schonberger, R .J. (1982)	*Japanese Manufacturing Techniques – Nine Hidden Lesson in Simplicity*	The Free Press, New York
Schonberger, R. J. (1986)	*World Class Manufacturing*	The Free Press, New York
Secretary's Commission on Achieving Necessary Skills (1991)	*What Work Requires of School*	US Department of Labor
Semler, R. (1993)	*Maverick*	Century, London
Sengenberger, W. (1992)	*Lean Production: The Way of Working and Production in the Future*	International Institute for Labour Studies, Geneva
Shingo, S. (1988)	*Non-Stock Production*	Productivity Press, Oregon
Sloan, R. and N. Jackson (1997)	*Sharing in Success*	Bacon & Woodrow
Smilansky, J. (1992)	'How Not to Implement TQM'	'Re-thinking Quality' – *The Economist* Conferences. (Dec)
Smith, A. (1776; repr. 1980)	*The Wealth of Nations*	Methuen, London
Stalk, G. Jnr. and T. M. Hout (1990)	*Competing Against Time*	The Free Press, New York
Stayer, R. (1990)	'How I Learned to Let My Workers Lead'	*Harvard Business Review* (Nov.–Dec.)
Steele, M. and A. Brown (1990)	*Leadership*	Cranfield Press, Cranfield
Storey, J., P. Edwards and K. Sissons (1997)	*Managers in the Making*	Sage, London
Tannenbaum, A. S. (1966)	*Social Psychology of the Work Organisation*	Wadsworth, California
Tannenbaum, A. S. (1968)	*Control in Organisations*	McGraw-Hill, New York
Taylor, F. W. (1911)	*The Principles of Scientific Management*	W.W. Norton, New York

Thompson, M. (1994)   'Paying for Performance', in R. Heller (ed.), *Managing 1994: The Competitive Edge*   Sterling Publications, London

Thurow, L. (1993)   *Head to Head*   Nicholas Brealey, London

Tichy, N. M. and S. Sherman (1993)   *Control Your Destiny or Someone Else Will*   Currency Doubleday, New York

Towers Perrin (1997)   *Learning from the Past: Changing for the Future*   Towers Perrin UK, London

Trades Union Congress (1993)   *The Future of Trade Unions*   TUC, London

Trades Union Congress (1994)   *Human Resource Management*   TUC, London

Trades Union Congress (1997)   *Partners for Progress*   TUC, London

Trist, E. L. (1981)   'The Socio-Technical Perspective', in A. van der Ven and W. F. Joyce (eds), *Perspectives on Organisational Design and Behaviour*   Wiley-Interscience, New York

Trist, E. L. and K. W. Bamforth (1981)   'Some Social and Psychological Consequences of the Long Wall Method of Coal Getting'   *Human Relations* (vol. 4, no. 1)

Tuckman, B. W. (1965)   'Development Sequence in Small Group'   *Psychological Bulletin* (no. 3)

Unterweger, P. (1992)   *Lean Production: Myth and Reality*   International Institute for Labour Studies, Geneva

Vista (1997)   *Seventh Vista Survey of Managers' Opinions on Communication and Management Style*   Vista Communications Ltd

van Wolferen, K. (1989)   *The Enigma of Japanese Power*   Macmillan, London

Vroom, V. H. (1964)   *Work and Motivation*   John Wiley, New York

Walton, R. H. (1985)   'From Control to Commitment in the Workplace'   *Harvard Business Review* (Mar.–Apr.)

Waterman, R. (1994)   *The Frontiers of Excellence*   Nicholas Brealey, London

Weber, M. (1930)   *The Protestant Ethic and the Spirit of Capitalism*   Allen & Unwin, London

Weber, M. (1947)   *The Theory of Social and Economic Organisations*   The Free Press, New York

Wickens, P. D. (1987)   *The Road to Nissan*   Macmillan, London

Williams, K., C. Haslam, J. Williams and T. Cutler (1992)   'Against Lean Production'   *Employment and Society* (vol. 21, no. 3, August)

Wolf, M. J. (1984)   *The Japanese Conspiracy*   New English Library, Sevenoaks

Womack, J. P. and D. T. Jones (1996)   *Lean Thinking*   Simon & Schuster, New York

Womack, J. P., D. T. Jones and D. Roos (1990)   *The Machine that Changed the World*   Rawson Associates, New York

Zairi, M., A. Letza and J. S. Oakland (1994)   'Does TQM Impact on the Bottom Line?'   *The TQM Magazine* (vol. 6, no. 1)

Wyatt Company (1990)   *Performance Management 1990*   The Wyatt Company/ *Personnel Today*

Zuboff, S. (1988)   *In the Age of the Smart Machine*   Basic Books, New York

Index